EX LIBRIS
Irving Leffel

THE CHURCHILL YEARS

THE

By the editors of The Viking Press
Text by *The Times* of London
With a foreword by Lord Butler of Saffron Walden

1874-1965

CHURCHILL YEARS

NEW YORK

THE VIKING PRESS

Copyright © 1965 by The Times Publishing Company Limited, London
Copyright © 1965 by The Viking Press, Inc.
All rights reserved

First published in 1965 by The Viking Press, Inc.
625 Madison Avenue, New York, N.Y. 10022

Published simultaneously in Canada by
The Macmillan Company of Canada Limited

The italicized portions of the picture captions are in Churchill's own words. These and other quotations from Churchill are drawn from the books and speeches listed on pages 261-62, but principally from the following sources, by permission of: CASSELL AND COMPANY LTD. for material from *The Unwritten Alliance* and *War Speeches*, edited by Charles Eade; H.M. STATIONERY OFFICE for speeches delivered in Parliament and first published in Hansard; HOUGHTON MIFFLIN COMPANY and CASSELL AND COMPANY LTD. for material from *The Gathering Storm, Their Finest Hour, The Grand Alliance, The Hinge of Fate, Closing the Ring, Triumph and Tragedy, Sinews of Peace, Europe Unite,* and *Stemming the Tide;* CHARLES SCRIBNER'S SONS and ODHAMS BOOKS LIMITED for material from *My Early Life: A Roving Commission*, Copyright 1930 Charles Scribner's Sons, Renewal Copyright © 1958 Winston Churchill, and from *The World Crisis,* Volumes I and IV, Copyright 1923, 1927 Charles Scribner's Sons, Renewal Copyright 1951, 1955 Winston S. Churchill. G. P. PUTNAM'S SONS for *Blood, Sweat and Tears,* Copyright 1941 by Winston Churchill.

Edited, designed, and produced by the staff of The Viking Press under the direction of Bryan Holme, with special assistance from Catharine Carver, Katharine Tweed, Nicolas Ducrot, Christopher Harris, Mary Kopecky, Jane Turner, Beatrice Trueblood, Pamela J. Robertson, Jean I. Russell.

Special thanks are due to the following individuals and organizations for assistance in photographic research and preparation of caption material: *New York:* Milton Davidson, Underwood & Underwood; Ruth Isaacs, British Information Services Library; Elizabeth B. Drewry, Raymond H. Corry, Paul J. McLaughlin, and Clarice D. Morris, Franklin D. Roosevelt Library, Hyde Park; Helen Ruskell, New York Society Library; David Strout and the Hallmark Gallery; Mrs. Harrie George, Philip George Associates; John Looney, United Press International. *London:* Charles Pick and Roland Gant, William Heinemann Ltd.; Rathbone and Naomi Holme; Mark Boxer; Doris R. Bryen; J. F. Golding and the staff of the photo library, Imperial War Museum; Miss D. M. Moss, Radio Times Hulton Picture Library.

Library of Congress catalog card number: 65-23956

Printed in the U.S.A. by Herst Litho, Inc., in Magnavure; colour plates made under the supervision of J. H. Masui Associates, La Conversion, Switzerland, and printed in the U.S.A. by Davis, Delaney Inc.; binding by The Book Press.

Contents

Tribute to Sir Winston Churchill by Lord Butler of Saffron Walden	7
The Great Deliverer	11
The Churchill Line of Descent	15
I. A Statesman in the Making: 1874-1913	16
II. World Crisis and Aftermath: 1914-1935	56
III. The Second World War: 1936-1945	89
IV. The Shaping of the Future: 1945-1965	179
Epilogue: January 30, 1965	239
Attendance at the Funeral Service	257
Chronological Summary of the Life of Sir Winston Churchill	260
Churchill's Books and Speeches	261
Photographic Credits	262
Index	263

Tribute to Sir Winston Churchill

I served Sir Winston Churchill throughout the whole of his two periods as Prime Minister and also during his period of Opposition, when he asked me to formulate the policy-making for our Party. During these fifteen years it was like living under an enormous spreading tree, and enjoying the shelter and the strength which came from his vast might.

I cannot write of Sir Winston as one of his generals or immediate collaborators in the war although, as a member of his wartime Government, I was able to value what Lord Attlee described as his unique gifts as a war leader. Lord Attlee has compared him to Oliver Cromwell and Lord Chatham. He vied with the one as a strategist and with the other as an orator and national leader. Those whom he inspired in the Navy, Army, and Air Force knew that his life had been dedicated to learning and understanding the art of war.

I fought Churchill on the Indian issue in the 1930's. This increased rather than dimmed our friendship. When I joined him in the fateful year 1940, I was Under Secretary at the Foreign Office, and in that position had the privilege of meeting him frequently. Indeed, on one occasion, I remember his striding up and down the garden of No. 10, Downing Street, while rehearsing his world famous speech, "We shall fight on the beaches". By the time his great speeches were delivered they had been frequently rehearsed, committed to paper and then learned by heart. Aneurin Bevan, himself perhaps the greatest socialist orator, thought the speeches would burn their mark into the records of history even more deeply than they moved his hearers. I would say that Churchill's voice in his broadcasts not only put a ramrod down the backs of his own countrymen but sustained and comforted the subject peoples of Europe.

Judging from the minutes addressed to his colleagues in the Government (and these are attached to his war memoirs), Churchill was a fierce Prime Minister. But I think his most loved characteristic was the manner in which he got together with his friends to make up any quarrel engendered by his determined manner.

As a war leader he steadily forbore from interfering with the detailed conduct of the war by the Chiefs of Staff. He knew that he was not a general himself and he did not attempt to be. But on the vital occasions, such as the eve of the Battle of El Alamein, he himself intervened and appointed Montgomery to win the battle. He told me on many an occasion that a proper war leader should not attempt to be a general himself. One can read in Lord Alanbrooke's memoirs and elsewhere how pathetically pleased he was, in either of the Great Wars, to be asked to the front by the general commanding.

He always relished danger, and this is true of his remarkable early life, his charge at Omdurman, his gallantry and courage which came through in all his activities whether in peace or war.

Not enough is written about Winston Churchill's record in home affairs. He had a singularly distinguished period at the Board of Trade in his early Liberal days. This will be remembered alike by the trade unions and the trading community.

I remember well when I introduced my first Budget in 1952 how he besought me to introduce "compassion" for the old age pensioners. The very morning I delivered the speech he telephoned me and said, "Remember the compassion. I am thinking of what my father, Lord Randolph, intended for the working people of this country." He was desperately anxious to justify his father's record, and bitter against those who had criticized or opposed Lord Randolph. His life of his father stands out as one of the great biographies of the language, written before Winston Churchill had perfected his rounded style but illustrating his power of handling a mass of material.

His attitude to social affairs was well summed up in his broadcast in 1943. He asked me to help him with this, since I was then busy at work on the Education Act. He showed his intense interest in the young people of the country, many of whose first enterprises "started so fair and ended so foul". He saw the advantage of reframing the whole education system of the country as the bombs were falling. He was confident of victory, and felt with Disraeli that on the future education of Great Britain the greatness of the country depended. His sole fear of the Education Act was that we should get into controversies as fierce as those of 1902, when the religious issue led to bitter division between the Parties. When, in the wartime Coalition Government, I arranged a settlement of the religious issue Churchill was deeply grateful.

It is as well to remember these aspects of so many-sided a man. His second period as Prime Minister, in which he was chiefly involved in matters of interest on the home front, ended in April 1955. He did not resign as was expected on his eightieth birthday, after the simple and moving ceremony in Westminster Hall when Graham Sutherland's portrait was presented to him. His last speech as Prime Minister was on the subject of the H bomb. He concluded with the characteristic words, "Meanwhile, never flinch, never weary, never despair".

Unfamiliar as they were, I believe he enjoyed his years of retirement. He finished his *History of the English Speaking Peoples,* thereby putting a seal on his reputation as a Nobel Prize Winner for Literature.

On April 9th, 1963, Sir Winston was proclaimed an Honorary Citizen of the United States, "Son of America though a subject of Britain", and President Kennedy paid tribute to a "Champion of liberty who, serving six monarchs of his native Great Britain, has served all men's freedom and dignity".

This, framed against the backcloth of his classic funeral ceremony, is the best epitaph for Churchill. He knew that Britain's destiny was and is indissolubly tied with that of America. His whole life was dedicated to perpetuating that fusion.

Churchill was great in everything which he undertook, as statesman, orator, writer, painter, and exponent of the art of friendship. Those of us who lived with him live on inspired by his words, "In War: Resolution; in Defeat: Defiance; in Victory: Magnanimity; in Peace: Good Will".

March, 1965
              LORD BUTLER OF SAFFRON WALDEN,
                  P.C., C.H., M.A., F.R.G.S.,
                     formerly Mr. R. A. Butler

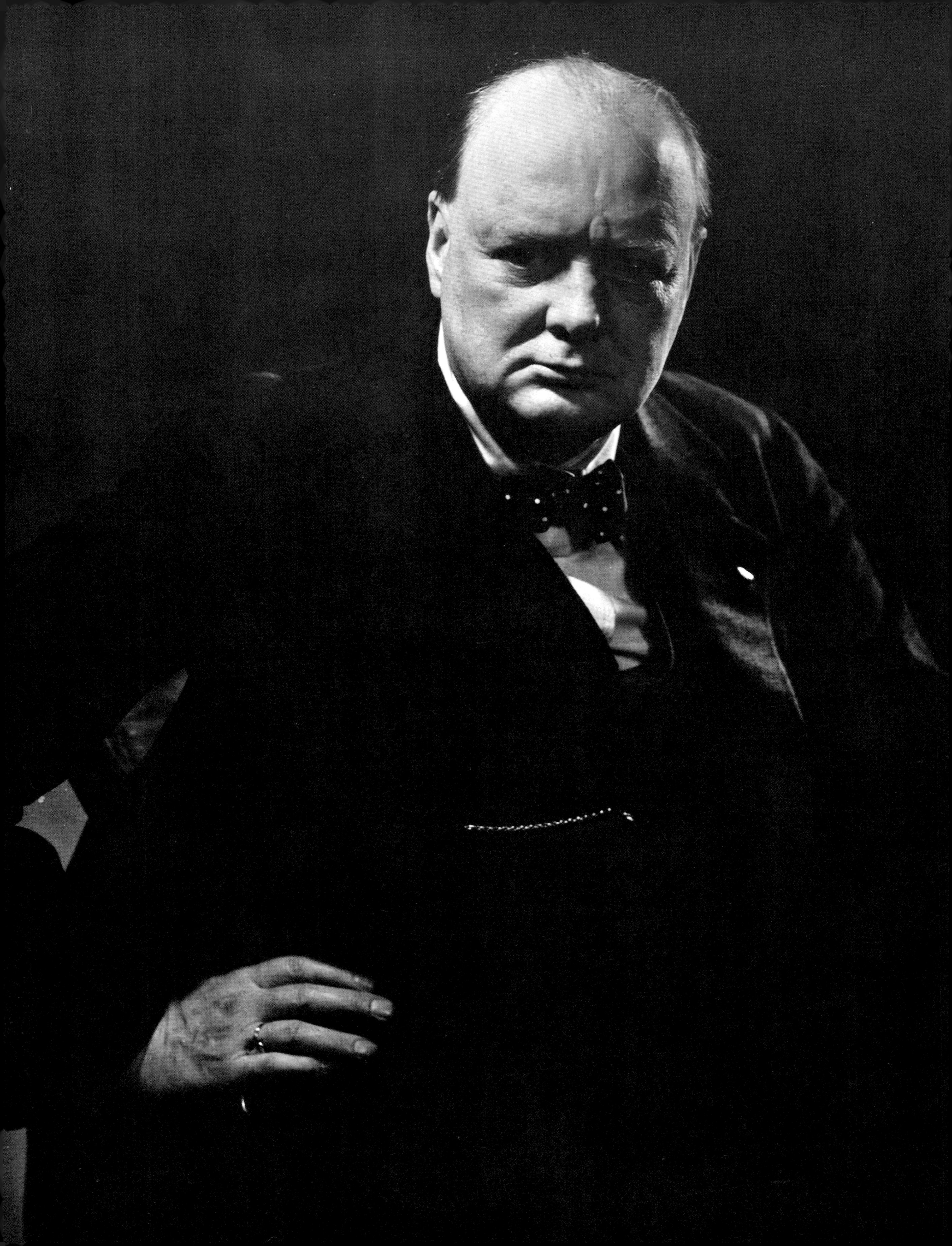

THE GREAT DELIVERER

"And he died in a good old age, full of days, riches, and honour."

There is a patriarchal grandeur and completeness about the life of Sir Winston Churchill such as the Chronicler saw in the career of King David, who had leapt into fame while still a stripling, had contended in the forefront of domestic conflict, had led a united people against overwhelming odds, had never faltered, never lost faith in their cause and their destiny, and came out with them at last into a little space of tranquillity before the end. He drank delight of battle, whether with shot and shell against the forces of tyranny that he hated, or in the bloodless contests of the Parliament he loved; but he never struck a foul blow. He outlived all his enemies, save the very many whom he converted into friends. None of those with whom he was from time to time at issue has any power, or today any wish, to diminish his towering stature. He is secure of his fame among the great deliverers. He belongs to his country; he belongs to the Commonwealth; he belongs to the world; and now he belongs to the ages.

"His personality", as Bagehot said of Palmerston, "was a power." "Winston is back", cabled the Admiralty to the King's ships at sea in September, 1939; and from the outset the Germans recognized as clearly as did the Navy that here was the dauntless and implacable enemy of all their designs. Around him, as one by one the free peoples were swept into the whirlpool of total war, the greatest leaders of the United Nations gathered and declared their faith. With far less material force at his back than either of his partners at the head of the alliance, he could match the authority of Roosevelt even in the Capitol and carry the same prestige of leadership in war and politics to Moscow. He stood at the very heart and centre of the confederacy for freedom, as the younger Pitt once stood; and he has this in common with Pitt, that he had the capacity and the ambition to be a great peace Minister, had not his times summoned him to the direction of war. He shared with his senior colleague Lloyd George the honour of founding the welfare state. When his own time for pre-eminence came, his ascendancy over his colleagues was greater than that even Pitt achieved.

In that respect, as in much else, his closer affinity is with Pitt's father, the Great Commoner. Like Chatham he was ardent and imperious, spoke with a commanding force that gave to his very words the quality of deeds, embodied the vigour and resolve of a supreme national tradition and, drawing his strength from the contemporary life of his people, possessed the genius to interpret that people to itself and then to address the world with its authentic voice. He controlled every faculty of the orator, from the majestic and moving appeal to the imagination, to the forcefulness of direct, unadorned and even colloquial trenchancy. He could use the homeliest language without ever descending below the level of the grand style. His dramatic instinct gave him an impeccable sense of timing and contrast: he could draw even the unseen audience of his broadcasts into a sense of active communion with himself. His speeches will live, and not only in the memory of his contemporaries still under the spell of glowing phrases. Never has the spoken word taken the colour of a greater cause or served it more decisively. In the hour when all but courage failed, Churchill made courage conscious of itself, plumed it with defiance and rendered it invincible.

No War Minister in British history has brought to his task the training and experience with which Churchill was armed. He began, like Chatham, as a cornet of horse, and, unlike Chatham, had led his men in battle. He remained a lifelong student and critic of war, whose estimates were sharpened by the memory of war itself. His insight into strategy, which no civilian statesman has rivalled, was proved in his monumental biography of his ancestor, the greatest of English soldiers. His military sense and spirit were exercised not only in two world wars but in preparation for them both. It was mainly due to the memorable partnership of Churchill and Prince Louis of Battenberg at the Admiralty that the Navy was ready in 1914; it was no fault of a statesman in the wilderness, who spared no exertion to give warning of a greater menace than the Kaiser's, that the nation was unready in 1938 and 1939. In both conflicts he planned greater enterprises of offensive war which challenged controversy and led to his being accused of meddling with matters beyond his comprehension. But, on the whole, military historians of the First World War have confirmed Churchill's judgment, holding that the defence of Antwerp made victory possible on the Marne, and that the abortive attack on the Dardanelles, if it had been prosecuted according to Churchill's own design, might have deflected the whole course of war. On his conduct of the latter conflict, which he directed, so far as his allies would permit, on Chatham's principle of holding the enemy in the grip of sea power and using it to sap their strength at the remoter fringes of their dominion, the verdict is still in suspense. All the world now knows, what only a few in places of high responsibility knew at the time, that his apparently effortless authority over the whole conduct of war was in fact exercised through a daily conflict of wills with his chief professional advisers, who on occasion opposed him not only on tactical detail but on major strategic principle. Whether risks were needlessly taken, whether victory could have been achieved at less cost in blood and treasure, whether a different kind of victory, leaving a better world order than we now enjoy, might by other means than Churchill's have been won—these are questions that cannot yet be finally answered. What cannot be doubted is that the nation's ablest captains of war, the men whom Churchill chose as supreme commanders and staff officers and whose choice the fact of victory and the consensus of their professions have ratified, including the men whose day-to-day differences with the Prime Minister have been most canvassed, were all agreed that they would rather suffer the strain of constant disagreement with their political chief, and see their skilled advice overruled even in matters of strategical life and death, than accept the direction of any other man.

Churchill's demonic energy and driving power seemed only to increase with the advancing years. His long journeys to Washington, Quebec, Moscow, Casablanca, Yalta, Cairo and Teheran, which contributed decisively to the war effort and to the unity of the alliance, would have taxed a much younger man. Yet he was not careless of his strength. His working day—and night—may have been the despair at times of colleagues who ordered their lives by a more conventional time-table. It was, however, well designed to conserve his physical and mental energies. It was popularly supposed that a man so incisive in action must have a corresponding power of quick decision. On the contrary, Churchill was cautious in his approach to the greater problems, and sometimes his hesitation imposed irksome delays on men of quicker if narrower judgment. At times he could be intolerant of opposition and resentful of even friendly criticism. But he had a right to masterful ways, even if he had not constantly disarmed his opponents by inviting them to share a sly smile at his own expense.

Not the least endearing of his qualities was an individual sense of humour engagingly mischievous at times, and part of that eternal youth of which he seemed to have been granted the secret. Over the House of Commons in wartime he established an ascendancy that no other statesman of his day approached. Yet with all his feeling for the great institution of Parliament, and with all his deep loyalty to its tradition and purpose, he was never the complete master of the mood of British politics. He had been known—and that long before the catastrophe in the election of 1945—profoundly to misjudge the people whose undisputed leader he was to become. There came, however, a season when, rising above himself and identifying himself with them and their whole history, he was the inspiration of their national resistance at its greatest. He drew his incomparable courage from all he knew and felt about the British people, and at that tremendous climax he gave it back in fullest measure. He became one with his country as few Englishmen since Alfred had been —and as Washington had been one with that other nation of Englishmen to whom he was so proud to be affiliated. It is as a great Englishman that he will hold his imperishable place in the history of the Empire and the world. Never will the name of Winston Churchill be separable from the "finest hour", from the pride and heroism of 1940.

Yet even as he led his country and the Empire through the shadows of total disaster towards the light of victory, he was aware that they were advancing into a world in which patriotism, even imperial patriotism, was not enough. The sense of dedication to something larger than this, which had sustained him as with Roosevelt he formulated the terms of the Atlantic Charter and the United Nations, enabled him to bear what seemed to him the bitterness of ingratitude when the British electorate, in deciding to whom to entrust the vast, intricate and crucial business of reconstruction, turned abruptly from the man to whom, more than anyone, they owed their freedom to choose. It was not in his character to withdraw from the battle to the tranquil role of an elder statesman in the House of Lords: he would continue in the thick of the political conflict until he could win back the confidence of his countrymen. But meanwhile, if he was not permitted to lead his country, he could still lead the world. The authority of his name was international, and he used it internationally. He had always been at heart a romantic, and now he was inspired by the romantic vision of the Europe that might be, of the harmony of the English-speaking nations that must be, if the practical choice of life or death for western civilization, the threats to which he understood better than any man, was to be surmounted. The great speeches in which he turned the thoughts of Europeans and Americans to the idea of giving concrete shape and organization to their common inheritance, though they were not of a kind to yield a full harvest in a short term of years, may yet come to be remembered in the perspective of the ages as being equal to his grandest services to his own time. The sense of communion in the larger movement of humanity remained with him while he continued to lead his party in Opposition; and when he was at last called back to power his deepest thinking remained devoted to the building, in a darkening international atmosphere, of combinations for peace comparable with the Grand Alliance that had won the war, and to finding a way for western civilization as a whole to come to terms with the antipathetic civilization that had arisen in the east.

This romantic-practical hope was the chief preoccupation of his last political years; one other element of romance had inspired him always, his intensely personal dedication to the service of the Throne. The distant devotion he had felt for the venerable Queen who had given him his first commission, nourished through half a century of service to four successive royal masters, was laid in warmest affection and loyalty at the feet of the young girl to whom he surrendered his last charge; and when with the tendance of his vast public experience he had guided her first steps and seen her taken to the heart of all her peoples, his public work was done. By her, when the end was in sight, he was admitted into the noble fellowship of the Order of the Garter. He had been offered the same great honour by King George VI on the morrow of his electoral defeat; but Winston Churchill did not accept consolation prizes. Yet this, to his romantic heart, was a prized and appropriate reward, for it set him in the immemorial tradition of the worthies of England, installed him beneath "armoury of the invincible knights of old", and wedded to the splendour of their achievements his own services to country and Commonwealth, in peace and war, in office and out of office, in counsel, speech, and action, in politics and in literature. He dies sure of his majestic place in history, and leaves to his countrymen a name inseparable from their proudest and bravest memories.

The Churchill Line of Descent

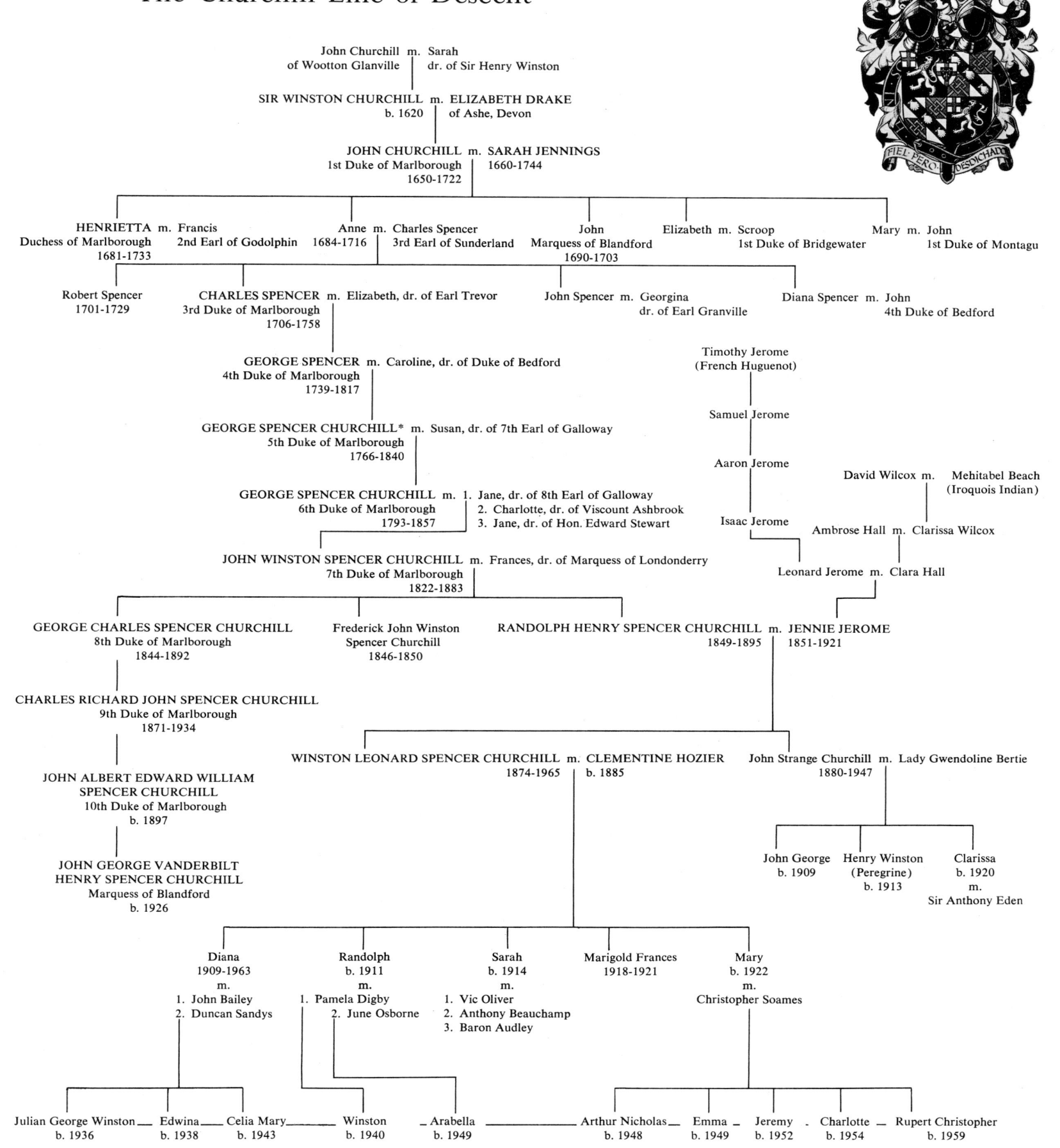

John Churchill m. Sarah
of Wootton Glanville | dr. of Sir Henry Winston

SIR WINSTON CHURCHILL m. ELIZABETH DRAKE
b. 1620 | of Ashe, Devon

JOHN CHURCHILL m. SARAH JENNINGS
1st Duke of Marlborough | 1660-1744
1650-1722

- HENRIETTA m. Francis
  Duchess of Marlborough — 2nd Earl of Godolphin
  1681-1733
- Anne m. Charles Spencer
  1684-1716 — 3rd Earl of Sunderland
- John
  Marquess of Blandford
  1690-1703
- Elizabeth m. Scroop
  1st Duke of Bridgewater
- Mary m. John
  1st Duke of Montagu

Robert Spencer
1701-1729

CHARLES SPENCER m. Elizabeth, dr. of Earl Trevor
3rd Duke of Marlborough
1706-1758

John Spencer m. Georgina
dr. of Earl Granville

Diana Spencer m. John
4th Duke of Bedford

GEORGE SPENCER m. Caroline, dr. of Duke of Bedford
4th Duke of Marlborough
1739-1817

GEORGE SPENCER CHURCHILL* m. Susan, dr. of 7th Earl of Galloway
5th Duke of Marlborough
1766-1840

GEORGE SPENCER CHURCHILL m. 1. Jane, dr. of 8th Earl of Galloway
6th Duke of Marlborough   2. Charlotte, dr. of Viscount Ashbrook
1793-1857   3. Jane, dr. of Hon. Edward Stewart

JOHN WINSTON SPENCER CHURCHILL m. Frances, dr. of Marquess of Londonderry
7th Duke of Marlborough
1822-1883

Timothy Jerome
(French Huguenot)

Samuel Jerome

Aaron Jerome

David Wilcox m. Mehitabel Beach
(Iroquois Indian)

Isaac Jerome

Ambrose Hall m. Clarissa Wilcox

Leonard Jerome m. Clara Hall

- GEORGE CHARLES SPENCER CHURCHILL
  8th Duke of Marlborough
  1844-1892
- Frederick John Winston
  Spencer Churchill
  1846-1850
- RANDOLPH HENRY SPENCER CHURCHILL m. JENNIE JEROME
  1849-1895 | 1851-1921

CHARLES RICHARD JOHN SPENCER CHURCHILL
9th Duke of Marlborough
1871-1934

WINSTON LEONARD SPENCER CHURCHILL m. CLEMENTINE HOZIER
1874-1965 | b. 1885

John Strange Churchill m. Lady Gwendoline Bertie
1880-1947

JOHN ALBERT EDWARD WILLIAM
SPENCER CHURCHILL
10th Duke of Marlborough
b. 1897

- John George
  b. 1909
- Henry Winston
  (Peregrine)
  b. 1913
- Clarissa
  b. 1920
  m.
  Sir Anthony Eden

JOHN GEORGE VANDERBILT
HENRY SPENCER CHURCHILL
Marquess of Blandford
b. 1926

- Diana
  1909-1963
  m.
  1. John Bailey
  2. Duncan Sandys
- Randolph
  b. 1911
  m.
  1. Pamela Digby
  2. June Osborne
- Sarah
  b. 1914
  m.
  1. Vic Oliver
  2. Anthony Beauchamp
  3. Baron Audley
- Marigold Frances
  1918-1921
- Mary
  b. 1922
  m.
  Christopher Soames

Julian George Winston — Edwina — Celia Mary — Winston — Arabella — Arthur Nicholas — Emma — Jeremy — Charlotte — Rupert Christopher
b. 1936 | b. 1938 | b. 1943 | b. 1940 | b. 1949 | b. 1948 | b. 1949 | b. 1952 | b. 1954 | b. 1959

* Authorized in 1817 to use the name of Churchill in addition to that of Spencer, to perpetuate the surname of the 1st Duke. (Some members of the family used the hyphenated form, Spencer-Churchill.)

I

A Statesman in the Making: 1874-1913

Sir Winston Churchill, who died at his London home on Sunday, January 24, 1965, led Great Britain from the peril of subjugation by the Nazi tyranny to victory; and during the last four years of his active political life he directed his country's efforts to maintain peace with honour, to resist another tyranny, and to avert a war more terrible than the last. In character, intellect, and talent he had the attributes of greatness.

An indifferent schoolboy, he was indifferent at nothing else which he attempted. Inheriting Lord Randolph Churchill's energy and political fearlessness, and being granted almost twice as many years, he carried to fulfilment a genius that in his father showed only brilliant promise. As a leader of men and multitudes, strategist, statesman of high authority in the councils of nations, orator with a command of language that matched the grandeur of his themes, able parliamentary tactician, master of historical narrative, his renown is assured so long as the story of these lands is told.

The great war leader of his age, he lived through the fastest transformation of warfare the world has ever known, charging with the 21st Lancers at Omdurman in his youth, and in his old age arming his country with the hydrogen bomb.

He first entered Parliament in the sixty-fourth year of the reign of Queen Victoria. Sixty-four years later, in the thirteenth year of the reign of her great-great-granddaughter, he retired from it. Through more than half a century of British history there was not a year —barely a month—in which he was not actively and prominently engaged in public affairs.

Churchill's outstanding political virtue, which never deserted him, was his courage.

"At Blenheim I took two very important decisions: to be born and to marry. I am happily content with the decisions I took on both those occasions." Blenheim Palace (OPPOSITE), birthplace of Sir Winston Churchill, the gift of Queen Anne to the first Duke of Marlborough.

Anne, Queen of Great Britain and Ireland (1665–1714)

John Churchill, first Duke of Marlborough, K.G. (1650–1722)

The Great Hall (ABOVE) in the vast palace Vanbrugh designed for the Victor of Blenheim. TOP RIGHT: Tapestries in the Second State Room. BOTTOM RIGHT: The Red Drawing Room, with portraits by Reynolds and others.

18

"Thanks, Sir, cry'd I, 'tis very fine
But where d'ye sleep, or where d'ye dine?"
wrote Dr. Abel Evans of Blenheim. ABOVE: The Saloon, with murals by Laguerre and carvings by Grinling Gibbons.

There was the sheer physical courage which led him to seek more risks on active service before he was 25 than many professional soldiers know in a lifetime; and which gave him the will, when he was past 75, to overcome an affliction which would have laid other men low from the start. But there was moral and intellectual courage in equal degree. He served in Kitchener's Army in the Sudan—but attacked Kitchener publicly for his desecration of the Mahdi's tomb. He was returned as a Conservative in the "Khaki Election" of 1900—only to devote a passage in his maiden speech to a generous tribute to the Boers. No sooner was his maiden speech over than he shocked the Conservative front bench again by turning on one of his own party leaders, the Secretary of State for War, with a scorn which would have been startling even in a member of the Opposition.

He was still under 30 when, finding himself at odds with the tariff reform policy of Joseph Chamberlain, he crossed the Floor of the House. So it continued all through his life —the habit of following his own judgment, his own intuition, and his own impulses. When he resigned from the Conservative "Shadow Cabinet" in 1931, as a protest against its attitude to India, he was acting with the same courage and independence which—they were inherited from his father—he had displayed from the very beginning. His independence frequently baffled his contemporaries, who tended to conclude, as did Margot Asquith in 1908, that he was a man of "transitory convictions". But the point is not that they were transitory but that they were his own. His mind was always restlessly surveying the political scene. He was for ever testing, courting, encouraging new ideas. No politician of this century has been less conservative and less hidebound.

This adventurousness, of course, had its disadvantages, of which his colleagues were often painfully aware. His mind never stopped roaming, and Asquith's Cabinet was described by one of its members as "very forbearing to his chatter". During the 1939-45 War—as the famous memoranda published as appendices to his history of *The Second World War* show—any question however trivial or however far removed from the central direction of the war might gain his attention. He seized on new ideas so indiscriminately that it became necessary for some of those closest to him to act as a sieve, and so prevent valuable time from being wasted on the wilder schemes. Yet, when the dross had fallen through, there remained in the sieve one or two nuggets. There is in Printing House Square a letter written early in the 1914-18 War by a high personage accusing Churchill of madness because of some impracticable scheme which he was pressing through in the face of much expert opposition. The "scheme" was the tank.

The independence of his ideas always made it difficult to define Churchill's political position. He was more of a Tory than a Conservative. The symbols of Toryism—Crown, Country, Empire—which might seem abstractions to some were to him realities. There was, indeed, always a personal element in the service he gave to his Sovereigns, which found quite different expressions in his attitude to the abdication of Edward VIII and in the tributes he paid when George VI died and Queen Elizabeth II was crowned. But it was a Toryism infused by another abstraction which to him was equally a reality: the People. He believed deeply that the People existed—not different and warring classes of people. In an earlier age he would have stood committed to the idea of the King and the People

THE ATTRIBUTES OF GREATNESS

"An Italian palace in an English park. The palace is severe in its symmetry and completeness . . . yet there is no violent contrast, no abrupt dividing line between the wildness and freshness of the garden and the pomp of the architecture." OPPOSITE: Blenheim from the air.

against the great Whig magnates—the cardinal principle of Disraelian Toryism. He was, in brief, a Tory Democrat, and in a speech to the Conservative conference in 1953 he proclaimed again the creed of his father, the first prophet of Tory Democracy.

Least of all was he a "Little Englander". No statesman has ever been more aware of his country's position in the world and its responsibility to the world. It was not merely his awareness of the facts of Germany's rearmament which made him speak so clearly from the beginning of the thirties: it was, even more (as befitted a descendant of Marlborough), his fundamental assumption that Britain was a part of Europe. He could no more have talked of Czechoslovakia as a far-away country than of Blenheim and Ramillies as far-away towns.

His politics were infused with a sense of history. It was a common gibe of his opponents that he lived in the past—that he was, in the words of Harold Laski, a "gallant and romantic relic of eighteenth-century imperialism". Nothing could be farther from the truth. He was as aware of the present, its opportunities and its challenges, as any of his contemporaries. But he drew from the past a profound conviction in the greatness of Britain, her people and her heritage. Romantic? It may be. But it was from this reserve that he drew the inspiration which he communicated to his fellow-countrymen in their and his finest hour. He was the symbol of British resistance, but of how much more as well. In his voice spoke the centuries which had made Britain as they had made him, and those who heard him in those days will never forget the echoes of Burghley, of Chatham, of Pitt, and countless more. "The last of the great orators to reach the heights."

BIRTH AND EDUCATION

The Right Honourable Sir Winston Leonard Spencer-Churchill, K.G., O.M., C.H., F.R.S., M.P., was born on St. Andrew's Day, 1874, at Blenheim Palace. He was the elder son of Lord Randolph Churchill and a grandson of the seventh Duke of Marlborough. His mother was the beautiful and talented daughter of Leonard Jerome, a New York businessman. Surviving her husband until 1921, she lived to see her son's fame firmly established.

The year 1874 had been an eventful one for Lord Randolph. Apart from marriage and the birth of a son and heir, it had begun with his election as Conservative M.P. for Woodstock and included a maiden speech which drew from Disraeli, who had a good eye for a duke's son, a warm commendation. Lord Randolph's rise to power and influence was to be rapid, but his decline was even more rapid, and when he died in 1895 he left his son with memories of defeat and failure which carried a moral he was often to remember. Winston Churchill's education was conventional in its pattern: from a preparatory school at Ascot, to a small school at Brighton, to Harrow in 1888, and then, after twice failing to gain admission, to the Royal Military College at Sandhurst. But his verdict on Harrow was individual, for he left there, as he later confessed, convinced that he was "all for the public schools, but I do not want to go there again".

"Where does a family start? It starts with a young man falling in love with a girl. No superior alternative has yet been found." OPPOSITE: Churchill's father, Lord Randolph Churchill, fell in love in 1873 with a beautiful American girl, Jennie Jerome, overcame the objections of his father, the seventh Duke of Marlborough, to the match, and married her the following year. Leonard Jerome, Jennie's father, a stockbroker and sportsman, was part owner of *The New York Times*. Lord Randolph's father—*"the old Duke, the formidable grandpapa, talking loudly to the crowd"*—was Lord President of the Council and Viceroy of Ireland under Disraeli. His brilliant son, who became leader of the House of Commons and in 1886 Chancellor of the Exchequer, *"was of the temper that gallops until it falls"*; his political career was cut short, and he died at 46.

Leonard Jerome (1819–1891)

Lady Randolph Churchill, the former Jennie Jerome

Lord Randolph Churchill

John Winston Spencer Churchill, seventh Duke of Marlborough, K.G. (1822–1883)

BELOW: Winston Churchill, aged 7. "He rather resembles a naughty little bulldog," said his American grandmother. His schoolmates called him "Carrots" because of his red hair.

At Harrow in 1889.

My dear mama
I am so glad
you are coming
to see us I had
such a nice
bathe in the
sea to day.
love to papa
your loving
winston

His first letter to his mother: "She shone for me like the Evening Star."

After three tries, and much cramming in mathematics —"*Depth beyond depth was revealed to me—the Byss and the Abyss*"—he qualified as a cavalry cadet (RIGHT) at the Royal Military College at Sandhurst.

"*I was delighted at the prospect of soldiering on horseback. Also the uniforms of the cavalry were far more magnificent.*" LEFT: At 21, in the full-dress uniform of the 4th Hussars. ABOVE: As a lieutenant attached to the 21st Lancers in the Sudan, 1898.

Queen Victoria breakfasting with her daughters, the Princesses Beatrice and Victoria (LEFT), in 1897, the year of her Diamond Jubilee. BELOW: The Queen's carriage in the City during the Jubilee.

A SOLDIER IN THE FIELD

In 1895, soon after his father's death, he entered the 4th Hussars at Aldershot, and immediately obtained leave to go to Cuba for the *Daily Graphic* to watch the Spanish Army at work. While he was there he participated in the repulse of the insurgents who tried to cross the Spanish line at Trocham. After enjoying the London Season in 1896 he embarked for India, where he relieved the monotony of morning parades and evening polo by indulging his delight in reading. He was back in London for the Season in 1897, and then left in September to join the Malakand Field Force on the North-West Frontier of India. After being mentioned in dispatches for "making himself useful at a critical moment", he had to return to the 4th Hussars at Bangalore early in 1898, and there he occupied himself with the writing of his first history, *The Story of the Malakand Field Force,* which had considerable success at the time and is still consulted.

While he was at Bangalore he also wrote his only novel, *Savrola, a Tale of the Revolution in Laurania,* which he later urged his friends not to read. It contained, however, the sentence which seems to be as autobiographical as any he wrote: "Under any circumstances, in any situation, Savrola knew himself a factor to be reckoned with; whatever the game, he would play it to his amusement, if not to his advantage." During these early years Lieutenant Churchill, enjoying a liberty not likely to be granted nowadays to a serving officer, was able to combine the roles of a soldier and a newspaper correspondent, and it was as the representative of the *Morning Post* that at last, after three rebuffs from Kitchener, he joined the Sirdar's Army in the Sudan. He reached Cairo in time to take part in the advance south into the Mahdi's country, and was present at the final victory at Omdurman.

The strategy, tactics, and what a later generation has learnt to call the logistics of the campaign were set out by Churchill in *The River War, an Account of the Reconquest of the Sudan,* which was immediately successful when it was published in 1899. His early military writings showed a grasp, remarkable in a man of his years, of the operations of war, which was best revealed in the clear separation of the essential from the accidental. They were also distinguished by a dogmatic self-confidence which never hesitated in its criticism of senior officers. His outspokenness did not improve his prospects and he was doubtless wise to resign his commission after wearing the Queen's uniform for only four years. Moreover, his success as a journalist had enabled him to think of giving up the Army as a career, and he had even turned his attention to politics, addressing a Conservative garden party at Bath (his first political speech) and fighting a by-election (unsuccessfully) at Oldham.

It was as a correspondent, again for the *Morning Post,* that he left for South Africa within a fortnight of the outbreak of war in the autumn of 1899. There he met with sensational adventures very much to his taste. Taken prisoner on an armoured train expedition by a Boer by the name of Louis Botha he succeeded in escaping from the prison camp at Pretoria within three weeks, "jumped" a train, and after an extraordinary journey reached Delagoa Bay. He saw the campaign out until he could reenter Pretoria with the victorious Army, and when he returned to England he was received tumultuously at Oldham, where, in the "Khaki Election" of 1900, he won the seat from Walter Runciman. He was not yet 26, and contemporary accounts record that Joseph Chamberlain nudged his neighbour on the front bench when, in his maiden speech, Churchill declared: "If I were a Boer fighting in the field—and if I were a Boer, I hope I should be fighting in the field . . ."

The year of the Queen's Jubilee, Churchill was at Rawalpindi in India:
"*I have got tunes in my head for every war I have been to, and . . . I remember well the songs the soldiers sang.*
　　'Great White Mother, far across the sea,
　　Ruler of the Empire may she ever be.
　　Long may she reign, glorious and free,
　　In the Great White Motherland.'"

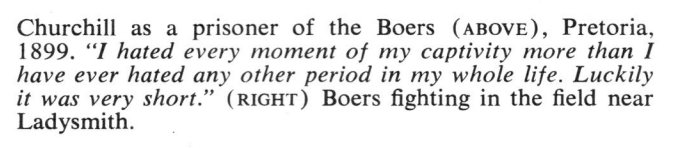

Churchill as a prisoner of the Boers (ABOVE), Pretoria, 1899. *"I hated every moment of my captivity more than I have ever hated any other period in my whole life. Luckily it was very short."* (RIGHT) Boers fighting in the field near Ladysmith.

At Durban, December, 1899, after his spectacular escape from Pretoria. *"I was received as if I had won a great victory. Whirled along on the shoulders of the crowd, I was carried to the steps of the town hall* (LEFT), *where nothing would content them but a speech, which after a becoming reluctance I was induced to deliver* (ABOVE)." Meanwhile, the Boers were offering £25 reward for an Englishman, dead or alive, "about 25 years old, about 5 feet 8 inches tall, indifferent build, walks with a forward stoop, pale appearance, red-brownish hair, small and hardly noticeable moustache, talks through his nose and cannot pronounce the letter 'S' properly." Churchill's own account of his capture and his escape is on the following page.

South Africa, 1899-1900

The Armoured Train: Natal, November 15, 1899

Upwards of forty persons, of whom the greater part were streaming with blood, were crowded on the engine and its tender, and we began to move slowly forward. The shells burst all around, some striking the engine, others dashing the gravel of the track upon it. At last I got down on to the line and went back to find Captain Haldane.

But I had not retraced my steps 200 yards when, instead of Haldane and his company, two figures in plain clothes appeared upon the line. "Plate-layers!" I said to myself, and then with a surge of realization, "Boers!" My mind retains its impression of these tall figures, full of energy, clad in dark, flapping clothes, with slouch, storm-driven hats, poising on their levelled rifles hardly a hundred yards away. I turned again and ran back towards the engine, the two Boers firing as I ran between the metals. Their bullets, sucking to right and left, seemed to miss only by inches. I jigged to the left, and scrambled up the bank. The earth sprang up beside me. I got through the wire fence unhurt. Outside the cutting was a tiny depression. I crouched in this, struggling to get my breath.

About 200 yards away was the rocky gorge of the Blue Krantz River; there was plenty of cover there. I determined to make a dash for the river. I rose to my feet. Suddenly on the other side of the railway, separated from me by the rails and two uncut wire fences, I saw a horseman galloping furiously, a tall, dark figure, holding his rifle in his right hand. He pulled up his horse almost in its own length and shaking the rifle at me shouted a loud command. We were forty yards apart. I thought I could kill this man, and after the treatment I had received I earnestly desired to do so. I put my hand to my belt, my pistol was not there. It came safely home on the engine. I have it now! But at this moment I was quite unarmed. Meanwhile, I suppose in about the time this takes to tell, the Boer horseman, still seated on his horse, had covered me with his rifle. The animal stood stock still, so did he, and so did I. I looked towards the river. The Boer continued to look along his sights. I thought there was absolutely no chance of escape, if he fired he would surely hit me, so I held up my hands and surrendered myself a prisoner of war.

I Escape From the Boers: Pretoria, December 12, 1899

Now or never! I stood on a ledge, seized the top of the wall with my hands, and drew myself up. Twice I let myself down again in sickly hesitation, and then with a third resolve scrambled up and over. My waistcoat got entangled with the ornamental metal-work on the top. I had to pause for an appreciable moment to extricate myself. Then I lowered myself lightly down into the adjoining garden and crouched among the shrubs. I was free! The first step had been taken, and it was irrevocable. I said to myself, *"Toujours de l'audace,"* put my hat on my head, strode into the middle of the garden, walked past the windows of the house without any attempt at concealment, and so went through the gate and turned to the left. I passed the sentry at less than five yards. Most of them knew me by sight. Whether he looked at me or not I do not know, for I never turned my head. I restrained with the utmost difficulty an impulse to run. But after walking a hundred yards and hearing no challenge, I knew I was at large in Pretoria.

I walked on leisurely through the night, humming a tune and choosing the middle of the road. The streets were full of burghers, but they paid no attention to me. Gradually I reached the suburbs, and on a little bridge I sat down to reflect and consider. I was in the heart of the enemy's country. I knew no one to whom I could apply for succour. My escape must be known at dawn. Pursuit would be immediate. Yet all exits were barred. The trains were searched, the line was guarded. But when hope had departed, fear had gone as well. I formed a plan. I would find the Delagoa Bay Railway. Without map or compass, I must follow that in spite of the pickets. I looked at the stars. Orion shone brightly. Scarcely a year before he had guided me when lost in the desert to the banks of the Nile. He had given me water. Now he should lead to freedom. I could not endure the want of either.

from *My Early Life. A Roving Commission* (1930)

BELOW: At Bloemfontein in 1900, in the uniform of the South African Light Horse, in which he served after his return from captivity.

TOP RIGHT: British infantry crossing the Modder River with the aid of lifelines. RIGHT: Canadians storming a kopje near Sunnyside.

Late in 1900, Churchill went on a lecture tour to earn money so that he could devote himself thereafter solely to politics. In December he crossed the Atlantic to lecture in the United States and Canada on his South African adventures and his escape from the Boers.

"My opening lecture in New York was under the auspices of no less a personage than 'Mark Twain' himself (RIGHT). He was now very old and snow-white, and combined with a noble air a most delightful style of conversation. Of course we argued about the war.... I think however I did not displease him; for he was good enough at my request to sign every one of the thirty volumes of his works for my benefit."

LEFT: Fifth Avenue, New York, at the turn of the century. BELOW: Churchill arriving in New York to begin his tour. He found American audiences *"cool and critical, but also urbane and good-natured. . . . A great many of them thought the Boers were in the right."*

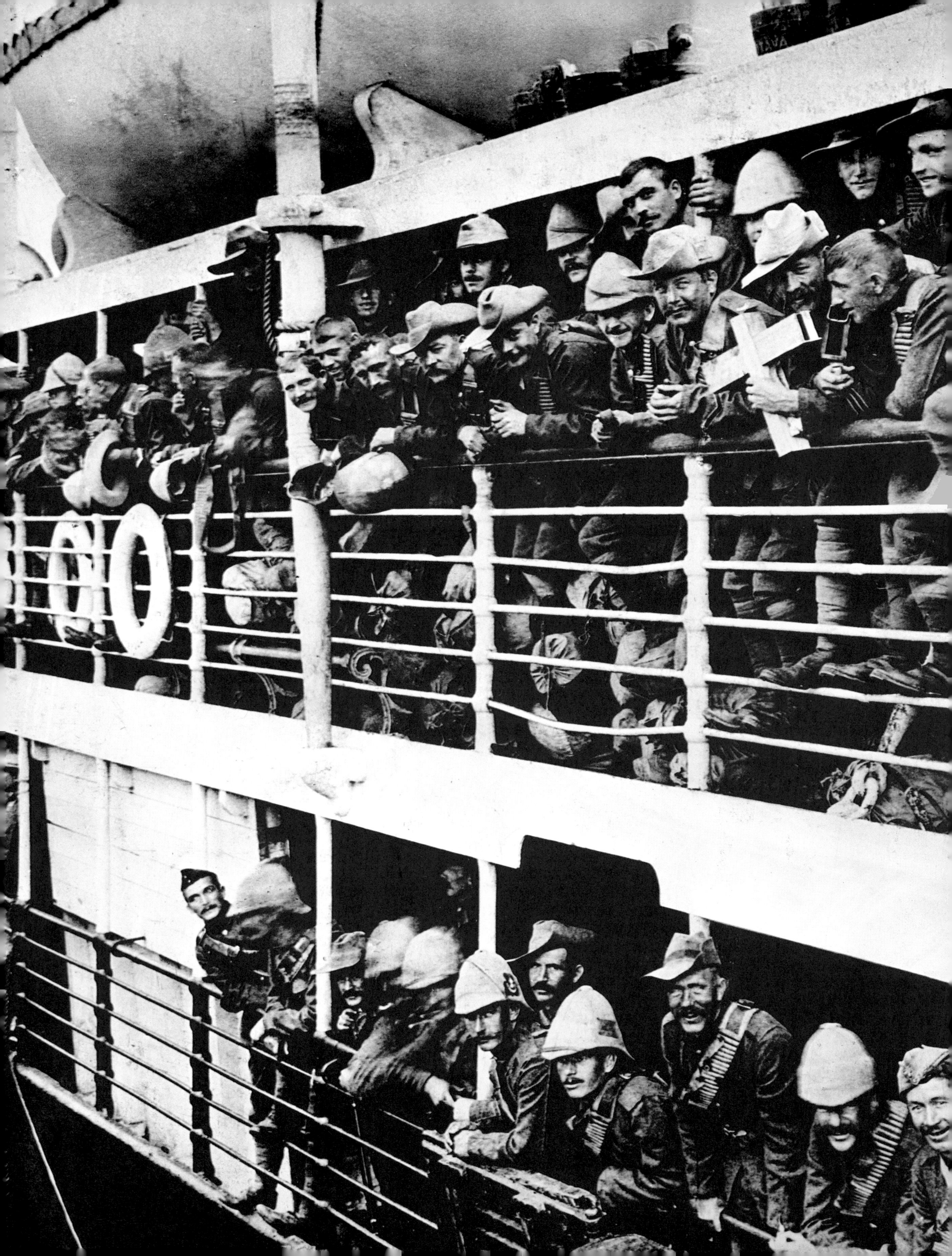

Maiden Speech in the House of Commons, 1901

I understood that the hon. Member [for Caernarvon Boroughs, Mr. D. Lloyd George] to whose speech the House has just listened, had intended to move an Amendment to the Address. The text of the Amendment, which had appeared in the papers, was singularly mild and moderate in tone; but mild and moderate as it was, neither the hon. Member nor his political friends had cared to expose it to criticism or to challenge a division upon it, and, indeed, when we compare the moderation of the Amendment with the very bitter speech which the hon. Member has just delivered, it is difficult to avoid the conclusion that the moderation of the Amendment was the moderation of the hon. Member's political friends and leaders, and that the bitterness of his speech is all his own. It has been suggested to me that it might perhaps have been better, upon the whole, if the hon. Member, instead of making his speech without moving his Amendment, had moved his Amendment without making his speech. . . .

Moreover, I do not believe that the Boers would attach particular importance to the utterances of the hon. Member. No people in the world received so much verbal sympathy and so little practical support as the Boers. If I were a Boer fighting in the field—and if I were a Boer I hope I should be fighting in the field—I would not allow myself to be taken in by any message of sympathy, not even if it were signed by a hundred hon. Members. . . .

I invite the House to consider which form of government—civil government or military government—is most likely to be conducive to the restoration of the vanished prosperity of the country [South Africa] and most likely to encourage the return of the population now scattered far and wide. I understand that there are hon. Members who are in hopes that representative institutions may directly follow military government, but I think they cannot realize thoroughly how very irksome such military government is. I have the greatest respect for British officers, and when I hear them attacked, it makes me very sorry, and very angry too. Although I regard British officers in the field of war, and in dealing with native races, as the best officers in the world, I do not believe that either their training or their habits of thought qualify them to exercise arbitrary authority over civil populations of European race. I have often myself been very much ashamed to see respectable old Boer farmers—the Boer is a curious combination of the squire and the peasant, and under the rough coat of the farmer there are very often to be found the instincts of the squire—to see such men ordered about peremptorily by young subaltern officers, as if they were private soldiers. . . .

I earnestly hope that the right hon. Gentleman the Colonial Secretary will leave nothing undone to bring home to those brave and unhappy men who are fighting in the field that whenever they are prepared to recognize that their small independence must be merged in the larger liberties of the British Empire, there will be a full guarantee for the security of their property and religion, an assurance of equal rights, a promise of representative institutions, and last of all, but not least of all, what the British Army would most readily accord to a brave and enduring foe—all the honours of war. . . .

If the Boers remain deaf to the voice of reason, and blind to the hand of friendship, if they refuse all overtures and disdain all terms, then, while we cannot help admiring their determination and endurance, we can only hope that our own race, in the pursuit of what they feel to be a righteous cause, will show determination as strong and endurance as lasting. . . .

I think if any hon. Members are feeling unhappy about the state of affairs in South Africa I would recommend them a receipt from which I myself derived much exhilaration. Let them look to the other great dependencies and colonies of the British Empire and see what the effect of the war has been there. Whatever we may have lost in doubtful friends in Cape Colony we have gained ten times, or perhaps twenty times, over in Canada and Australia, where the people—down to the humblest farmer in the most distant provinces—have by their effective participation in the conflict been able to realise, as they never could realise before, that they belong to the Empire, and that the Empire belongs to them. I cannot sit down without saying how very grateful I am for the kindness and patience with which the House has heard me, and which have been extended to me, I well know, not on my own account, but because of a certain splendid memory which many hon. Members still preserve.

M. P. at 26: *"I am a child of the House of Commons."*

OPPOSITE: A troopship returning from South Africa.

IN HIS FATHER'S
FOOTSTEPS

Chamberlain was right to take notice of Churchill's maiden speech; its words had an ominous smack, and in his first session in the House not only did Churchill speak vehemently against the Conservative Government's plan for Army reform—and their unfortunate advocate, Mr. Brodrick—but he voted against them as well. His unorthodoxy had deep roots. He was at work on his life of his father, who had remained in a party with whose orthodox leaders he was at war and had suffered in the end only isolation and defeat. At the very beginning of his political career Churchill was in much the same position. He was as much a Tory Democrat as his father, in a party led by Balfour, who had always seemed to Lord Randolph to be the main opponent of Tory Democracy. Moreover, there was little intellectual adventure to be found in the Conservative Party of 1902, and Churchill, who always retained a great respect for the academic and cultured intellect, felt drawn to the company of Morley, Asquith, Haldane, and Grey.

Then, in the summer of 1903, Joseph Chamberlain made his great effort to revive protection—"playing Old Harry with all party relations", as Campbell-Bannerman excitedly remarked. With the Duke of Devonshire and Lord Hugh Cecil, Churchill declared himself a Unionist Free Trader, and by September, when it became clear that the Protectionists in the Cabinet had won, he was publicly exclaiming to a meeting at Halifax, "Thank God for the Liberal Party". Not unreasonably, the Oldham Conservative Association took exception to this and disowned him, and in the following year he crossed the floor of the House. How many who were there on that May 31, 1904, could foresee the irony in the incident as Churchill took his seat by the side of none other than David Lloyd George?

Before the end of 1905 Churchill had completed the life of his father. It stands, over half a century later, as one of the most brilliant political biographies of all time. The prose was perhaps never excelled by Churchill—later in his life the influence of the platform and the House of Commons made his prose too rhetorical—and the bringing to life of the political scene is so vividly and precisely done that the reader never loses his interest.

No sooner was this work of filial vindication done than Balfour—after months of trying to pacify his party and the House by "expressing no settled conviction where no settled conviction exists"—threw in his hand, and Campbell-Bannerman took office. Churchill accepted the office of Under-Secretary of State for the Colonies and was the spokesman of his department in the House of Commons. A month later, at the general election, Churchill was returned as a Liberal for North West Manchester—while Balfour was defeated in the adjacent seat. In the House it fell to him to maintain the Government's decision to grant full self-government to the annexed Boer Republics—a controversial issue—and he began to develop his parliamentary style in the thick of a major parliamentary battle. At the same time his mind was moving to a new outlook on home affairs. Before leaving the Conservative Party he had looked back to the time "when it was not the sham it is now, and was not afraid to deal with the problem of the working classes". Now he confidently declared that the Liberal Party's cause was "the cause of the left-out millions".

The Member for Oldham in 1904 (OPPOSITE), the year he crossed the Floor to join the Liberals.

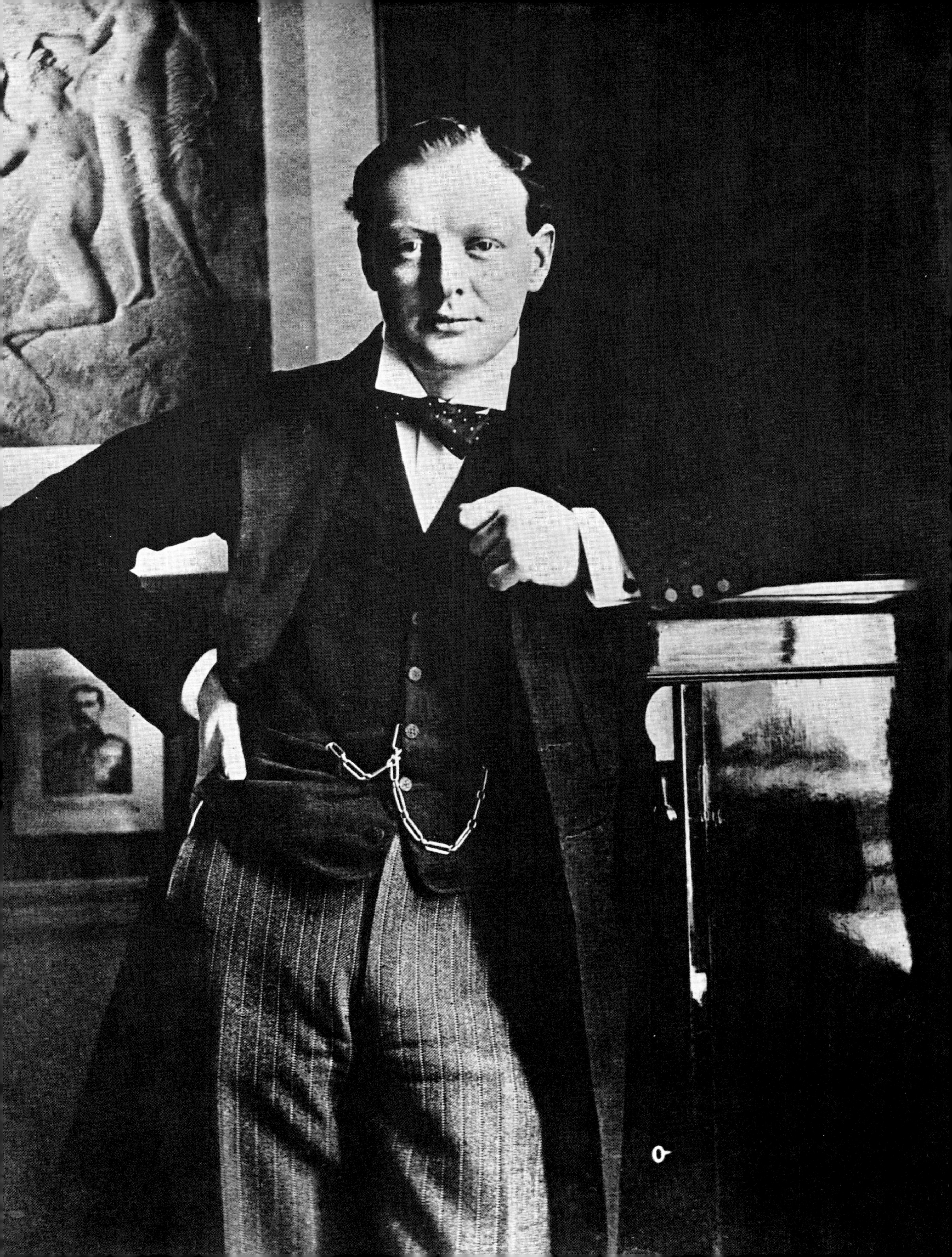

As Under-Secretary of State for the Colonies (BELOW), he did not have Cabinet rank; when he was offered it, as President of the Board of Trade in Asquith's Government, he had to stand in a by-election at North West Manchester. He toured the constituency in a motor-car fitted with a small ladder by which he climbed to the roof to address voters (RIGHT). *"The contest was unusually difficult, and all the forces hostile to the Government concentrated upon one of its most aggressive representatives."* He lost, but won a seat for Dundee.

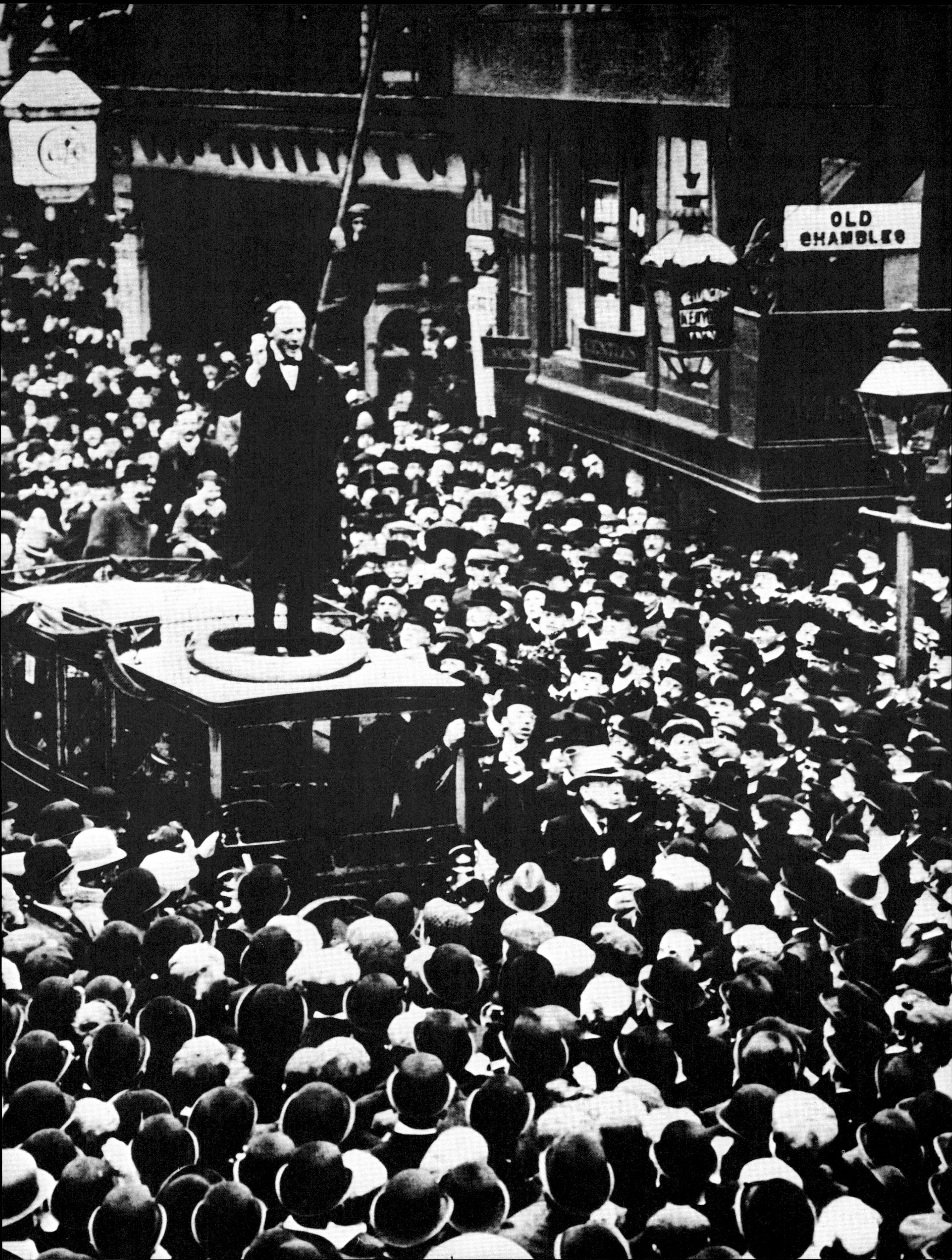
OLD
CHAMBLES

MARRIAGE AND
A PROMOTION

He was a Radical, describing the obstructive attitude of the House of Lords as "something very like an incitement to violence". In 1908, when Asquith succeeded Campbell-Bannerman, Churchill was promoted to the Cabinet as Lloyd George's successor at the Board of Trade, having turned down the Local Government Board on the ground that he refused "to be shut up in a soup-kitchen with Mrs. Sidney Webb". Under the law then still in force his promotion forced him to submit himself for reelection and a tempestuous by-election ended in his defeat by Mr. Joynson-Hicks. But he was found a seat at Dundee, and he returned to London, his official career uninterrupted, to marry Miss Clementine Hozier.

"My marriage was much the most fortunate and joyous event which happened to me in the whole of my life." BELOW: Arriving at Caxton Hall to get his marriage licence.

ABOVE: Churchill and his fiancée, the beautiful 23-year-old Clementine Hozier. OPPOSITE PAGE, BOTTOM LEFT: With his best man, Lord Hugh Cecil, at St. Margaret's for the wedding, September 12, 1908.

Edward VII's wedding present to the new President of the Board of Trade was a gold-mounted walking stick engraved with the Marlborough arms. LEFT: The King (right) with Queen Alexandra; the Princess of Wales, who became Queen Mary; and Prince Albert, later George VI. Earlier, Churchill had shocked the courtiers at Windsor by appearing in a cutaway (BELOW) when the King made him a Privy Councillor, shortly before he set off to tour the African colonies.

Clementine Churchill, 1910.

At a pheasant shoot, 1910.

A LEADING MEMBER OF THE GOVERNMENT

In the political field he became a less conspicuous figure in the House of Commons, but in the country was second only to Lloyd George in his advocacy of the new Liberalism. A natural association developed between these two dissimilar men. Side by side they tried to check the rising naval expenditure, for, war-leaders though they were both to be, in 1908-09 their whole interest was focused on the first experiments in the "welfare state".

Churchill hesitated for a moment when Lloyd George introduced his People's Budget in 1909, but then threw himself into the fight in the country. Bitterly he denounced the House of Lords—especially the backwoods peers "all revolving the problems of Empire and Epsom"—and as president of the Budget League he enthusiastically praised the social policies which had made the Budget necessary. There were Conservatives who, though they could have overlooked his treason to his party in 1904, never could forgive his treason to his class, as they saw it, in 1909. They were later to have their revenge. He was now becoming—though still only 35—one of the leading members of the Government. In Cabinet, where one of his colleagues thought him "as long-winded as he was persistent", he distributed long memoranda to the rest of the members on all subjects—however far removed from the affairs of his own department. (In the Board of Trade he was teaching his subordinates the duties which now belong to the Ministry of Labour.) "Winston", recorded Grey, "will very soon become incapable from sheer activity of mind of being anything in a Cabinet but a Prime Minister."

After the bitter general election of 1910 Churchill was promoted to the Home Office, where his interest in the future welfare of prisoners helped to launch the movement for penal reform. But the most famous episode of his term at the Home Office was the Sidney Street "siege", which he characteristically insisted on witnessing personally. Germany's intervention in Morocco had made it imperative to put a term to the controversy over the British naval programme which was dividing the Liberal Party, and Asquith took what proved to be the decisive step of inviting the First Lord of the Admiralty (Reginald McKenna) and the Home Secretary to exchange offices. Churchill went to the Admiralty, with a mandate to maintain the Fleet in constant readiness for war with Germany.

In silk hat and astrakhan-collared overcoat, the Home Secretary takes command (ABOVE) at the battle of Sidney Street, January 3, 1911. Churchill was criticized for helping the police lay siege to a house in London's East End where two Anarchists wanted for murder had barricaded themselves. When his friend C.P.G. Masterman berated him over this, he replied in his characteristic lisp: "Now Charlie. Don't be croth. It was such fun."

RIGHT: On his way to the House of Commons with Lloyd George, who had become his mentor and model. *"Naturally such a man greatly influenced me."* They were to work together, *"not indeed without differences . . . but in practically continuous association, for nearly twenty years."*

BELOW: Churchill and his cousin, the Duke of Marlborough, at Buckingham Palace after the death of Edward VII, 1910.

The Churchills at the Coronation of George V, June 22, 1911.

Edward, Prince of Wales, and his sister Mary (ABOVE) at the Coronation of their father. The reign of George V (RIGHT, with Queen Mary in their Coronation portrait), from 1910 to 1936, *"was one of the most important and memorable in the whole range of English history."*

Westminster Bridge, decorated for the Coronation of George V, June, 1911. RIGHT: Indian princes, in England for the Coronation, at Hampton Court.

Their Majesties King George and Queen Mary at a Durbar in Delhi, during their visit to India, 1912.

At Portsmouth, February, 1912, the First Lord of the Admiralty awaits the return of his Sovereigns.

Speaking (RIGHT) to a group of Devonians in July, 1912, at an Earl's Court exhibition commemorating the defeat of the Armada; with him (and at his right, ABOVE) is his mother, then Mrs. Cornwallis West, who continued to play an active part in his career. *"We worked together on even terms, more like brother and sister than mother and son."*

48

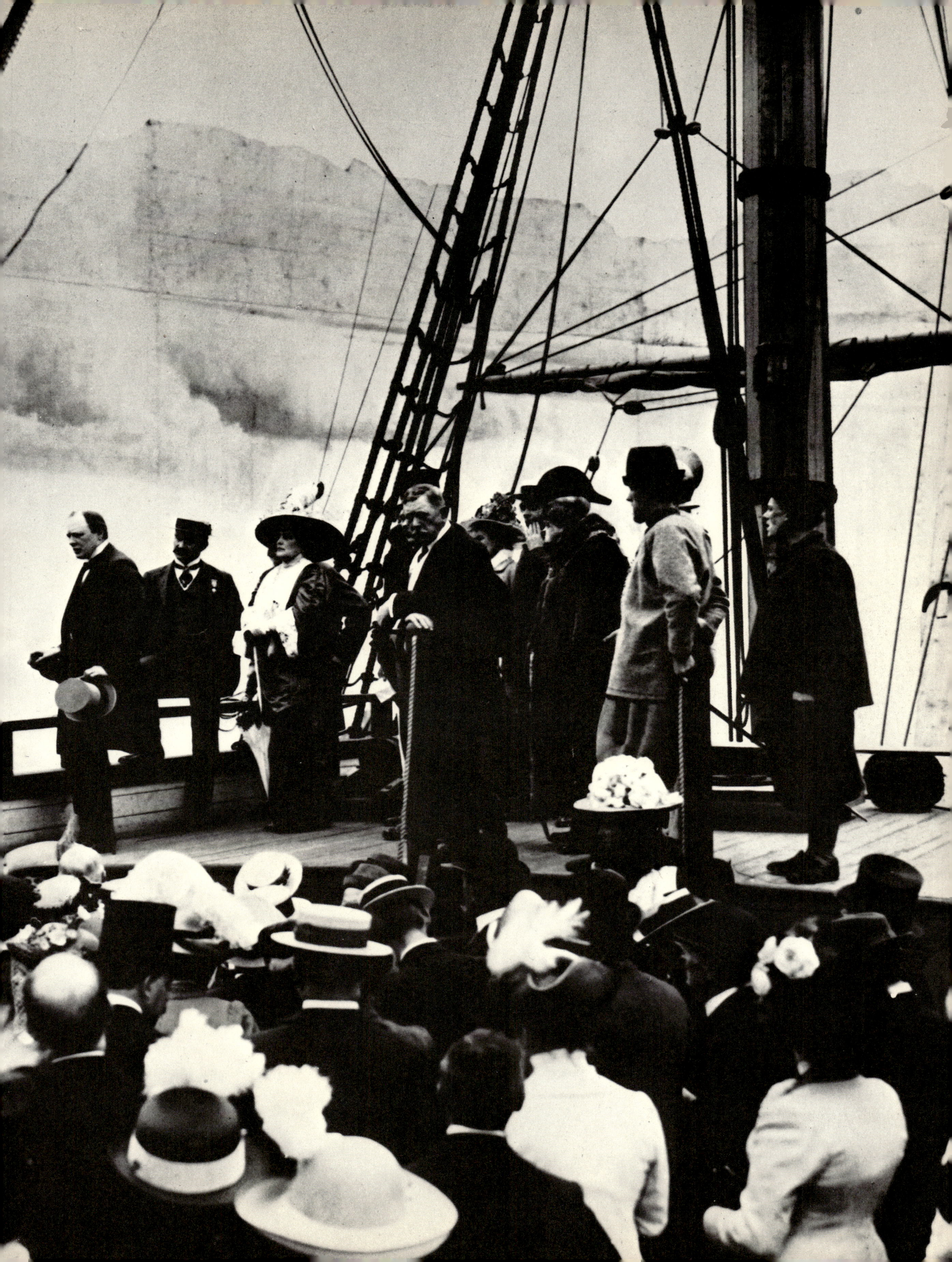

With Maxine Elliott on the golf links at Cannes. LEFT: With his wife, 1912, at the unveiling of a memorial, and (BELOW) at Portsmouth for the launching of a battleship, the *Iron Duke*.

On the Promenade at Monte Carlo in 1913 with Mrs. Churchill and Millicent, Duchess of Sutherland.

In 1913, the First Lord of the Admiralty took to the air; he learned to fly himself, and set up the Royal Naval Flying Corps. ABOVE: Inspecting a new model of seaplane. RIGHT: With Mrs. Churchill at Hendon aerodrome.

52

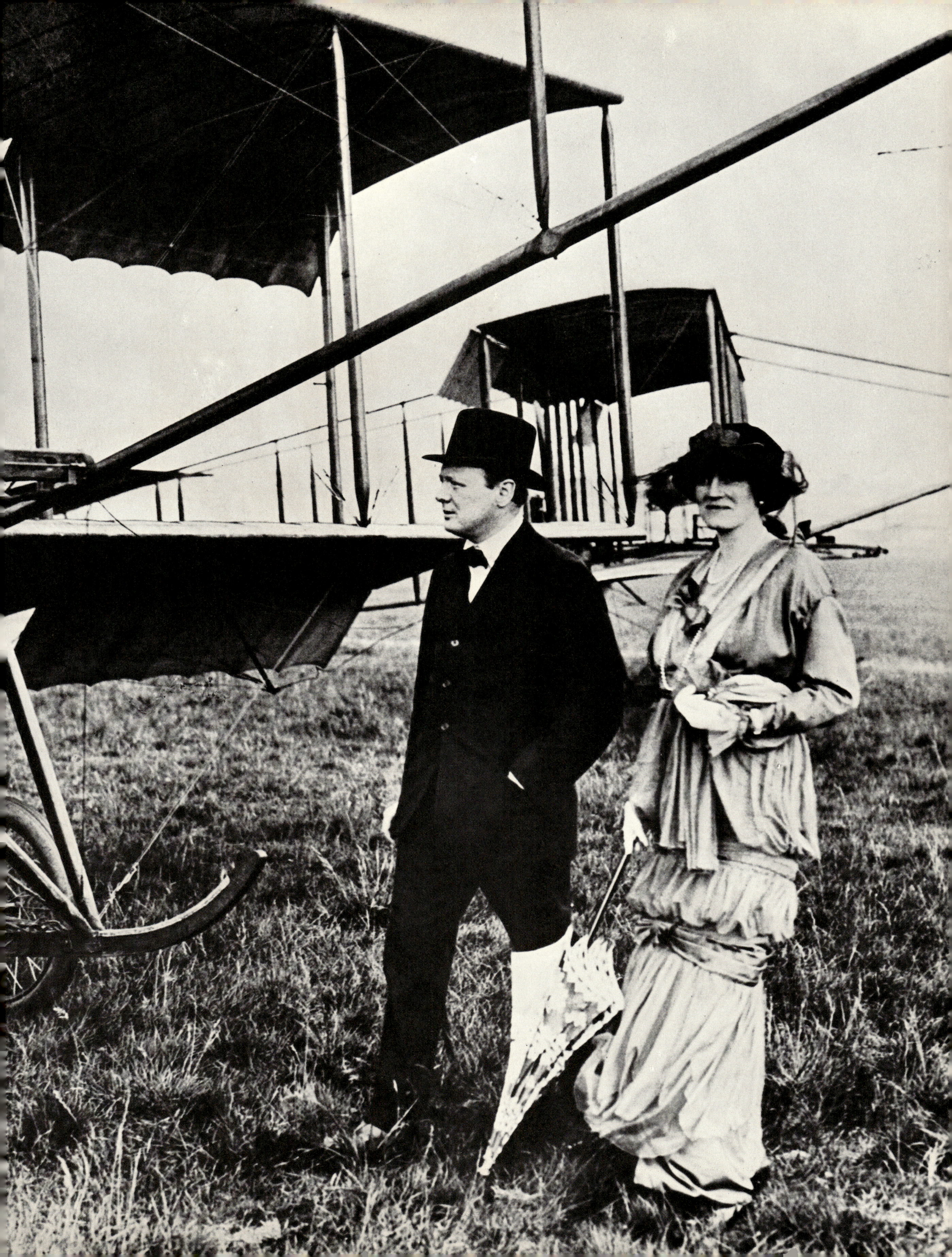

"Ah! foolish diligent Germans, working so hard, thinking so deeply, marching and counter-marching on the parade grounds of the Fatherland, poring over long calculations, fuming in new found prosperity, discontented amid the splendours of mundane success, how many bulwarks to your peace and glory did you not, with your own hands, successively tear down!" As Britain and Germany trod their cautious quadrille, the Kaiser (OPPOSITE PAGE, with George V) came to London for the Coronation, and reviewed his Army as Britain's First Lord of the Admiralty looked on (RIGHT, at manoeuvres in 1913). The British too held manoeuvres; Churchill watches (BELOW) with F. E. Smith, later Lord Birkenhead.

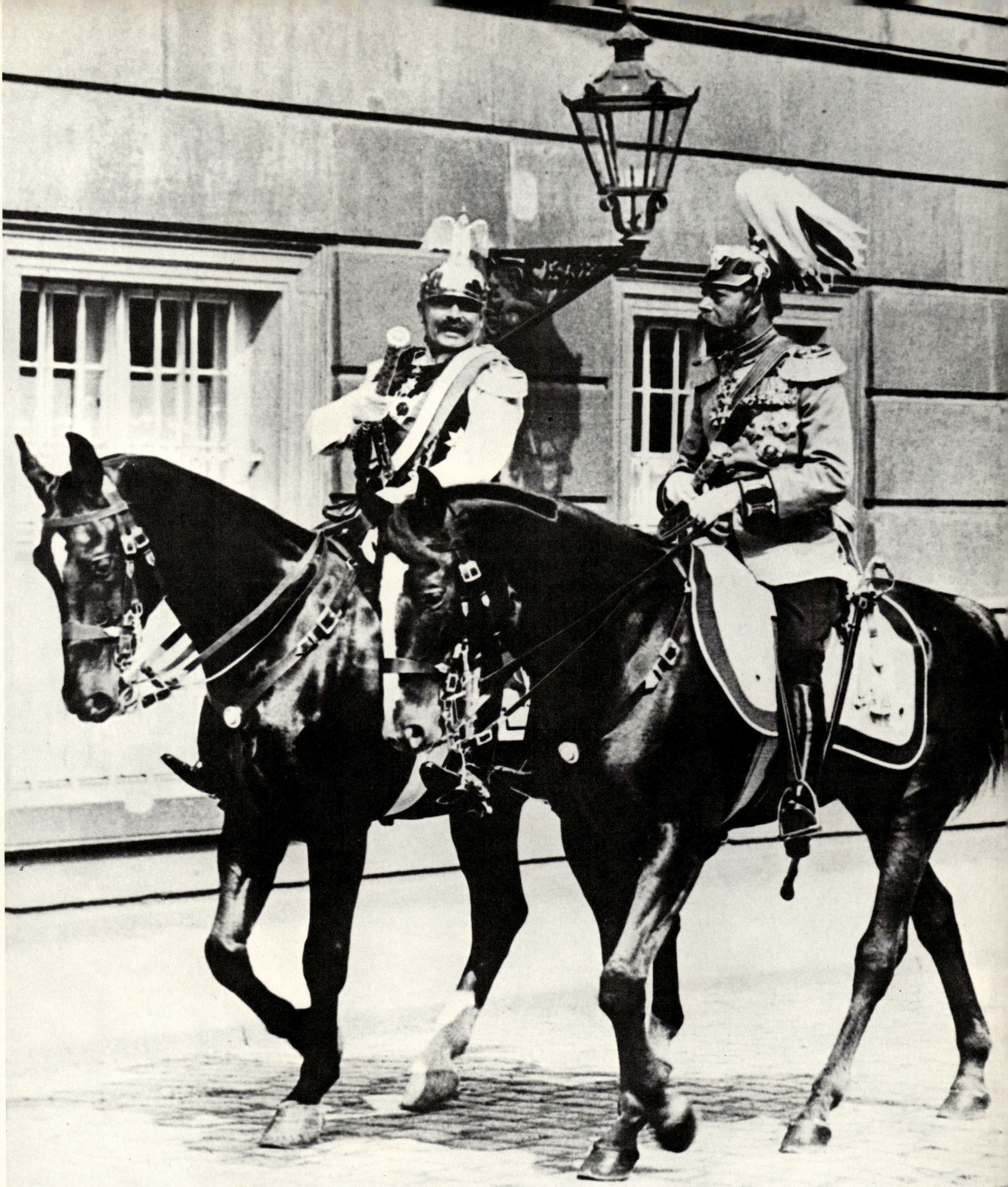

II

World Crisis and Aftermath: 1914-1935

The threat of war with Germany had completely changed Churchill's attitude to naval and military armaments, and he became (as 25 years later) a powerful advocate of preparedness, so much losing his interest in party differences and social policies that Lloyd George said he was apt to approach him with "Look here, David", and then "declaim for the rest of the afternoon about his blasted ships". In fact, the post of First Lord of the Admiralty, which he had assumed in October, 1911, exactly suited Churchill's temperament and gifts. His speeches in introduction of the Navy Estimates rank with Gladstone's Budgets as classical expositions of the relationship of policy to departmental practice. In the face of considerable service opposition he created a Naval War Staff. At weekends and when the House was in recess he familiarized himself with the work of the Navy, going everywhere, seeing everything, and exercising a magnificent judgment in his selection of officers.

When war came Churchill mobilized the Fleet on his own responsibility, forcing from Morley a sad reflection on "the splendid *condottiere* at the Admiralty". But two years later, when he was dismissed to satisfy the Conservative Party leaders, Kitchener took to him the personal message: "Well, there is one thing at any rate they cannot take from you. The Fleet was ready." Heads were to fall in the 1914-18 War which never should have fallen, and Churchill's was one of them.

"I had certain main ideas of what I was going to do and what, indeed, I was sent to the Admiralty to do. I intended to prepare for an attack by Germany as if it might come next day."

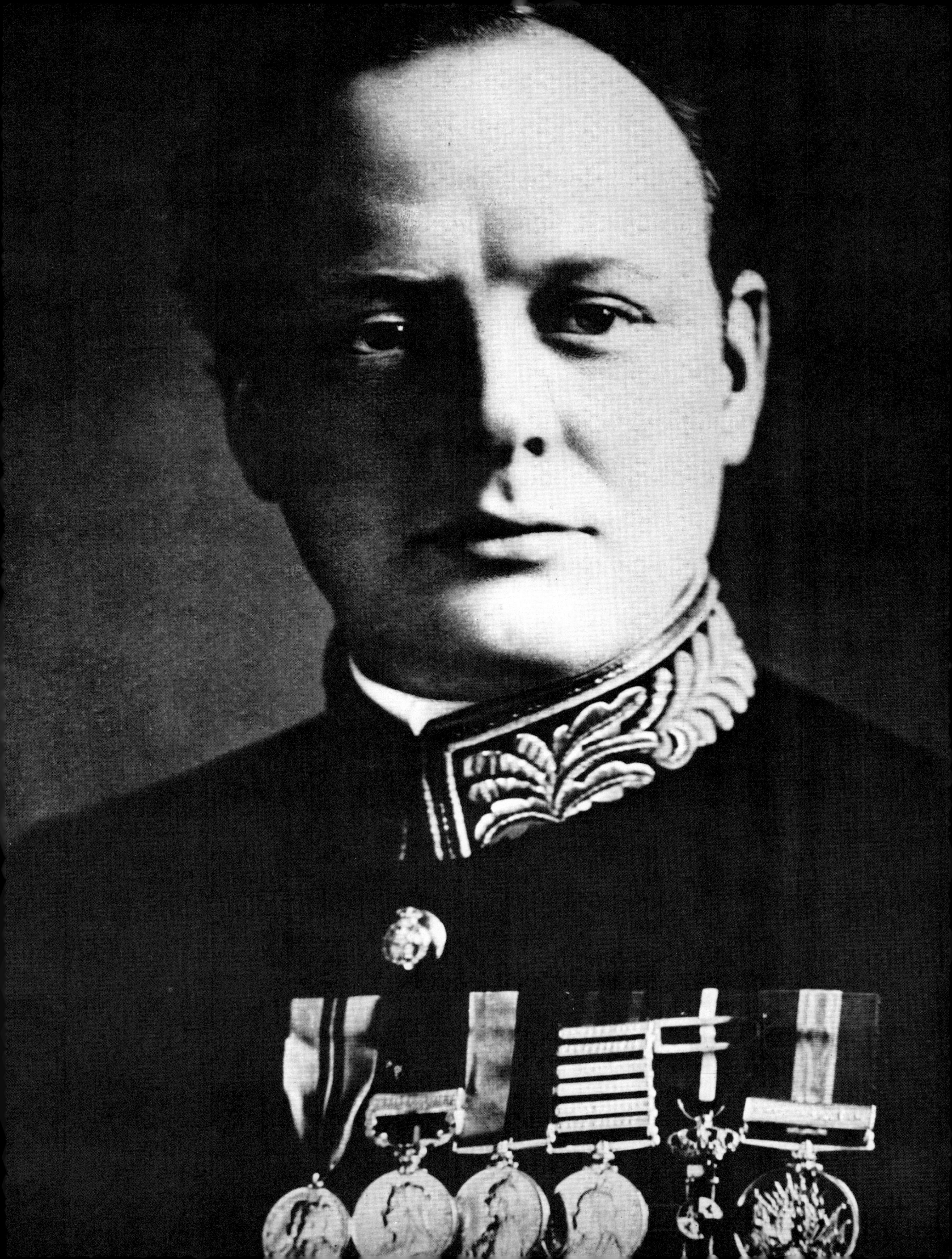

Bombardment of the Dardanelles by ships of the Allied Fleet, 1915.

Crossing Horse Guards Parade to the Cabinet Room, 1914.

He had carefully prepared for the Navy's first task—the carrying of the British Expeditionary Force to the Continent—and it was done well and without mishap. He had also foreseen the possibility of a German advance threatening the Channel ports, and in October it seemed that the way to them would be open unless Antwerp could be held—or, at least, not given up without a struggle. He himself organized and accompanied the expedition to Antwerp which not only delayed the fall of the city by five days, but by doing so saved the Channel ports and prevented the Germans from gaining a quick decision in the west.

Back in London Churchill took a decision which was eventually to involve him in misfortune. Although it was due to Prince Louis of Battenberg that the Fleet which was concentrated at Portland in the last fortnight of peace was not allowed to disperse, Churchill felt under the pressure of popular agitation that the Prince's name and origin deprived him of public confidence, and he suffered him to go into retirement.

In his place he recalled to active service Lord Fisher, a warrior after his own heart, dauntless and indefatigable, a master of every detail of the sea service. The Navy could confidently look for a direction equal to any emergency so long as these two men saw eye to eye. Together they brilliantly restored the British command of the sea, which had been compromised by the destruction of Cradock's squadron off the South American coast. But still there was no decisive victory over the main German fleet, and the shelling of Scarborough and Hartlepool brought public criticism of Churchill and the Admiralty to a focus.

He had, at the beginning of 1915, little public support—a relevant fact to keep in mind as one begins the confused story of the Dardanelles. The breach between Fisher and Churchill had come over a fundamental issue of the direction from which British sea power could make the most effective impact on the course of the war in Europe. Fisher favoured the Baltic, Churchill the Dardanelles. Few would now dispute the strategic insight underlying Churchill's conception of a swift, dramatic stroke at a vital point. Success might have been achieved by the employment of such a combination of sea and land forces as was eventually brought to bear—but only after the initial advantage of surprise had been lost.

The most important criticism of Churchill's role is that he persisted in the enterprise without securing the support of his own department and the cooperation of the War Office. The documents do not support the criticism. He was careful from the very beginning to seek and obtain the approval of those with whom he had to work, and when the idea of the operation was submitted to the War Council there was no expression of dissent. The Dardanelles did, in fact, become official policy, and the French and Russian Governments were informed of it. The two main causes of the failure were the late hour of the objections raised by the unpredictable Fisher and the War Council's inability to resolve the question of a divided command. The delays, hesitations, and postponements are in many cases directly traceable to Fisher's behaviour—he resigned shortly after the first military landings—and it was only at the very late stage of his resignation that the admirals turned against Churchill's plan.

FAILURE AT THE DARDANELLES

Five Allied battleships were lost at the Dardanelles in a single day, March 18, 1915, and infantry units which fought their way onto the Gallipoli peninsula (ABOVE) in April met heavy losses. As the campaign ground to a halt for lack of support and decisive action by the War Council, much of the blame fell on the First Lord of the Admiralty (RIGHT, as news of the losses reached him). *"Your commission may condemn the men who tried to force the Dardanelles,"* Churchill told the Dardanelles Commission, which in 1917 cleared him of sole responsibility for the fiasco, *"but your children will keep their condemnation for all who did not rally to their aid."*

THE CONSEQUENCES OF DEFEAT

Churchill took to heart the lessons of 1915. A notable feature of his direction during the 1939-45 War was his assumption of the post of Minister of Defence. In this capacity he was able to secure uninterrupted and effective liaison between the Chiefs of Staff themselves and between them and the Cabinet which he led. The 1939-45 War was singularly free of the disputes between commands, between the Services, and between the Services and the politicians which Lloyd George never succeeded in ending between 1916 and 1918.

The political consequences of the Dardanelles were immediate—so immediate that when Churchill crossed to Downing Street to inform the Prime Minister that Sir Arthur Wilson was ready to take Fisher's place he found that others had preceded him. Now was the hour of the Conservative Party's revenge. Bonar Law had informed Lloyd George that if Fisher had resigned Churchill must depart as well. Between them—and faced with a critical debate on the Dardanelles—Lloyd George and Asquith determined on their best way out: a Coalition Government formed at the cost of the resignation of Churchill. This was a hard political decision against which there could be no appeal, and in the new Government Churchill had to be satisfied with what the Conservatives were prepared to grant him—the Chancellorship of the Duchy of Lancaster. The public, then deeply suspicious of Churchill's talents, drew obvious conclusions. Six months of idleness and frustration were sufficient, and in November Churchill resigned his sinecure and rejoined the Army.

Stretcher bearers in the trenches, France, 1917.

A machine gun unit in action against the Germans in the Meuse-Argonne offensive. *"War, which used to be cruel and magnificent, has become cruel and squalid."*

WINDSOR CASTLE.

Soldiers of the United States, the people of the British Isles welcome you on your way to take your stand beside the Armies of many Nations now fighting in the Old World the great battle for human freedom.

The Allies will gain new heart & spirit in your company.

I wish that I could shake the hand of each one of you & bid you God speed on your mission.

George R.I.

April 1918.

Lieut.-Col. Winston Churchill of the Royal Scots Fusiliers, leaving London for the Front, 1916. LEFT: King George's welcome to American troops arriving in England on their way to join the Allied Forces in France.

Tanks—once called "Winston's folly"—were used in the breakthrough at Cambrai, November, 1917.

Within a few days he was at the Front, attached to the 2nd Grenadier Guards. A month later, with the rank of colonel, he was given command of a battalion of the Royal Scots Fusiliers. But his thoughts remained fixed on the conduct of the war, and in the spring of 1916 he was home on leave delivering a weighty speech in which, with the magnanimity which marked him all his life, he urged the recall of Fisher to the Admiralty. Later in the year his battalion was absorbed and he returned permanently to political life. Asquith had meanwhile refused all Lloyd George's attempts to place Churchill in the Ministry of Munitions, and even when Lloyd George replaced Asquith as Prime Minister the Conservatives were still firm that they would not admit him to the Cabinet. But, in February, 1917, in spite of all Asquith's protests, Lloyd George published the report of the Dardanelles Commission, which Asquith himself had appointed.

MINISTER OF MUNITIONS

Asquith's interest in the matter was soon apparent to the public, for it was Asquith who was severely condemned and Churchill who was exonerated. The commission could find no grounds on which to indict Churchill: his plan had been right and the delays and ill-organization had not been his fault. Churchill's stock rose immediately and, after a brilliant survey of the war situation during a secret session of May, 1917, Lloyd George (with Smuts's support) appointed Churchill Minister of Munitions. Established less than two years before, the Ministry had become the greatest directorate of industry in the country. No episode in the whole of Churchill's career is so eloquent of his exceptional capacity as a departmental head than the success with which he imposed unity and order on this vast organization and established himself as the source and controller of all its activities.

At Lille in October, 1918 (OPPOSITE), watching the march-past of the 47th Division; B. L. Montgomery, then Commander, at left. *"In these last days every soldier felt himself at once a Conqueror and a Deliverer."*

62

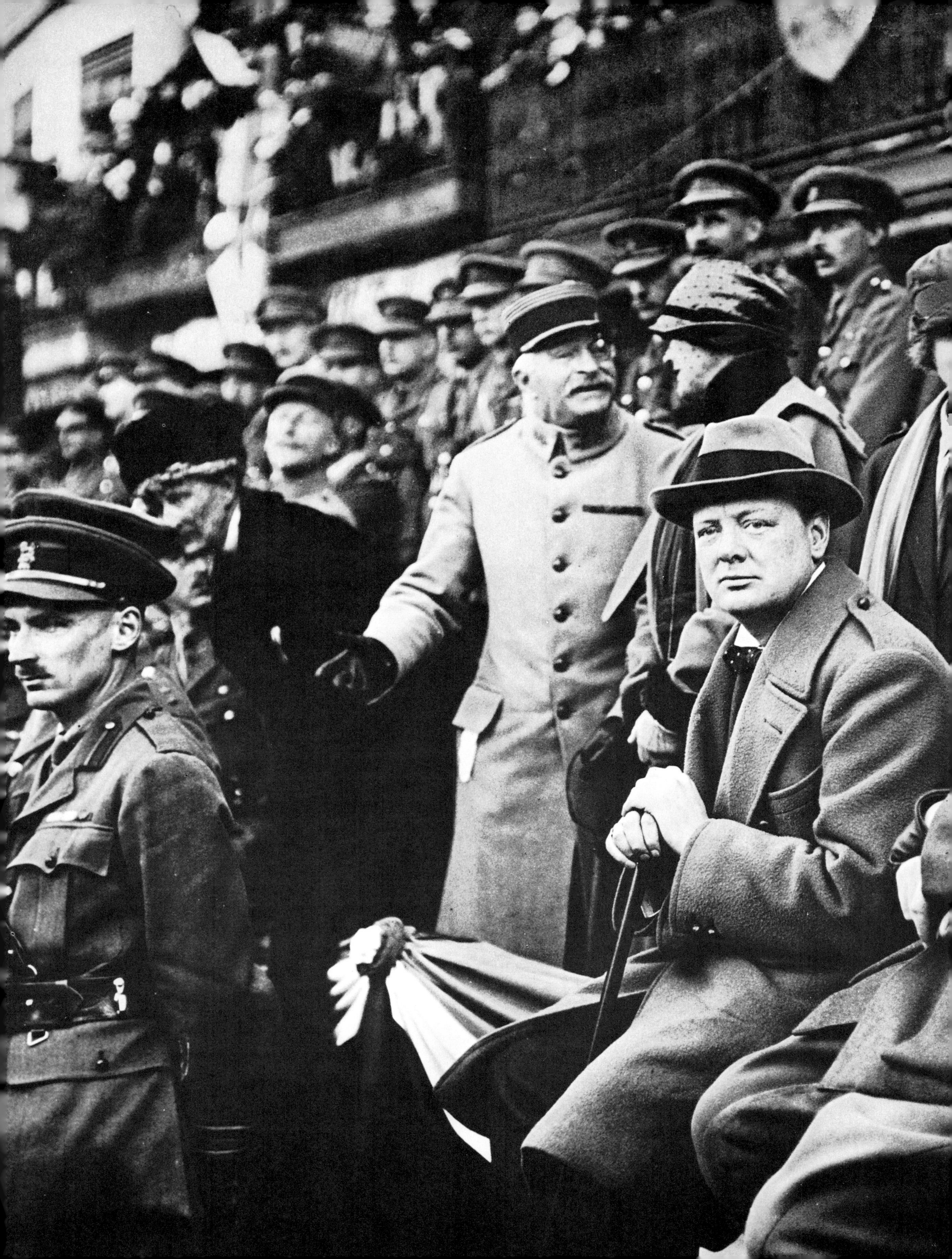

THE HOUR OF VICTORY

During the last months of the war Churchill became a close adviser of Lloyd George on its central direction. He was not in the War Cabinet, but Lloyd George consulted and used him frequently on matters far outside his departmental activities. Churchill's visits to the Continent, in fact, became so frequent that the backbench Conservative members, still harbouring their grudge, warned Lloyd George that he must not take the renegade into the War Cabinet. But Lloyd George still turned to Churchill and, after the German break-through in March, 1918, summoned him to a conference with Haig and Bonar Law. Haig found Churchill "a real gun in a crisis", and as the situation worsened Churchill slept at his Ministry so that he might be more closely in touch with the Prime Minister. He was Lloyd George's emissary at a meeting with Clemenceau, Foch, and Rawlinson—the prelude to the appointment of Foch as Supreme Commander—and at the hour of victory could feel that he had been at the heart of things, playing his part.

With Marshal Foch (TOP LEFT) as Supreme Commander, the Allies moved toward final victory. The Armistice ended the fighting on November 11, 1918: *"After fifty-two months of making burdens grievous to be borne and binding them on men's backs, at last, all at once, suddenly and everywhere the burdens were cast down."* The Council of Four (TOP RIGHT: Lloyd George, Orlando, Clemenceau, Wilson) met in Paris to frame the peace, and Churchill, as Secretary of State for War and Air, helped organize the demobilization of troops (LEFT, on a Rhine steamer in 1919, visiting British Army units in the Rhineland). OPPOSITE: With Edward, Prince of Wales, in June, 1919, after a luncheon honouring American airmen.

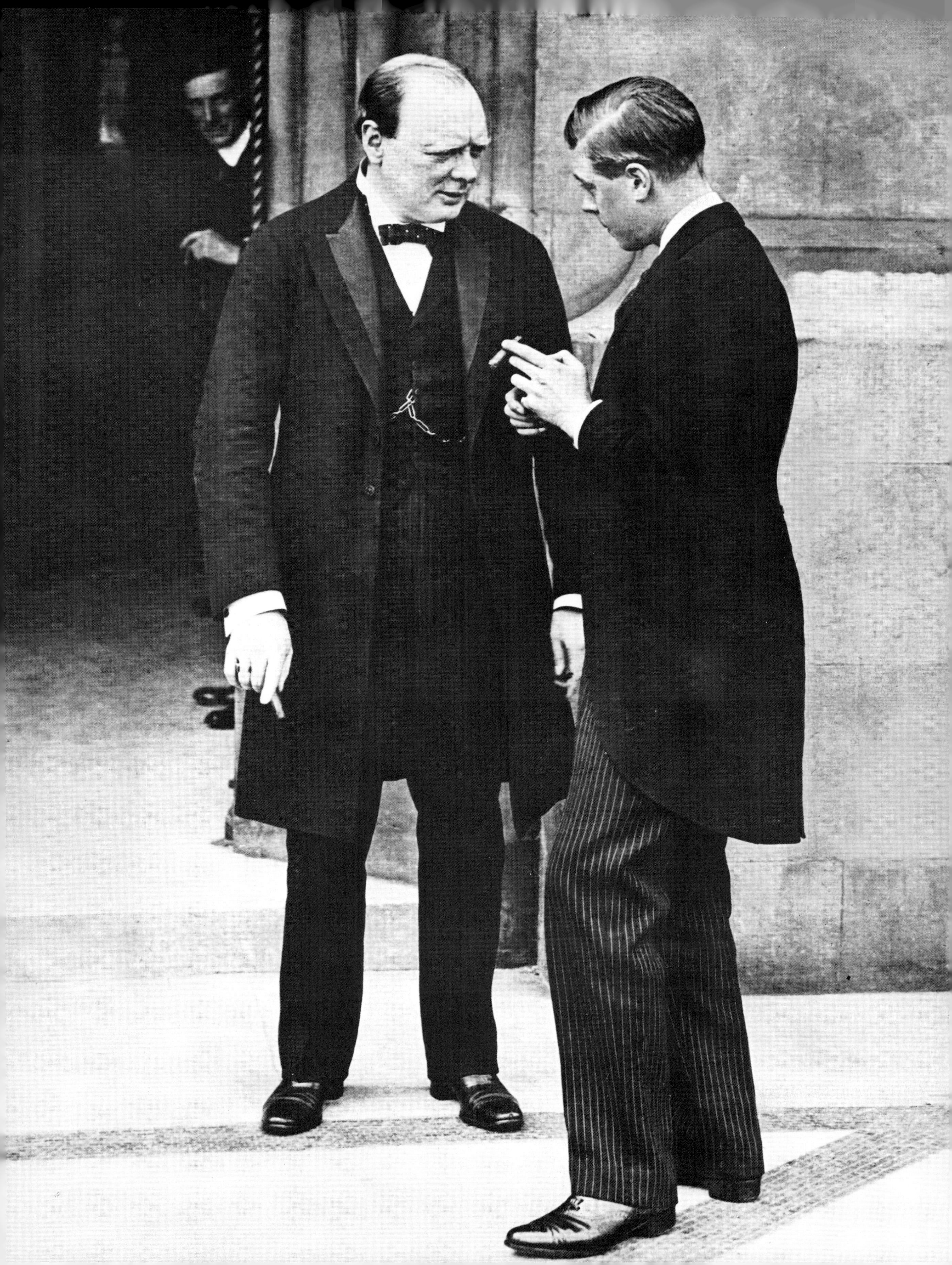

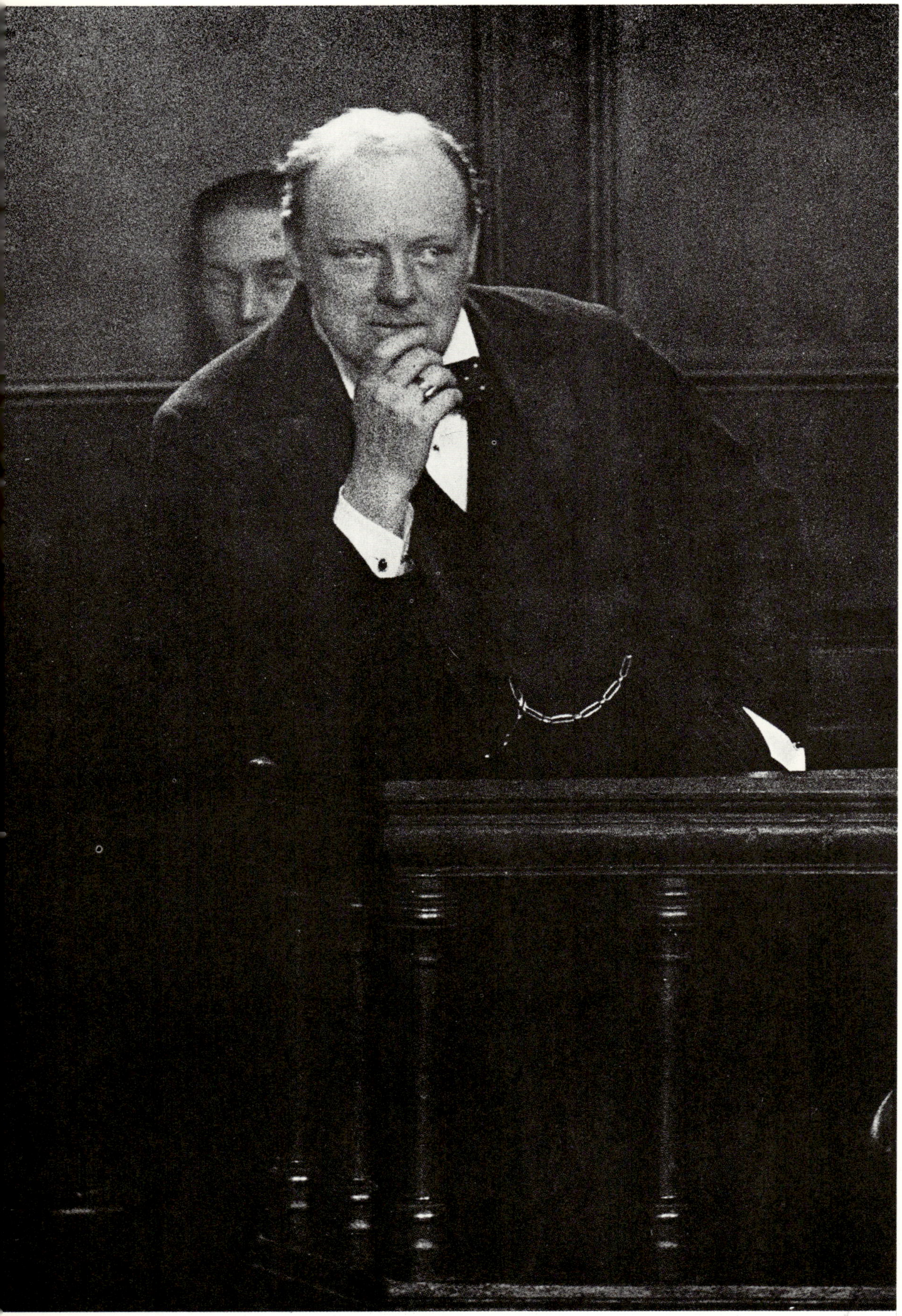

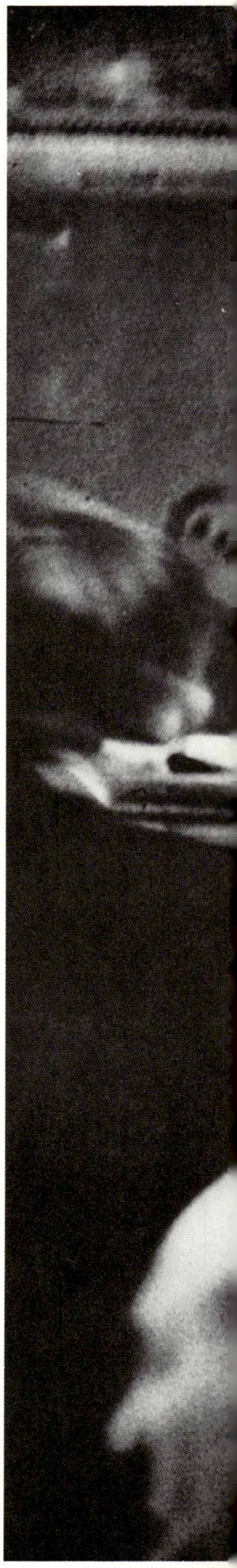

A Royal Commission recorded in 1919 "their view that it was primarily due to the receptivity, courage and driving force of the Rt. Hon. Winston Churchill that the general idea of the use of such an instrument of warfare as the tank was converted into practical shape." ABOVE and OPPOSITE: Churchill before the Commission, Lincoln's Inn Court.

68

Churchill had entered the war as a Liberal with an enviable popular reputation. He emerged from it a Coalition Liberal with a damaged reputation. As long as Lloyd George's Coalition held together Churchill was certain of office and could hope for promotion. But after that? The immediate tasks were, however, pressing. Lloyd George (who had been impressed by his departmental ability) asked him to move to the War Office (with which he combined the Air Ministry) to smooth away the friction which had at first attended demobilization. This he did in a fortnight. In this dual office Churchill became prominently involved in the question of Bolshevist Russia—eager, as he was, to continue the resistance to the Bolshevists. His appeal for a volunteer force to cover the withdrawal of British troops from Murmansk and Archangel—8,000 men were raised—lent weight to the suspicion that he was anxious to provoke a war with Russia.

Early in 1921 the growing difficulties in framing a policy suited to Britain's new position in the Eastern Mediterranean led to his transfer to the Colonial Office. In this capacity he was a member of the Cabinet Committee which in 1921 negotiated with the Irish leaders, and he played the role of peace-maker. "Tell Winston", said Collins afterwards, "we could never have done anything without him". But the pugnacity which he had kept in restraint during the Irish negotiations found new and unfortunate expression in 1922. The new Turkish state which was constituting itself under Mustapha Kemal clashed with British power in the Dardanelles. Thanks largely to the tact of the British Commander, Sir Charles Harington, a conflict was avoided, but Churchill's attitude, and especially his premature appeal to the Dominions, contributed both to the fall of the Government and to his own defeat at the ensuing election.

A MAKER OF POLICY

As Colonial Secretary, Churchill called a conference at Cairo in 1921 on the Middle East situation. "In a few weeks he made straight all the tangle," said T. E. Lawrence, his chief adviser. BELOW: On a camelback expedition to the Sphinx (OPPOSITE: as it was at that time), with Mrs. Churchill, the explorer and writer Gertrude Bell, and Lawrence.

At Roehampton in 1921.

If one wanted to "get at Churchill's angle in life," Patrick Thompson has said, one had to see him play polo. "He rides in the game like heavy cavalry getting into position for the assault. He trots about, keenly watchful, biding his time, a master of tactics and strategy. Abruptly he sees his chance, and he gathers his pony and charges in, neither deft nor graceful, but full of tearing physical energy—and skillful with it too. He bears down opposition by the weight of his dash, and strikes the ball. Did I say 'strikes'? He slashes the ball."

With the Prince of Wales, in 1924.

At Roehampton, with his right arm in a strap; he had dislocated his shoulder in India in 1895.

POLITICIAN
WITHOUT A PARTY

The Conservatives had for some time been restless under their allegiance to Lloyd George, and at a meeting at the Carlton Club on October 19, 1922, decided to end their association with him. Lloyd George immediately dissolved Parliament, and a confused general election gave the Conservatives power for the first time since 1905. Churchill was defeated—and for the first time since 1900 was out of the House of Commons with no certain hope of returning. He was politically isolated. He had severed himself from the Asquithian Liberals. He distrusted the Labour Party. And there was still much to divide him from the Conservatives: indeed all the more when, in the autumn of 1923, Baldwin appealed to the country on the issue of Protection—the very issue on which Churchill had left the Conservative Party 20 years before. He fought and lost the election as a Coalition Liberal—a term which barely had meaning any longer.

During 1923 Churchill completed the earlier portions of *The World Crisis,* though the whole work, together with its sequel, *The Aftermath,* was not completed until 1931. The volumes were not entirely successful. The style was too rhetorical and there was not the breadth of vision that marked his history of *The Second World War*. Balfour was not far wrong when he wrote to a friend: "I am immersed in Winston's brilliant autobiography, disguised as a history of the universe." In the following year Churchill severed his last links with Liberalism, and when, in February, a by-election was pending in the Abbey Division of Westminster he stood as an Independent Anti-Socialist. There was an official Conservative candidate in the field, but Churchill had the support of many of the more independent Conservatives, including Austen Chamberlain and Birkenhead. He was defeated by only 47 votes.

He fought the general election of 1924 as a Constitutionalist—and since there was no Conservative opponent was in effect the official Conservative candidate. He was returned to the House of Commons and (greatly to his surprise) was appointed Chancellor of the Exchequer. Baldwin had, in fact, decided to go outside the ranks of the safe and the orthodox: Austen Chamberlain and Birkenhead were also brought in. Even so, Churchill, as Asquith said, "towered like a Chimborazo or Everest among the sand-hills of the Baldwin Cabinet". His first Budget, brilliantly introduced, contained provisions for widows' pensions, but its most conspicuous feature was the decision to return to the gold standard.

After two years out of the House, Churchill won as a Constitutionalist in 1924 in the Epping Division of Essex. ABOVE: With Mrs. Churchill at Epping. BELOW: Campaigning in the Abbey Division by-election (OPPOSITE PAGE, LEFT) and in the general election of 1924.

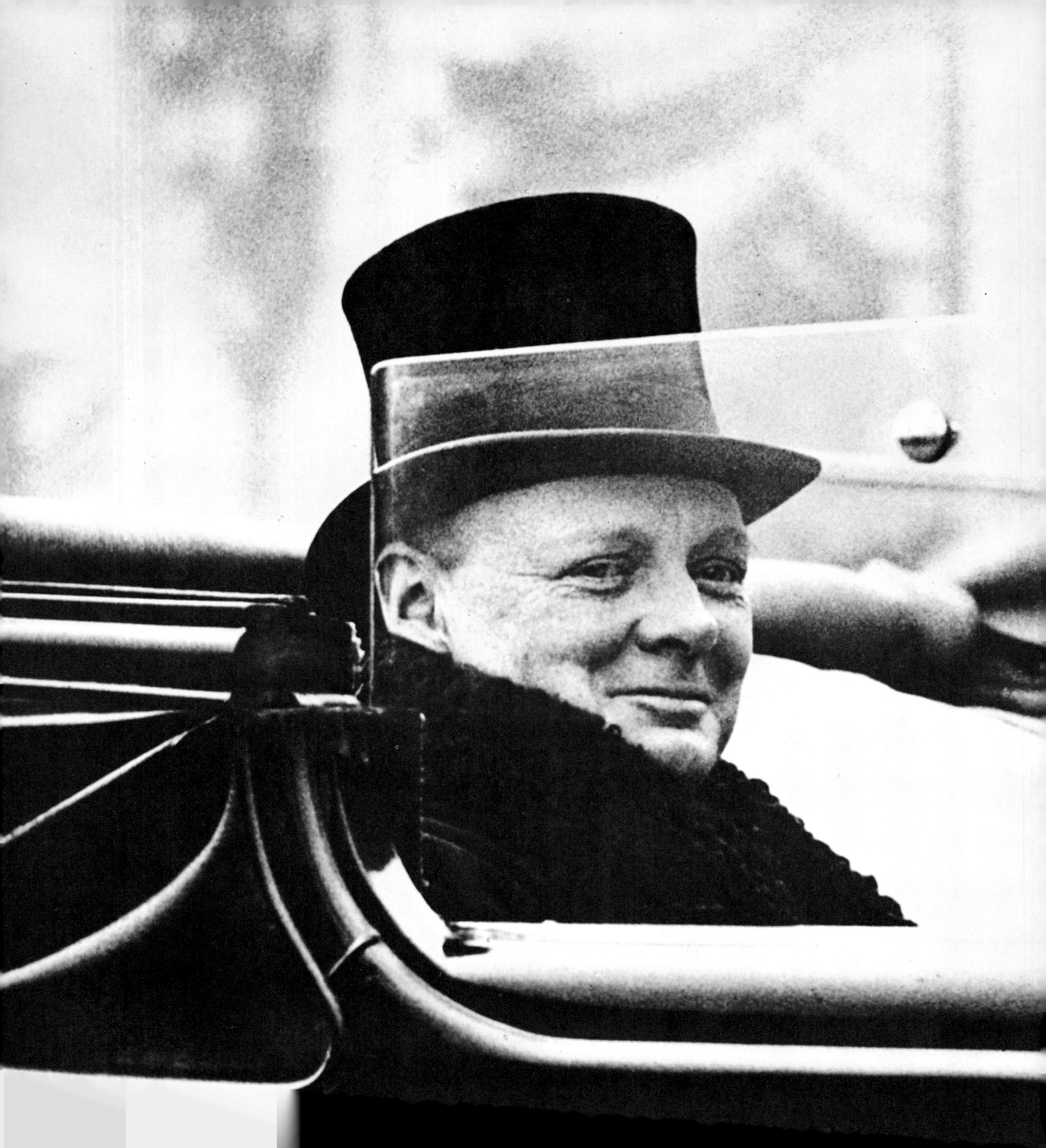

Driving to Buckingham Palace to receive the Seal of the Exchequer from George V, 1924. As a small boy he had said: *"My father is Chancellor of the Exchequer, and that's what I'm going to be, too."*

At Oxford, 1925, to receive an honorary degree.

ABOVE: With Mrs. Churchill at an International Army Polo Match, Hurlingham, 1925.
RIGHT: On his way to the House to present his first Budget, carrying Gladstone's famous red dispatch case.

With his daughter Mary, then 2, at Chartwell.

His policy on gold, though roundly condemned in the light of after events, was generally approved at the time by almost all except Keynes, who contributed a lively polemic entitled *The Economic Consequences of Mr. Churchill.*

    Keynes's warnings proved right. The mine-owners decided that in order to retain their markets in the world they must cut down their costs, and there followed the tragic course of events which led to the General Strike in 1926. Churchill's role was not a happy one. All the evidence suggests that he was not one of the more conciliatory members of the Cabinet, and his production of the *British Gazette* from the commandeered premises of the *Morning Post*—though the object was sound: the communication of information to the public—was marred by his eagerness to turn it into a partisan anti-strikers sheet, which could only inflame feelings still more on both sides. The remaining years of the Baldwin Government were quiet. In 1929 Baldwin appealed to the country and lost the general election. Churchill, however, was again returned at Epping. Two years later the National Government was formed, but Churchill was not a member, and he remained out of office until the outbreak of the 1939-45 War.

CHANCELLOR
OF THE EXCHEQUER

Churchill addressing a meeting of workers in 1926.

"People who are not prepared to do unpopular things and to defy clamour are not fit to be Ministers in times of stress." BELOW, LEFT: The first issue of the *British Gazette,* which Churchill published for the Government amid the clamour of the General Strike, May, 1926. ABOVE: Welsh Guards returning to their barracks from Victoria Embankment after a day on duty during the strike.

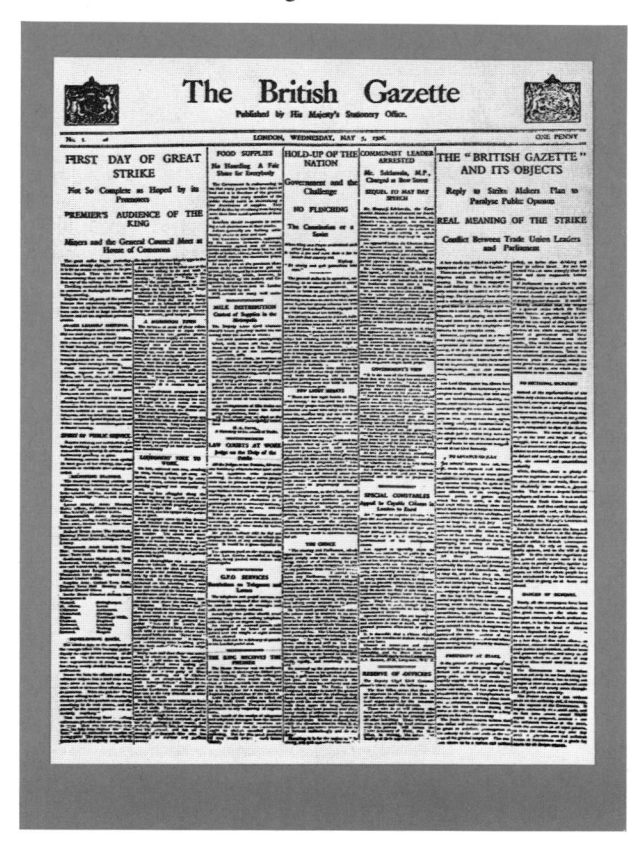

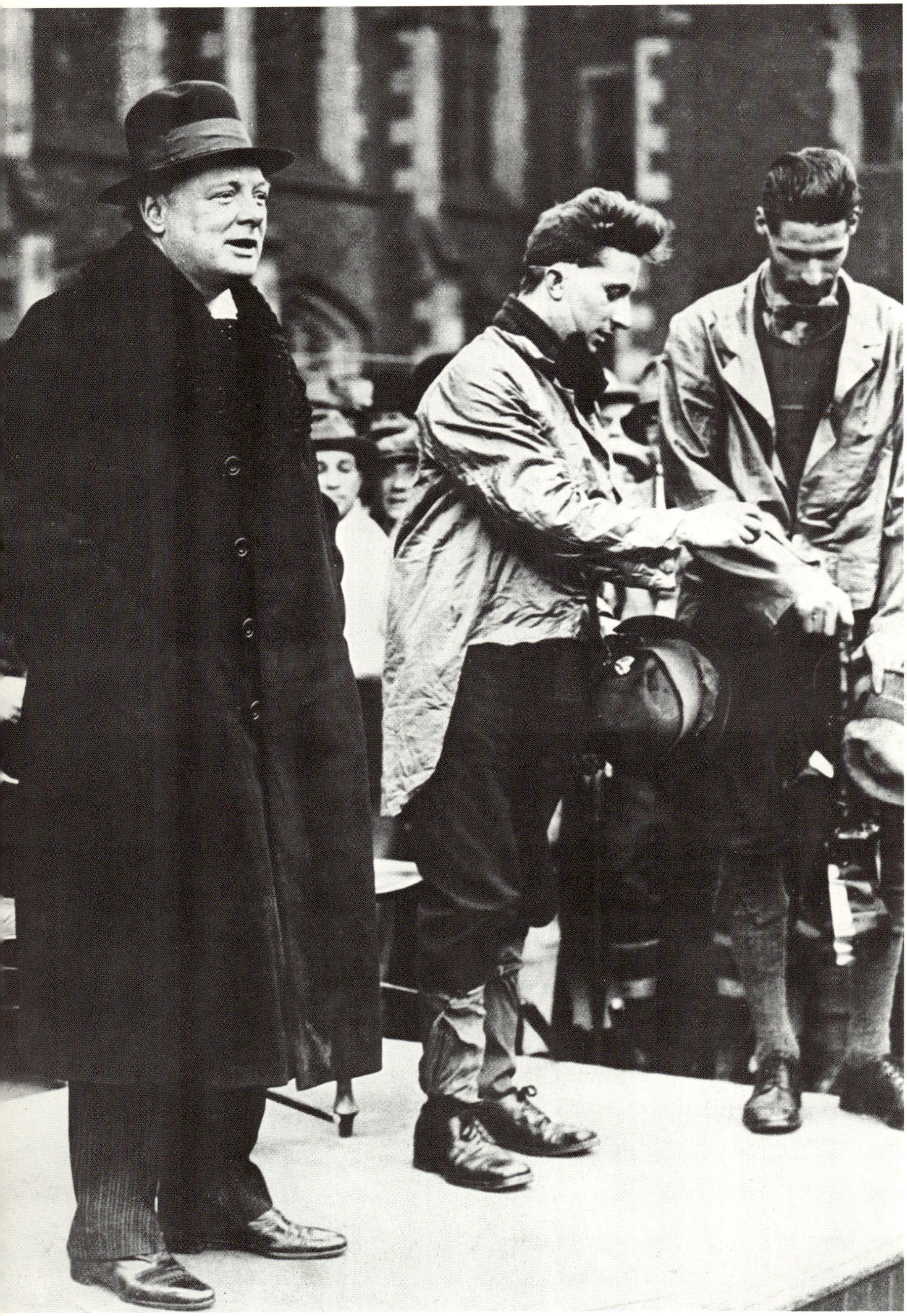
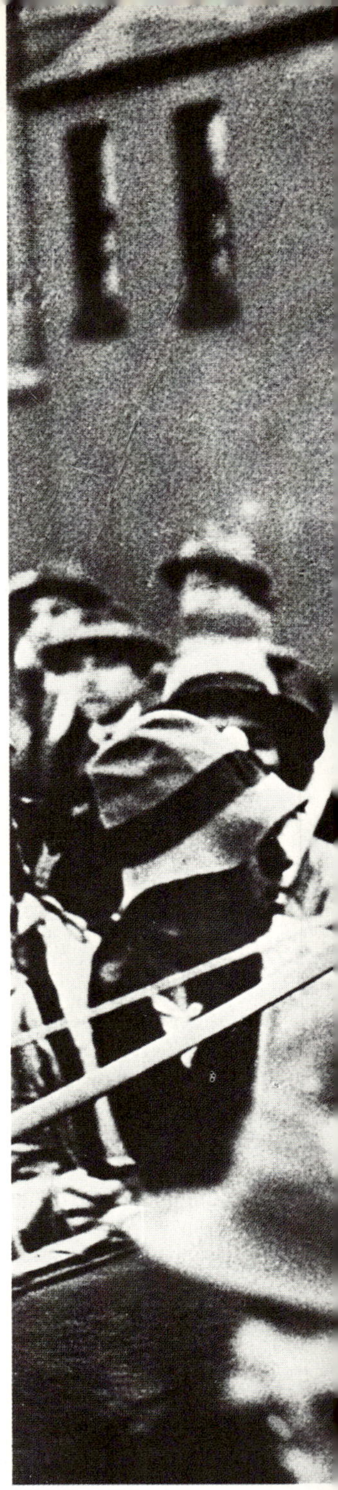
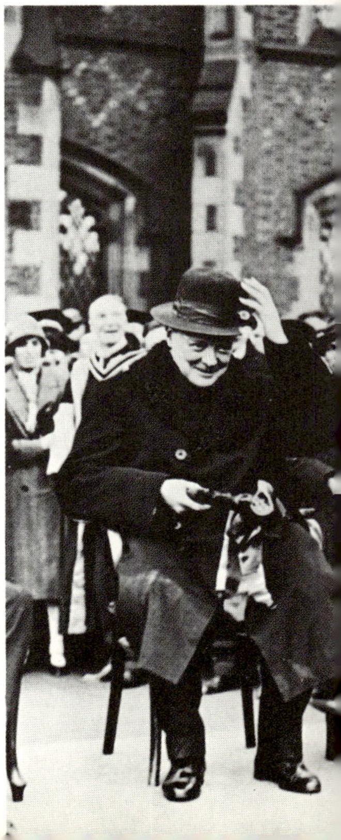

Presented with a "paddy" hat and a shillelagh by ragging students at Queen's University, Belfast, Churchill rides in a jaunting car (ABOVE), after receiving an honorary degree from the University, 1926.

ABOVE: Swathed in towels after a swim, during a holiday on the Riviera. RIGHT: At Deauville in 1927, with the Duke of Sutherland.

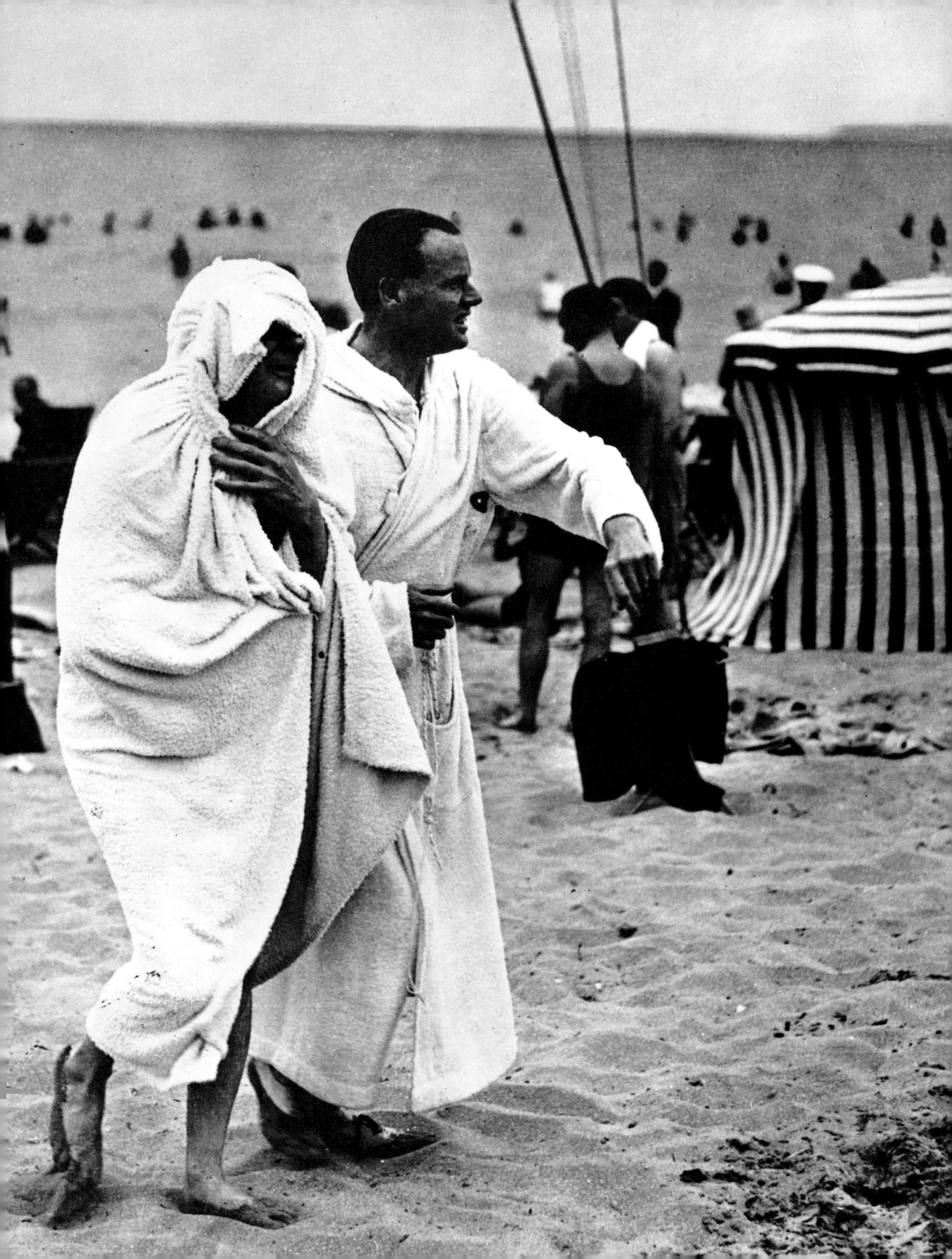

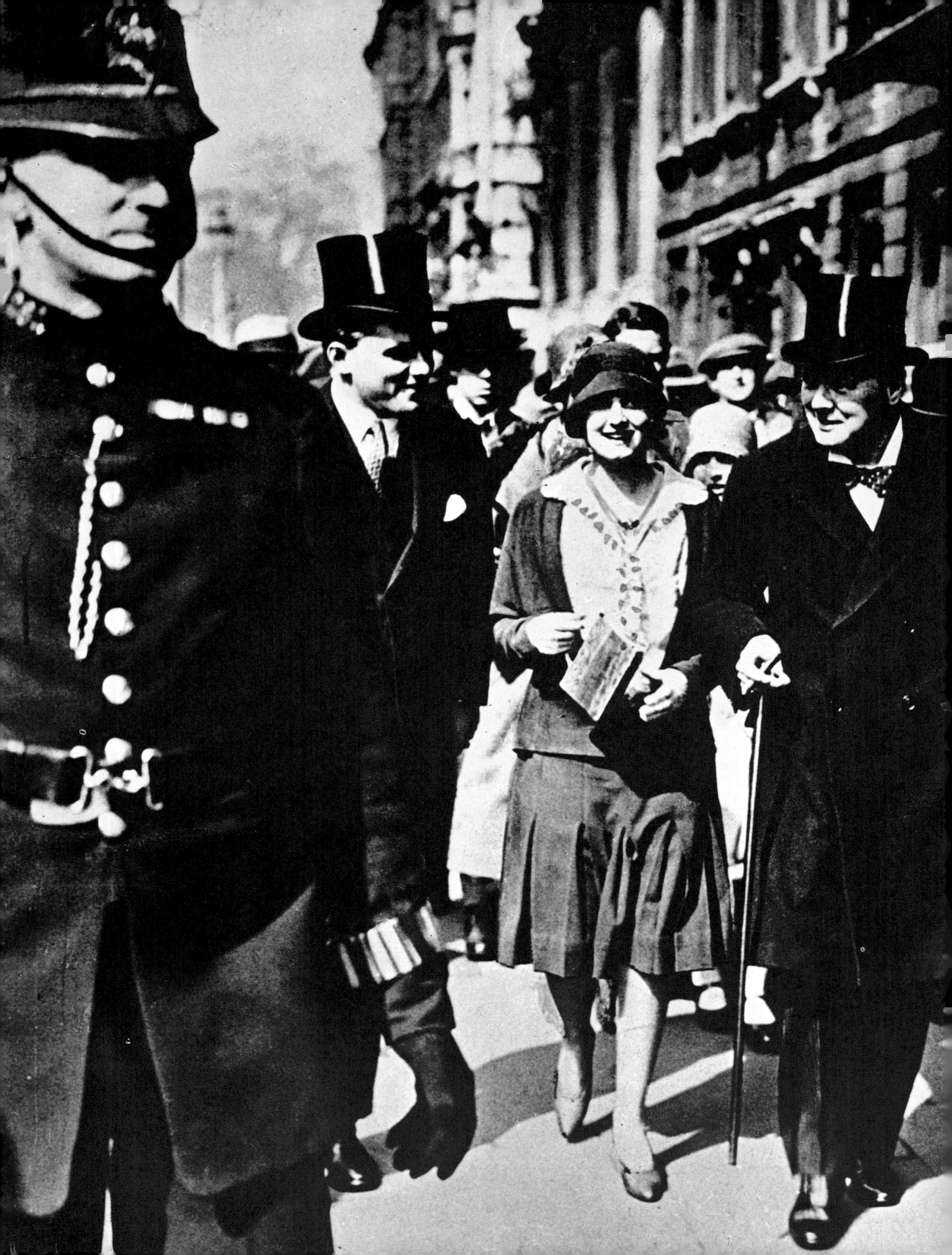

As Chancellor of the Exchequer, Churchill presented the Conservative Budget from 1924 to 1929. LEFT: With his daughter Diana on Budget Day, 1928. BELOW: With Mrs. Churchill, daughter Sarah, and son Randolph, on his way to the House of Commons to present his fifth and last Budget.

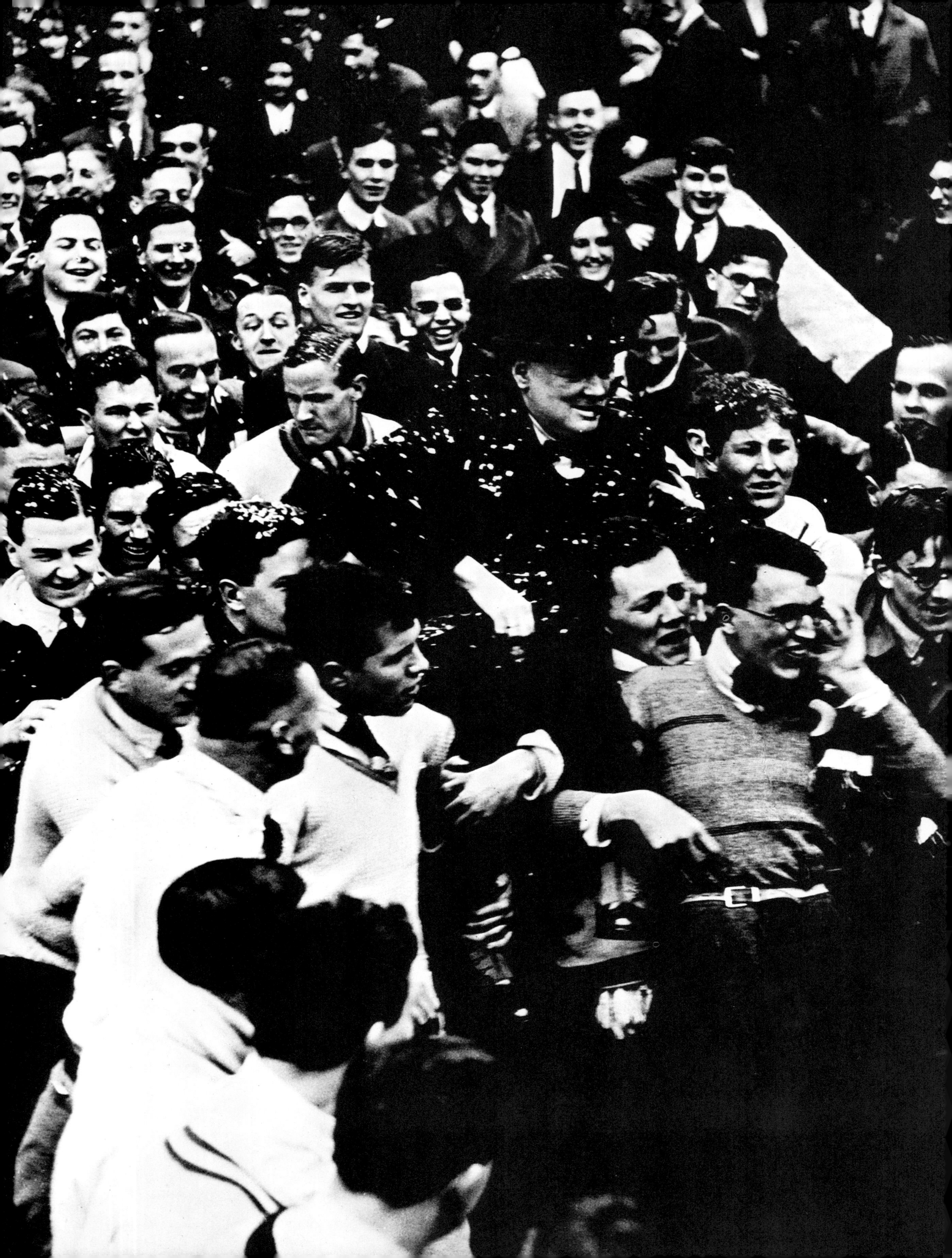

In 1930 the Simon Commission on India published its report, and the Round Table Conference was summoned the following autumn. Churchill opposed this moderately liberal policy, refusing to cast away "that most truly bright and precious jewel in the crown of the King"— an almost precise echo of a phrase used by his father, Lord Randolph. In January, 1931, he resigned from the Conservative "shadow Cabinet" as a protest against its support for the Labour Government's Indian policy. It was a courageous act whatever one may think of the merits of his views. Churchill's conduct of the opposition to the India Bill in the House of Commons—fighting it clause by clause in committee—was perhaps his most brilliant parliamentary performance. But even weightier issues were beginning to hold his attention. In 1932 there started his seven-year struggle to halt the drift to what he later called "the unnecessary war".

His freedom from office did, however, give him time to write the biography of Marlborough, which his cousin, the Duke of Marlborough, had long urged him to do. Based on a mass of material in the muniment room at Blenheim, the work was planned and completed on an ample scale, the last of its four volumes appearing just before the Munich crisis. Never restrained in the expression of his dislikes, Churchill pursued Macaulay with a rancour excused rather than justified by family loyalty. But no one else could have so brilliantly attempted to vindicate the qualities of a man of genius from the reproaches cast by a master of invective.

RESIGNATION FROM THE "SHADOW CABINET"

LEFT: The new Chancellor of Bristol University borne aloft by students; the same year, 1929, he became Rector of Edinburgh University. ABOVE: Mrs. Churchill in 1929. RIGHT: Randolph Churchill leaving Waterloo Station for America, 1930.

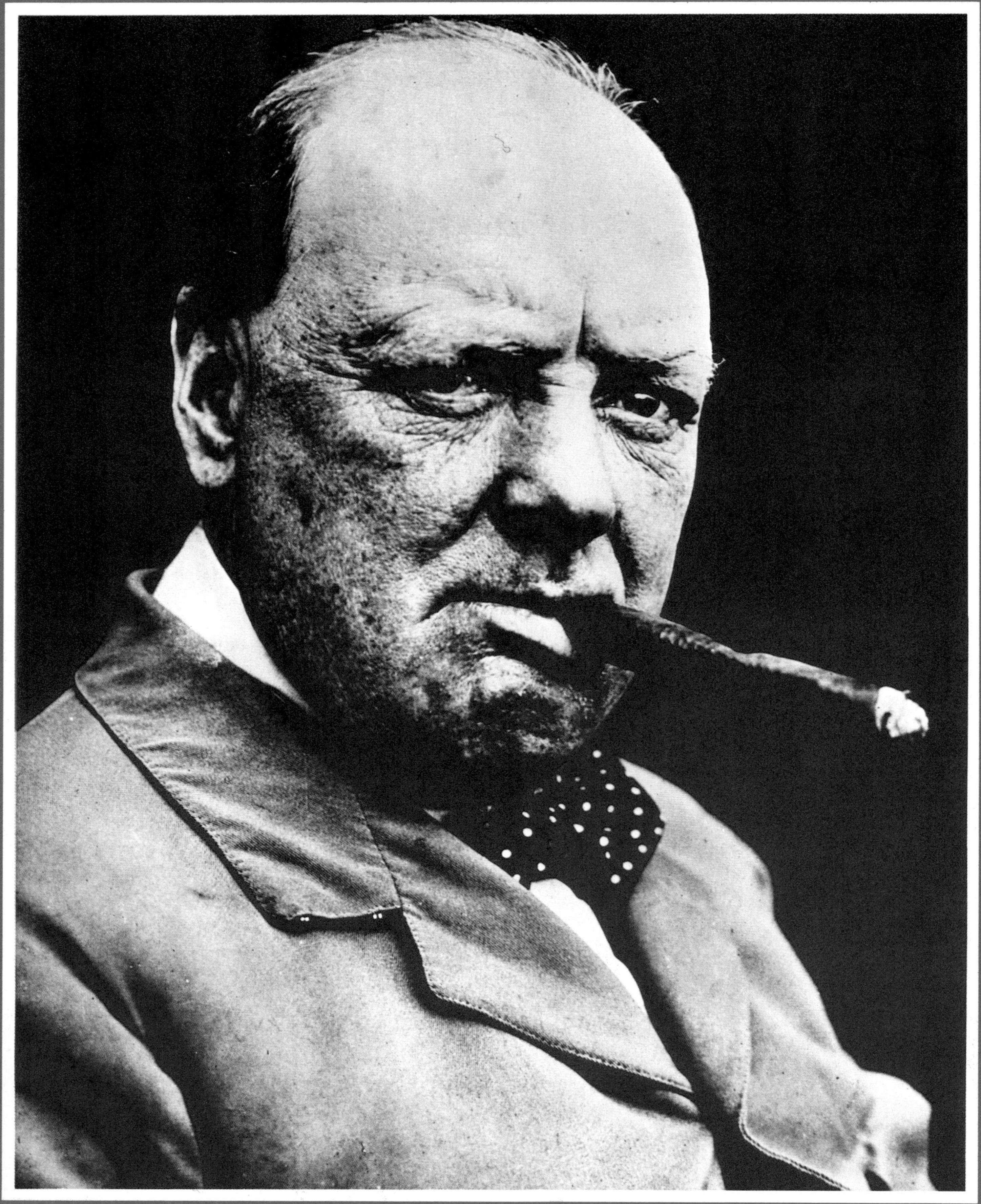

III

The Second World War: 1936-1945

Wherever the balance of advantage for foresight lies between the Conservative, Liberal and Labour Parties during the years leading up to the Second World War, Churchill's record is not open to even the smallest criticism. His views developed all the time—and consistently. As long as the Weimar Republic had endured he had urged the wisdom of encouraging Germany in a policy of peaceful cooperation with Europe through the revision of the Versailles clauses most obnoxious to German sentiment. Even after 1932, when he already saw that Hitler was "the moving impulse behind the German Government and may be more than that soon", he still demanded an effort to remove "the just grievances of the vanquished". But after Hitler's confirmation in power Churchill's theme changed. He sought, first, British preparedness—especially in the air—and carried on a persistent cross-examination of the Government's intentions in this respect. His warnings seemed to be dramatically confirmed by Baldwin's "confession" in 1936, and his influence in the country was steadily growing when an extraneous incident suddenly restored Baldwin's popularity and emphasized Churchill's isolation and unpredictable temperament. This was the abdication of Edward VIII.

During the crisis Churchill seemed sometimes on the verge of forming a "King's Party", and his actions and public utterances stood in unhappy contrast to the steady and wise guidance offered by Baldwin. This was undoubtedly a setback, but Churchill continued his campaign for preparedness, seeking the cooperation of all who agreed with him. He had never trusted the League of Nations as an instrument for general disarmament, but he looked to it now as the instrument of collective preparedness by all the non-aggressive Powers of Europe.

With Chaplin at Chartwell.

"I am perhaps the only man who has passed through both the two supreme cataclysms of recorded history in high Cabinet office."

When Edward VIII, who had become King in January, 1936, let it be known that he wished to abdicate in order to marry the American-born Wallis Warfield Simpson (TOP LEFT, with the then Prince of Wales at Ascot, June, 1935), Churchill was one of the few who supported him. *"I should have been ashamed if, in my independent and unofficial position, I had not cast about for any lawful means, even the most forlorn, to keep him on the Throne of his fathers."* When he took up the King's cause in the House he was hissed into silence. ABOVE: Edward broadcasting his abdication message, December 10, 1936.

INSTRUMENT OF ABDICATION

I, Edward the Eighth, of Great Britain, Ireland, and the British Dominions beyond the Seas, King, Emperor of India, do hereby declare My irrevocable determination to renounce the Throne for Myself and for My descendants, and My desire that effect should be given to this Instrument of Abdication immediately.

In token whereof I have hereunto set My hand this tenth day of December, nineteen hundred and thirty six, in the presence of the witnesses whose signatures are subscribed.

SIGNED AT
FORT BELVEDERE
IN THE PRESENCE
OF

LEFT: The Accession Council which met at St. James's on December 11, 1936, to proclaim George VI King; Churchill wears the uniform of an Elder Brother of Trinity House; Sir Herbert Samuel, the Liberal leader, is on his right. BELOW: The Royal Family at Buckingham Palace after the Coronation: (from left) Queen Elizabeth, Princess Elizabeth, the Queen Mother, Princess Margaret Rose, King George.

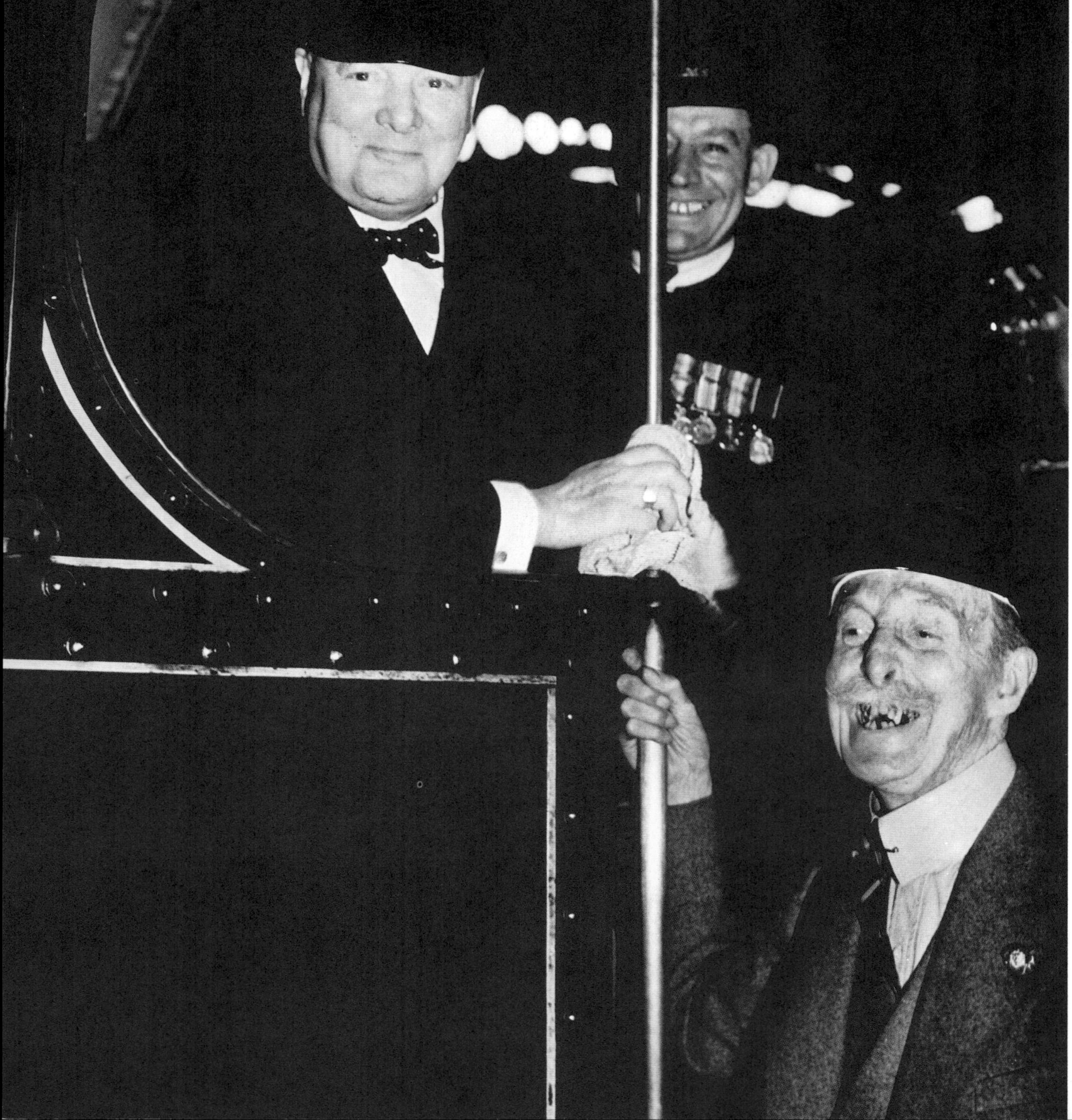

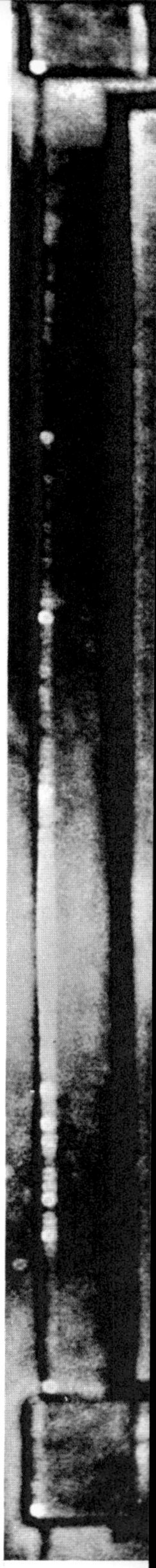

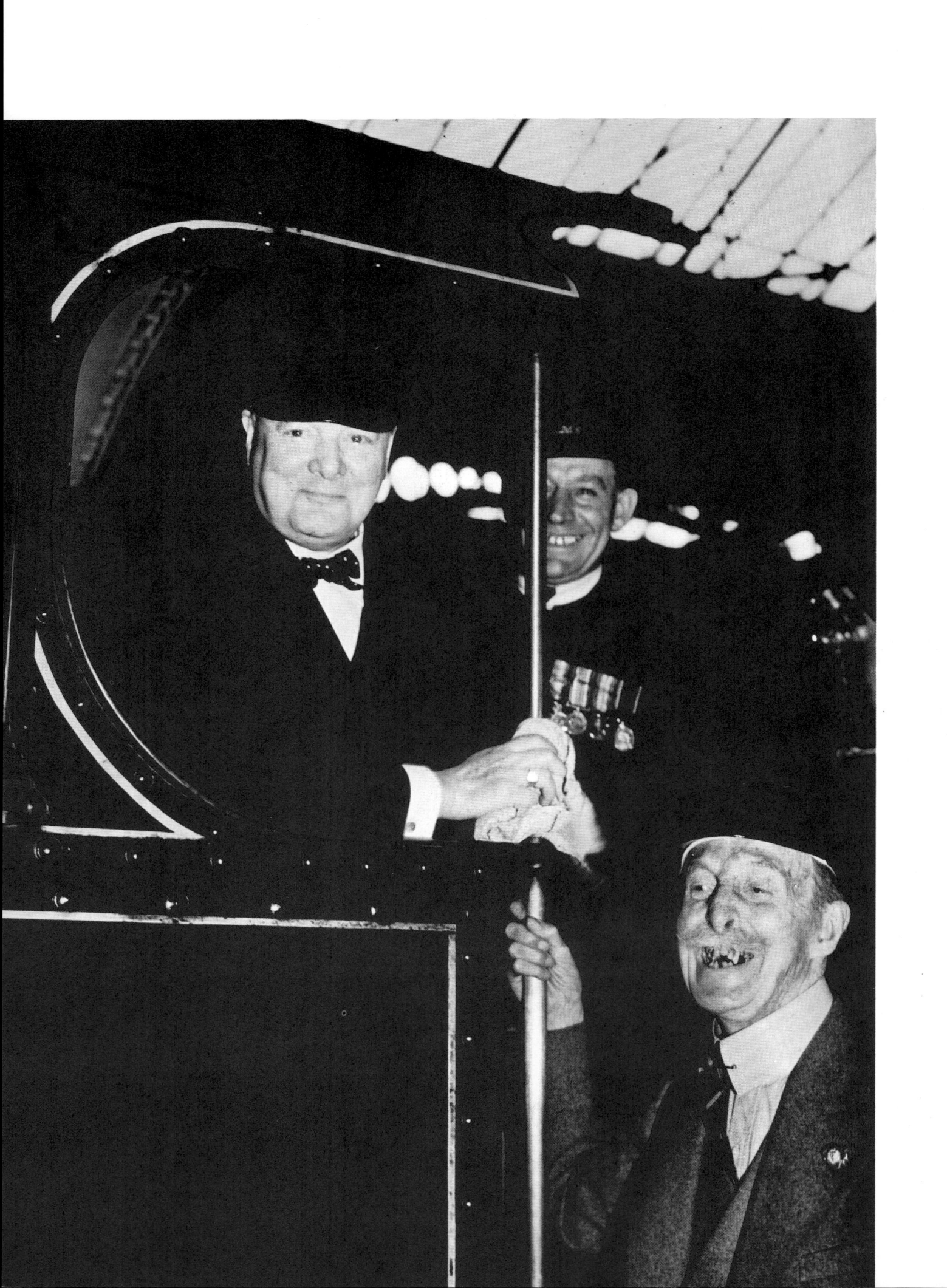

OPPOSITE: At the christening in June, 1937, of a new LMS engine, the *Royal Naval Division,* named for the force Churchill had raised in 1914; on the right is General Sir Ian Hamilton, commander of the Division, with whom he had served in South Africa in 1900. ABOVE: November, 1938: Leaving Guildhall after a reception for King Carol and Prince Michael of Roumania.

"I lived mainly at Chartwell (RIGHT), where I had much to amuse me. I built with my own hands a large part of two cottages and extensive kitchen-garden walls. . . . I never had a dull or idle moment from morning till midnight and dwelt at peace within my habitation."

At his desk (BELOW) at Chartwell, Churchill wrote most of the books he published after 1923. *"Already in 1900 I could boast to have written as many books as Moses, and I have not stopped writing them since, except when momentarily interrupted by war."*

The Gathering Storm: 1936-1939

Adamant for Drift

NOVEMBER, 1936. A PRIVATE MEMBER

My right hon. friend, the Minister for Defence, has argued as usual against a Ministry of Supply. The arguments which he used were very weighty, and even ponderous—it would disturb and delay existing programmes; it would do more harm than good; it would upset the life and industry of the country; it would destroy the export trade and demoralize the finances at the moment when they were most needed; it would turn this country into one vast munitions camp. Certainly these are massive arguments, if they are true. One would have thought that they would carry conviction to any man who accepted them. But then my right hon. friend went on somewhat surprisingly to say, "The decision is not final". It would be reviewed again in a few weeks. What will you know in a few weeks about this matter that you do not know now, that you ought not to have known a year ago and have not been told any time in the last six months? . . .

The First Lord of the Admiralty in his speech the other night went even farther. He said, "We are always reviewing the position". Everything, he assured us, is entirely fluid. I am sure that that is true. Anyone can see what the position is. The Government simply cannot make up their mind, or they cannot get the Prime Minister to make up his mind. So they go on in strange paradox, decided only to be undecided, resolved to be irresolute, adamant for drift, solid for fluidity, all-powerful to be impotent. So we go on preparing more months and years—precious, perhaps vital to the greatness of Britain—for the locusts to eat.

The Victors Are the Vanquished

MARCH, 1938. A PRIVATE MEMBER

All this time the vast degeneration of the forces of Parliamentary democracy will be proceeding throughout Europe. Every six weeks another corps will be added to the German army. All this time important countries, great rail and river communications will pass under the control of the German General Staff. All this time populations will be continually reduced to the rigours of Nazi domination and assimilated to that system. All this time the forces of conquest and intimidation will be consolidated, towering up soon in real and not make-believe strength and superiority. . . .

For five years I have talked to the House on these matters—not with very great success. I have watched this famous island descending incontinently, fecklessly, the stairway which leads to a dark gulf. It is a fine broad stairway at the beginning, but after a bit the carpet ends. A little farther on there are only flagstones, and a little farther on still these break beneath your feet. . . . Look back upon the last five years—since, that is to say, Germany began to rearm in earnest and openly to seek revenge. If we study the history of Rome and Carthage, we can understand what happened and why. It is not difficult to understand and form an intelligent view about the three Punic Wars; but if mortal catastrophe should overtake the British nation and the British Empire, historians a thousand years hence will still be baffled by the mystery of our affairs. They will never understand how it was that a victorious nation, with everything in hand, suffered themselves to be brought low and to cast away all that they had gained by measureless sacrifice and absolute victory—"gone with the wind"!

Now the victors are the vanquished, and those who threw down their arms in the field and sued for an armistice are striding on to world mastery. That is the position—that is the terrible transformation that has taken place bit by bit.

A Fuller, Less Burdened Life

MAY, 1938. A PRIVATE MEMBER; FREE TRADE HALL, MANCHESTER

But what is the purpose which has brought us all together? It is the conviction that the life of Britain, her glories and message to the world, can only be achieved by national unity, and national unity can only be preserved upon a cause which is larger than the nation itself. . . . We wish to make our country safe and strong—she can only be safe if she is strong—and we wish her to play her part with other Parliamentary democracies on both sides of the Atlantic Ocean in warding off from civilization while time yet remains, the devastating and obliterating horrors of another world war. We wish to see inaugurated a reign of international law, backed, as it must be in these turbulent times, by ample and, if possible, superabundant strength.

At this moment in history the broad toiling masses in every country have for the first time the opportunity of a fuller and less burdened life. Science is at hand to spread a more bountiful table than has ever been offered to the millions and to the tens of millions. Shorter hours of labour, greater assurances against individual misfortune: a wider if a simpler culture: a more consciously realized sense of social justice: an easier and a more equal society—these are the treasures which after all these generations and centuries of impotence and confusion, are now within the reach of mankind.

Are these hopes, are these prospects, are all the secrets which the genius of man has wrested from Nature to be turned only by tyranny, aggression and war to his own destruction? Or are they to become the agencies of a broadening freedom, and of an enduring peace?

Never before has the choice of blessings or curses been so plainly, vividly, even brutally offered to mankind. The choice is open. The dreadful balance trembles.

Bitter Waters Are Rising

APRIL, 1939. A PRIVATE MEMBER

The danger now is very near. A great part of Europe is to a very large extent mobilized. Millions of men are being prepared for war. Everywhere the frontier defences are manned. Everywhere it is felt that some new stroke is impending. If it should fall, can there be any doubt but that we shall be involved? We are no longer where we were two or three months ago. We have committed ourselves in every direction, rightly in my opinion, . . . having regard to all that has happened. . . . Surely then, when we aspire to lead all Europe back from the verge of the abyss on to the uplands of law and peace, we must ourselves set the highest example. We must keep nothing back. How can we bear to continue to lead our comfortable easy life here at home, unwilling even to pronounce the word "compulsion", unwilling even to take the necessary measure by which the armies that we have promised can alone be recruited and equipped? How can we continue—let me say it with particular frankness and sincerity—with less than the full force of the nation incorporated in the governing instrument? These very methods, which the Government owe it to the nation and to themselves to take, are not only indispensable to the duties that we have accepted but, by their very adoption, they may rescue our people and the people of many lands from the dark, bitter waters which are rising fast on every side.

The Tramp of Armies

AUGUST, 1939. A PRIVATE MEMBER; A BROADCAST TO THE UNITED STATES OF AMERICA

But to come back to the hush I said was hanging over Europe. What kind of a hush is it? Alas! it is the hush of suspense, and in many lands it is the hush of fear. Listen! No, listen carefully; I think I hear something—yes, there it was quite clear. Don't you hear it? It is the tramp of armies crunching the gravel of the parade-grounds, splashing through rain-soaked fields, the tramp of two million German soldiers and more than a million Italians—"going on manoeuvres"—yes, only on manoeuvres! Of course it's only manoeuvres—just like last year. After all, the dictators must train their soldiers. They could scarcely do less in common prudence, when the Danes, the Dutch, the Swiss, the Albanians—and of course the Jews—may leap out upon them at any moment and rob them of their living-space, and make them sign another paper to say who began it. Besides these German and Italian armies may have another work of liberation to perform. It was only last year they liberated Austria from the horrors of self-government. It was only in March they freed the Czechoslovak Republic from the misery of independent existence. It is only two years ago that Signor Mussolini gave the ancient kingdom of Abyssinia its Magna Charta. It is only two months ago that little Albania got its writ of Habeas Corpus, and Mussolini sent in his Bill of Rights for King Zog to pay. Why even at this moment, the mountaineers of the Tyrol, a German-speaking population who have dwelt in their beautiful valleys for a thousand years, are being liberated, that is to say, uprooted, from the land they love, from the soil which Andreas Hofer died to defend. No wonder the armies are tramping on when there is so much liberation to be done, and no wonder there is a hush among all the neighbours of Germany and Italy while they are wondering which one is going to be "liberated" next.

Neville Chamberlain (BELOW) with members of his Government on his return from Munich, September, 1938; and (BOTTOM LEFT) with Mussolini in Rome, January, 1939. *"We have sustained a defeat without a war; the whole equilibrium of Europe has been deranged, and the terrible words pronounced against the western democracies: 'Thou art weighed in the balance and found wanting.'"* RIGHT: Hitler speaking at Potsdam as his Wehrmacht (BELOW, CENTER) mobilized for war, 1939.

At Kenley, April 16, 1939 (ABOVE), after flying with No. 615 Auxiliary Squadron of the RAF, of which he was Honorary Air Commodore. *"If we had taken steps betimes to create an air force half as strong again, or twice as strong, as any that Germany could produce . . . , we should have kept control of the future."*

At the Admiralty again, September 4, 1939: *"The Board were kind enough to signal to the Fleet, 'Winston is back.'"*

Diplomatic efforts to halt German aggression were in vain, and on September 3, 1939, Britain was again at war. Churchill returned to office as First Lord of the Admiralty—an appointment greeted with relief by the public which had for so long been heedless of his warnings—and from the first he established himself as the popular war leader. At the Admiralty he took the first steps to combat the submarine menace which later became so formidable, but the main episode of his term was the brilliant operation in which Commodore Harwood, in command of *Ajax, Achilles,* and *Exeter,* drove the *Graf Spee* to its destruction. His voice meanwhile was strengthening the nerve of the British people—an invaluable task in the confusing days of the "phony war". There was the characteristic cockiness with which he offered "to engage the entire German Navy, using only the vessels which at one time or another they have declared they have destroyed". Meanwhile he was still pursuing his concept of collective security, urging the small European neutrals to understand the danger. But they did not heed either, and in the spring of 1940 Norway, Denmark, Belgium, and the Netherlands were all invaded.

On Churchill, as First Lord, fell the responsibility for the dispatch and disembarkation of the forces sent to strengthen Norway. Once more, as in 1915, an improvised undertaking ended in failure. The debate which followed—in which Churchill manfully defended the Government—decided the fate of Chamberlain's Government, and on May 10 Chamberlain resigned and advised the King to send for Churchill. The Labour and Liberal leaders agreed to serve with him, and so the great Coalition was formed which was to remain united until victory in Europe had been won.

In the first volume of his history of the war Churchill has described his feelings on that night in words which are as moving as they are simple: "During these last crowded days of the political crisis my pulse had not quickened at any moment. I took it all as it came. But I cannot conceal from the reader of this truthful account that as I went to bed at about 3 a.m. I was conscious of a profound sense of relief. At last I had the authority to give directions over the whole scene. I felt as if I were walking with destiny and that all my past life had been but a preparation for this hour and for this trial. . . . I thought I knew a good deal about it all, and I was sure I should not fail."

This undramatic confidence—recalling Chatham's "I know that I can save this country and that no one else can"—was quickly communicated to the people of Britain. "What is our aim?" he exclaimed when he first met the House of Commons as Prime Minister. "I can answer in one word: Victory—victory at all costs, victory in spite of all terrors, victory, however long and hard the road may be; for without victory there is no survival."

"Thus, then, on the night of the tenth of May, at the outset of this mighty battle, I acquired the chief power in the State, which henceforth I wielded in ever-growing measure for five years and three months of world war." LEFT: No. 10 Downing Street, where Churchill took up residence as Prime Minister in May, 1940, as the Nazis marched into the Low Countries.

Cecil Beaton

Their Finest Hour: 1940

Without Victory, No Survival

MAY, 1940. PRIME MINISTER

On Friday evening last I received His Majesty's Commission to form a new Administration. . . .

To form an Administration of this scale and complexity is a serious undertaking in itself, but it must be remembered that we are in the preliminary stage of one of the greatest battles of history, that we are in action at many points in Norway and in Holland, that we have to be prepared in the Mediterranean, that the air battle is continuous and that many preparations . . . have to be made here at home. In this crisis I hope I may be pardoned if I do not address the House at any length today. I hope that any of my friends and colleagues, or former colleagues, who are affected by the political reconstruction, will make all allowance for any lack of ceremony with which it has been necessary to act. I would say to the House, as I said to those who have joined this Government: "I have nothing to offer but blood, toil, tears and sweat."

We have before us an ordeal of the most grievous kind. We have before us many, many long months of struggle and of suffering. You ask, what is our policy? I will say: It is to wage war, by sea, land and air, with all our might and with all the strength that God can give us: to wage war against a monstrous tyranny, never surpassed in the dark, lamentable catalogue of human crime. That is our policy. You ask, What is our aim? I can answer in one word: it is victory, victory at all costs, victory in spite of all terror, victory, however long and hard the road may be; for without victory, there is no survival. Let that be realized; no survival for the British Empire, no survival for all that the British Empire has stood for, no survival for the urge and impulse of the ages, that mankind will move forward towards its goal. But I take up my task with buoyancy and hope. I feel sure that our cause will not be suffered to fail among men. At this time I feel entitled to claim the aid of all, and I say, "Come, then, let us go forward together with our united strength."

Broad, sunlit uplands

JUNE, 1940. PRIME MINISTER

However matters may go in France or with the French Government or with another French Government, we in this island and in the British Empire will never lose our sense of comradeship with the French people. If we are now called upon to endure what they have suffered we shall emulate their courage, and if final victory rewards our toils they shall share the gains, aye, and freedom shall be restored to all. We abate nothing of our just demands—Czechs, Poles, Norwegians, Dutch, Belgians, all who have joined their causes to our own shall be restored.

What General Weygand called the "Battle of France" is over. I expect that the battle of Britain is about to begin. Upon this battle depends the survival of Christian civilization. Upon it depends our own British life and the long continuity of our institutions and our Empire. The whole fury and might of the enemy must very soon be turned on us. Hitler knows that he will have to break us in this island or lose the war. If we can stand up to him all Europe may be free and the life of the world may move forward into broad, sunlit uplands; but if we fail then the whole world, including the United States, and all that we have known and cared for, will sink into the abyss of a new dark age made more sinister, and perhaps more prolonged, by the lights of perverted science. Let us therefore brace ourselves to our duty, and so bear ourselves that, if the British Commonwealth and Empire last for a thousand years men will still say, "This was their finest hour."

"The deadly, drilled, docile, brutish masses of the Hun soldiery plodding on like a swarm of crawling locusts."

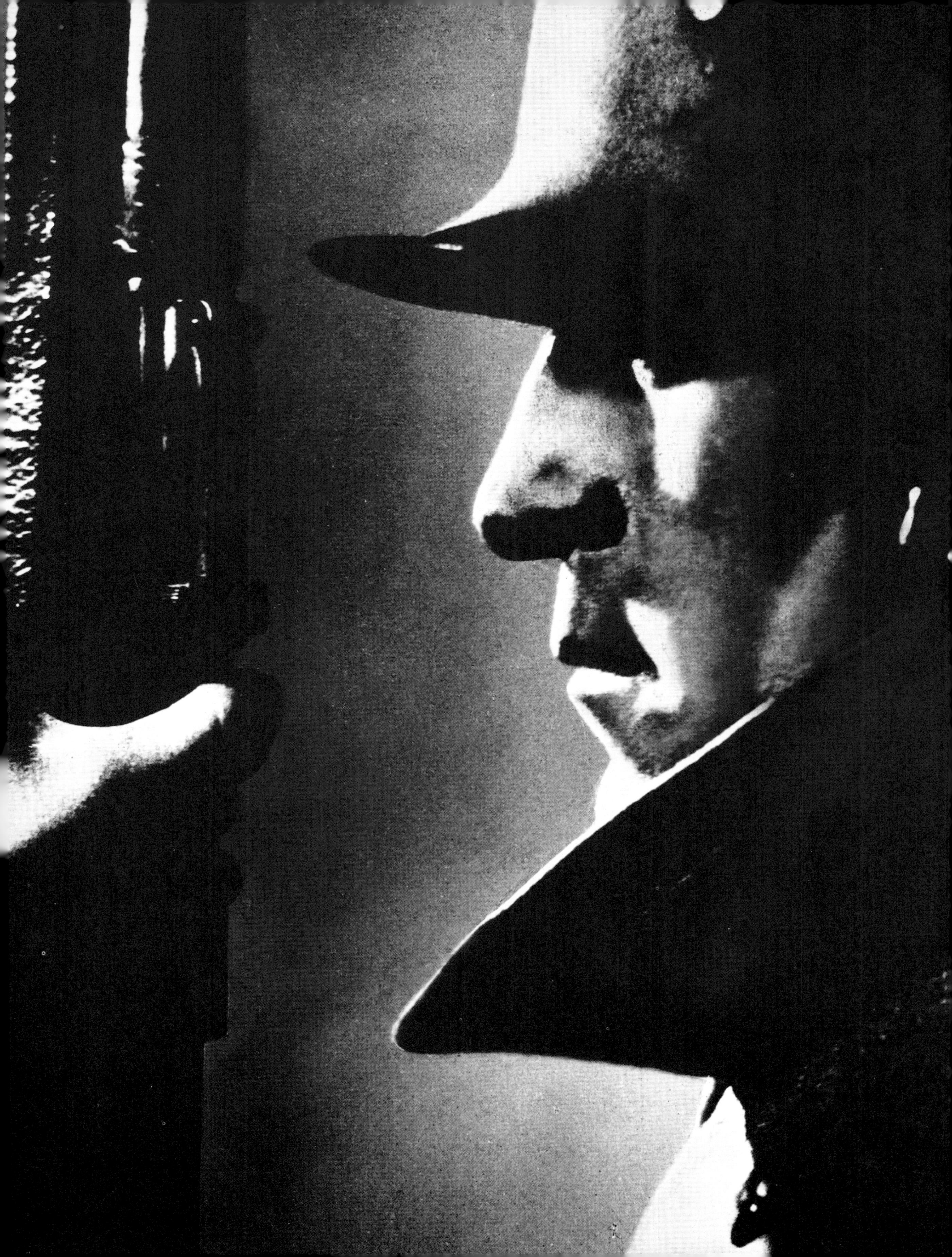

INVASION OF
THE LOWLANDS

Meanwhile, attacking through country which before the days of mechanization had been regarded as unsuitable for large-scale operations, the Germans drove a wedge between the Franco-British armies advancing north-eastwards and the main French Army. Holland surrendered after five days, Belgium held out until the allied troops were cut off both from their support and from the sea. There followed the unexpected success of the evacuation from Dunkirk, which so lifted the hearts of the British people that Churchill had to warn them that "Wars are not won by evacuations". It was at this point that Churchill ended a survey of the campaign with the words: "We shall not flag or fail. We shall go on to the end. . . . We shall defend our island whatever the cost may be. We shall fight on the beaches. We shall fight on the landing grounds. We shall fight in the fields and in the streets. We shall fight in the hills. We shall never surrender. And even if—which I do not for a moment believe—this island or a large part of it were subjugated and starving, then our Empire beyond the seas, armed and guarded by the British Fleet, would carry on the struggle until, in God's good time, the New World, with all its power and might, steps forth to the rescue and liberation of the old!"

Evacuation at Dunkirk: *"Out of the jaws of death and shame."*

The agony of France was now prolonged for another three weeks, heavy with disaster, during which Churchill himself carried the whole weight of the British effort to keep France in the war. He visited the French Ministers at Tours, and crossed the Channel again a few days later after he had already made his brave offer of a solemn Act of Union between the two countries. It was too brave for the Ministers at Bordeaux, and on June 21, 1940, France surrendered, without giving Churchill an undertaking not to allow the French fleet to fall into German hands. Churchill, bowing to the logic of necessity, then took what must have been one of the hardest decisions of his life. The French warships—constituting the flower of the French fleet—were fired on, with damage and destruction, by British vessels as they tried to make their way from a North African port to Toulon.

Britain was now alone and almost unarmed. For her immediate deliverance she relied upon the chosen band of her own young men flying a few machines. Churchill neither planned nor directed the Battle of Britain on which the future of human freedom depended; but it was he who had evoked and deployed the indomitable strength behind the British airmen which now inspired their unsleeping fight against enormous odds. It was fitting that he should stamp on men's minds the character and significance of this battle in the simplest of his phrases: "Never in the field of human conflict was so much owed by so many to so few." The bombing of London followed in September—with Churchill cheerfully calculating that "it would take 10 years at the present rate for half the houses of London to be demolished. After that, of course, progress would be much slower."

September, 1940: Surveying bomb damage to London (OPPOSITE) as the Battle of Britain began.

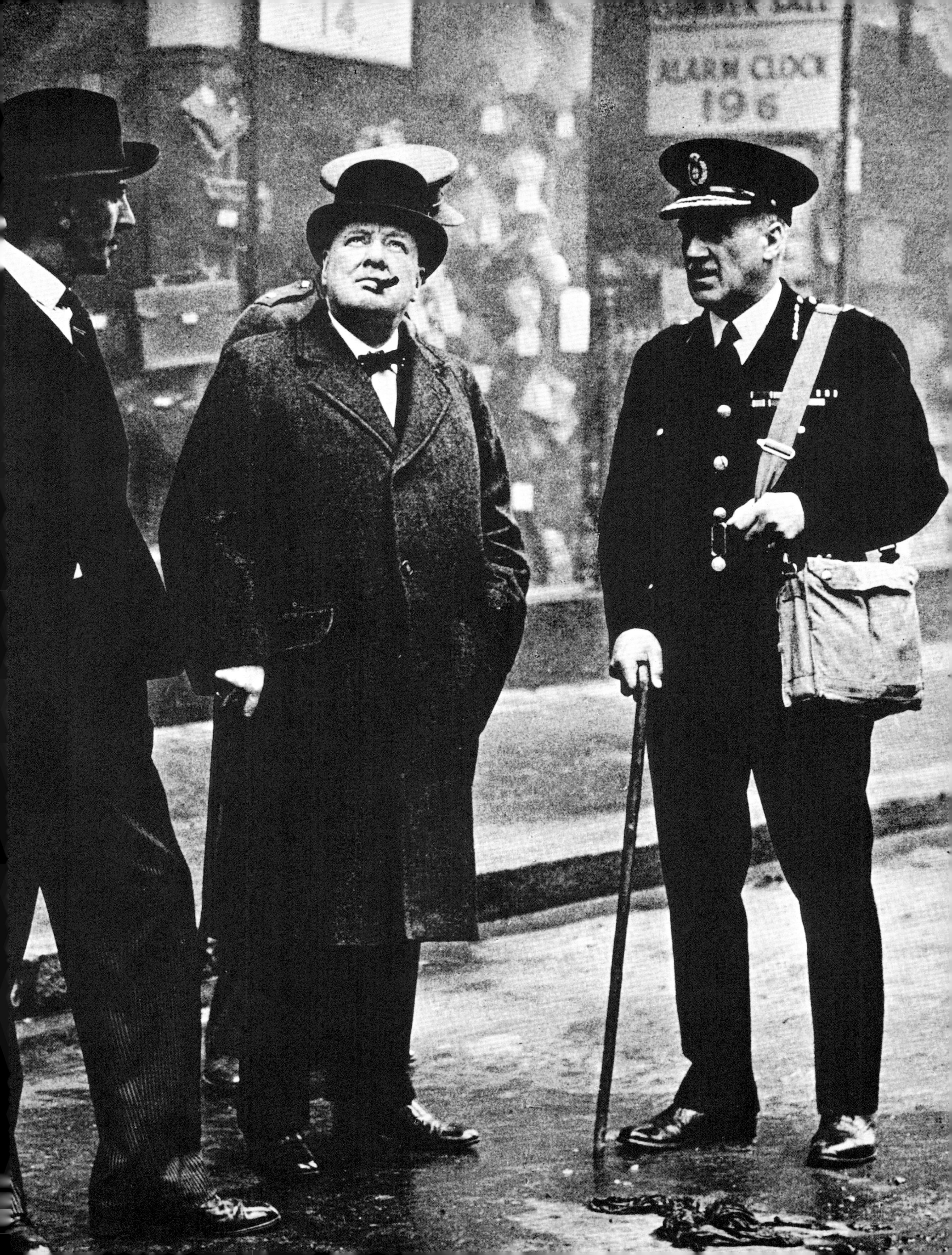
ALARM CLOCK
19 6

106

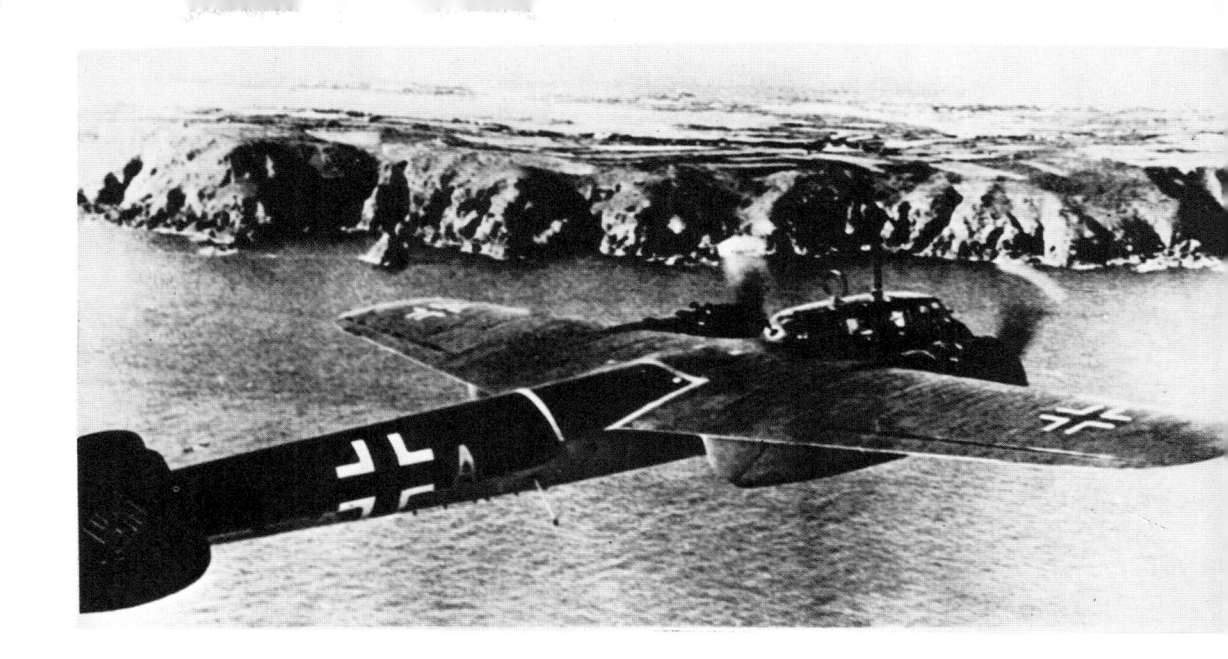

"Here in London, which Herr Hitler says he will reduce to ashes, and which his aeroplanes (ABOVE) are now bombarding . . ." Crowds in the Strand hurry towards shelters (OPPOSITE PAGE) as sirens sound; so many window panes were smashed by blast (as BELOW) that Churchill feared a glass famine.

"*. . . our people are bearing up unflinchingly.*" The Prime Minister scanning the skies for enemy bombers, as fire-watchers (RIGHT) stood guard on the roofs and millions of Londoners slept, night after night, in the Underground (BELOW).

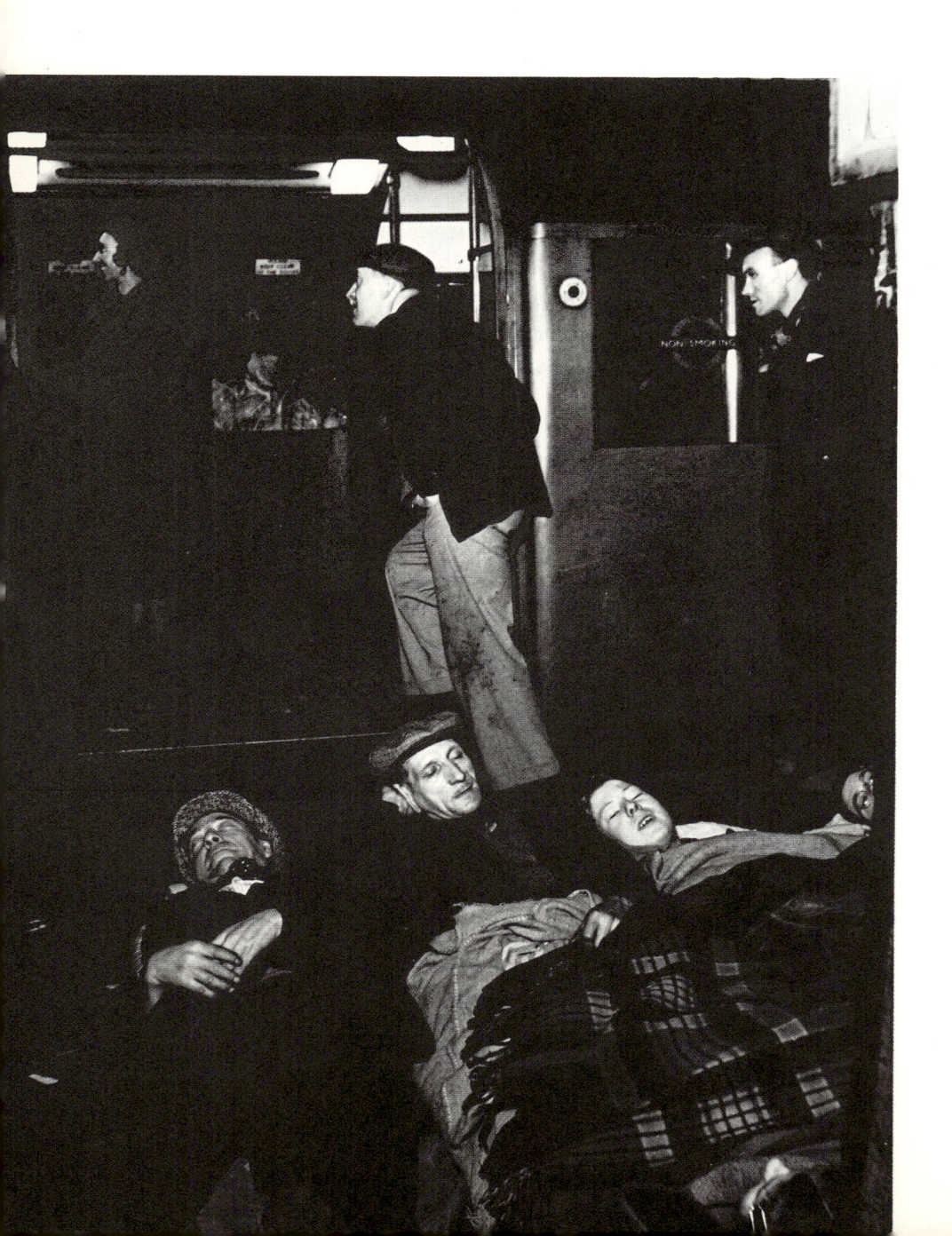

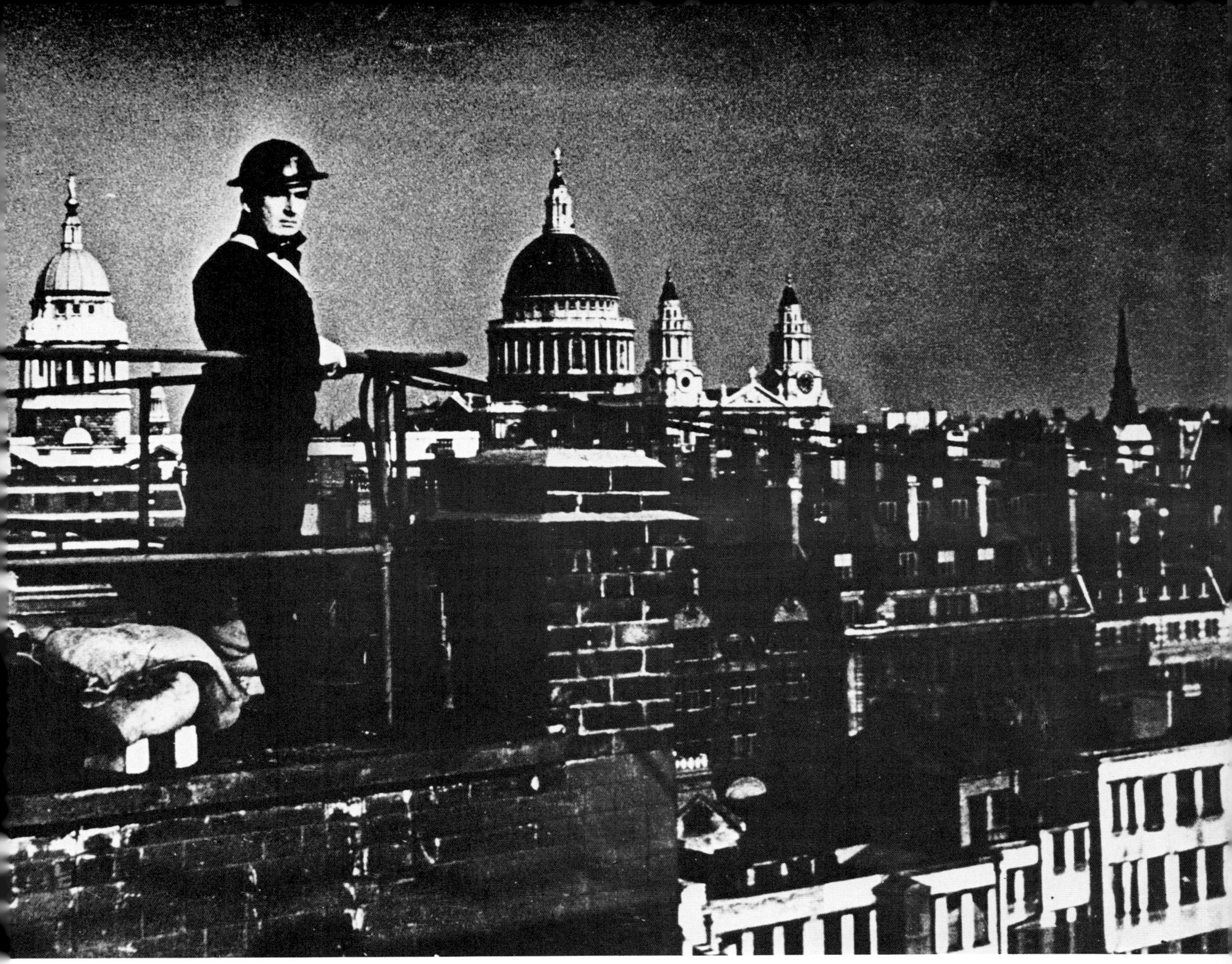
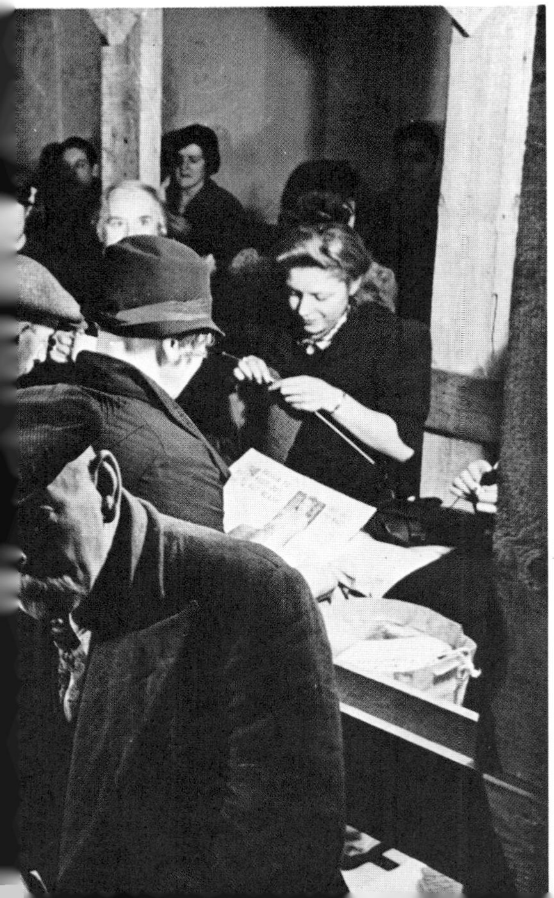
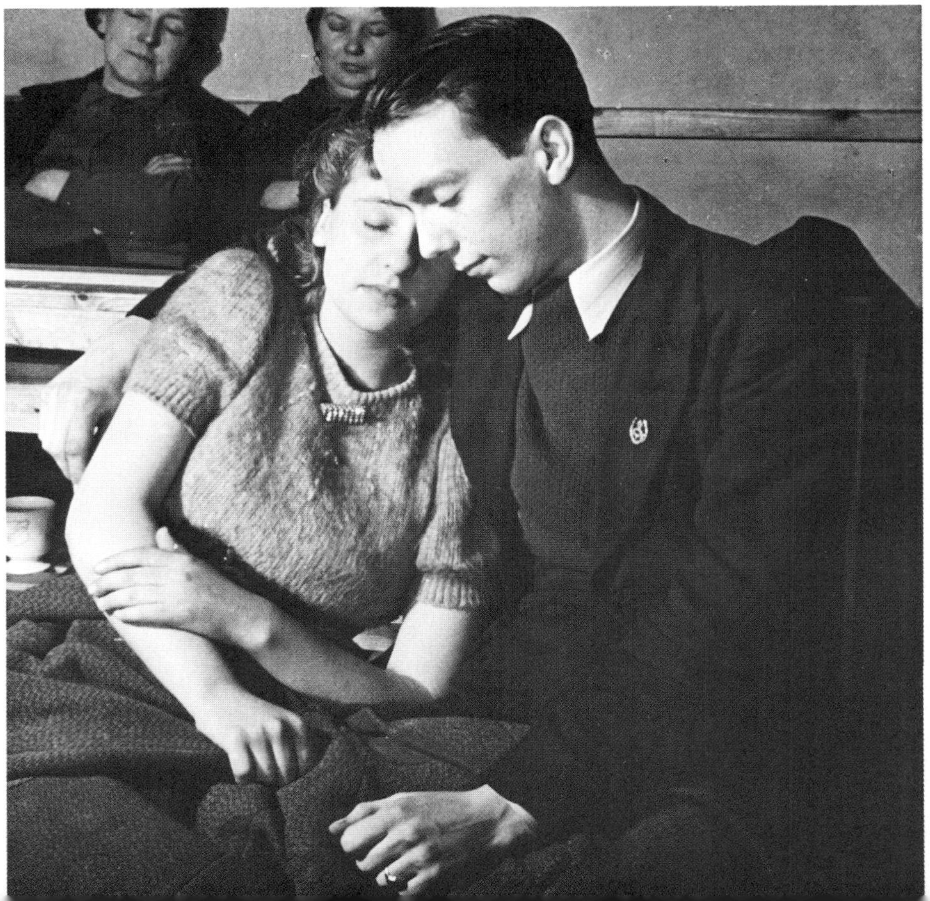

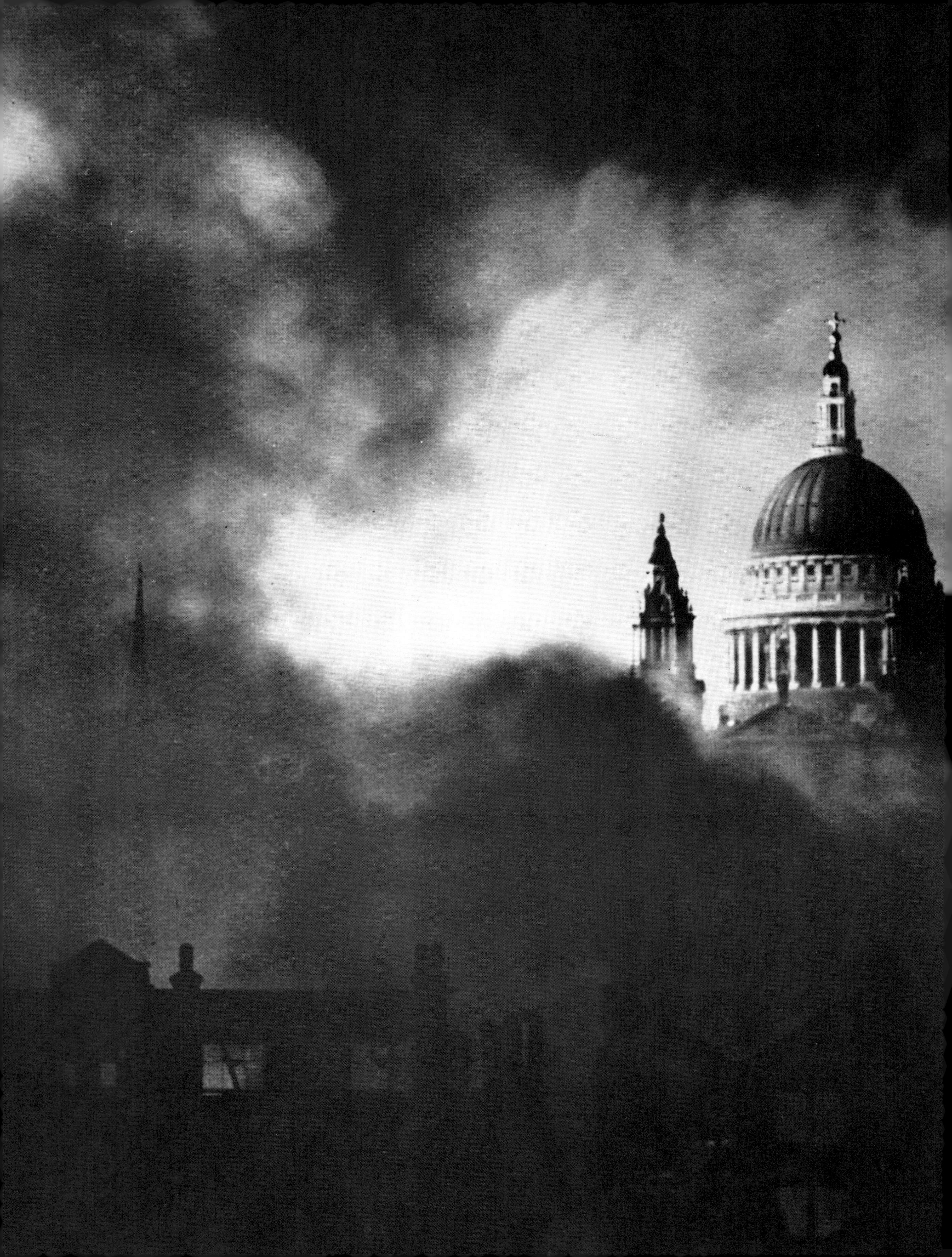

The City of London on fire (LEFT) after the climactic raid of Sunday, December 29, 1940, "... *an incendiary classic. Eight Wren churches were destroyed or damaged. The Guildhall was smitten by fire and blast, and St. Paul's Cathedral was only saved by heroic exertions. A void of ruin at the very centre of the British world gapes upon us.*"

With Mrs. Churchill, viewing from a launch the destruction along the Thames.

"London was like some huge prehistoric animal, capable of enduring terrible injuries, mangled and bleeding from many wounds, and yet preserving its life and movement. . . . Soon many of the bombs would fall upon houses already ruined and only make the rubble jump. Over large areas there would be nothing more to burn or destroy, and yet human beings might make their homes here and there, and carry on their work with infinite resource and fortitude. At this time anyone would have been proud to be a Londoner." RIGHT: January, 1941: Looking down from St. Paul's towards Newgate Street and Christ Church. ABOVE: A child looking up from the ruins in which his parents lie buried.

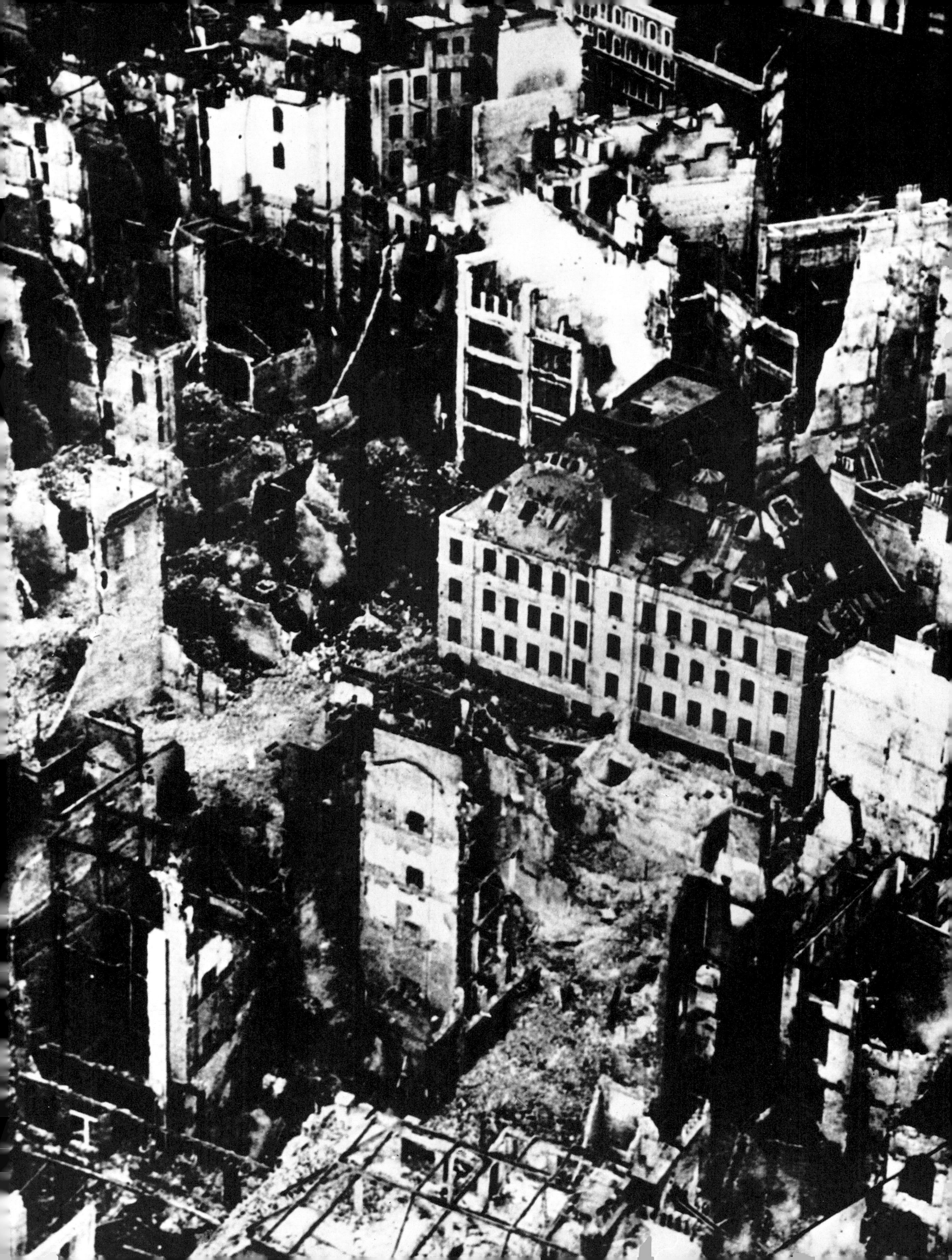

"All hearts go out to the fighter pilots, whose brilliant actions we see with our own eyes day after day." OPPOSITE: A formation of Spitfires over the Channel.

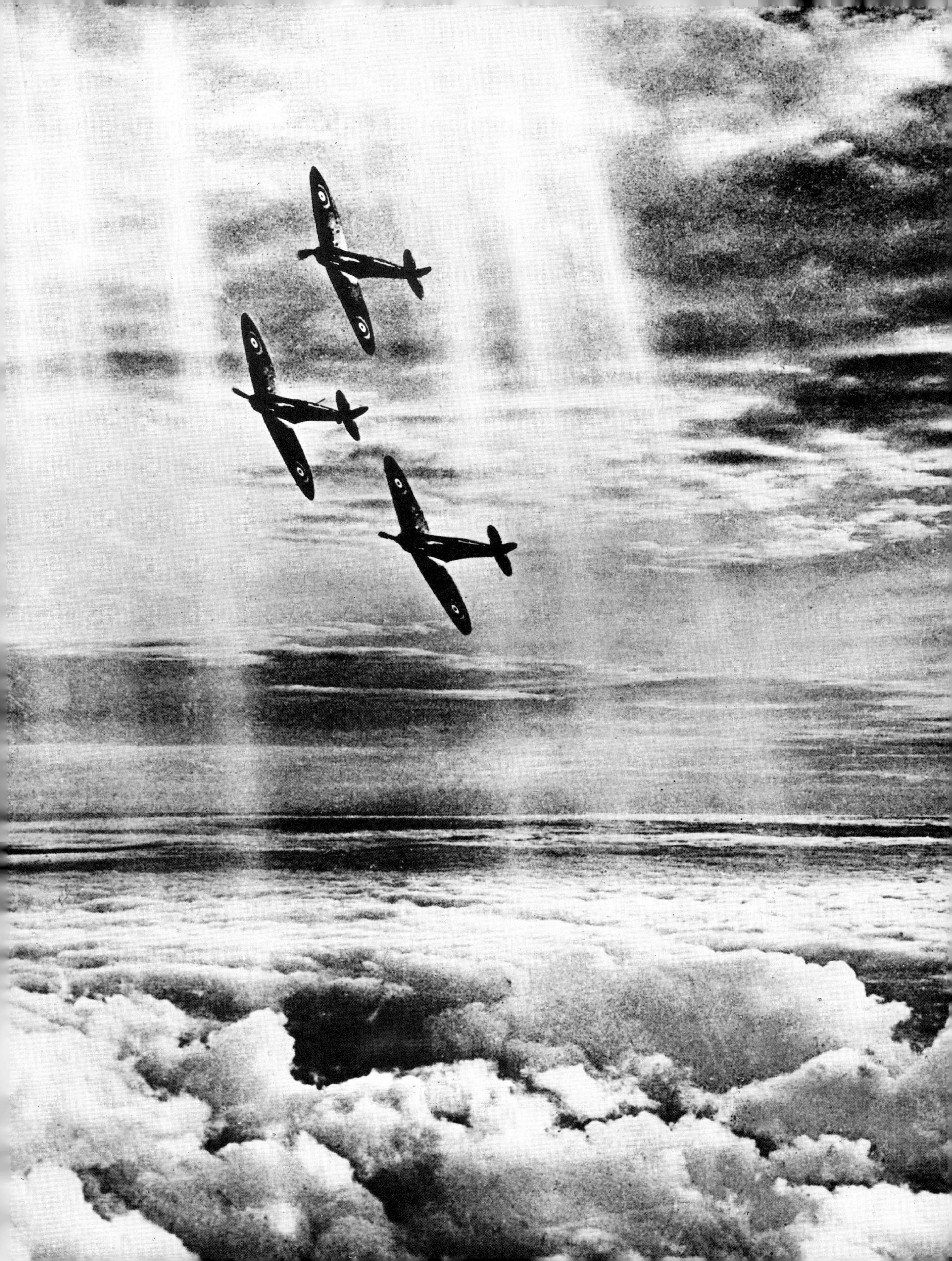

The War Cabinet, 1940: (seated from left) Sir John Anderson, Mr. Churchill, Mr. Clement Attlee, Mr. Anthony Eden; (standing) Mr. Arthur Greenwood, Mr. Ernest Bevin, Lord Beaverbrook, Sir Kingsley Wood.

THE WAR CABINET

The organization through which every department of Government consciously worked under Churchill's superintending eye and felt the drive of his personality was built up gradually in the light of experience. When first constructed his administration was modelled on Lloyd George's War Cabinet, and of the Prime Minister's four colleagues, Mr. Chamberlain, Mr. Attlee, Mr. Greenwood, and Lord Halifax, only the last carried, as Foreign Secretary, the burden of heavy departmental responsibilities. But three months later the intimate relationship already apparent between the issue of the war and the activities of the Ministry of Aircraft Production—itself one of Churchill's creations—led to the inclusion in the War Cabinet of its head, Lord Beaverbrook. As the war developed the Prime Minister brought in the Ministers in charge of other departments most directly concerned with its conduct, so that in its later form the War Cabinet had a membership of eight or nine, and included the Chancellor of the Exchequer and the Ministers of Labour, Production, and Home Security. Gradually, too, Churchill worked out his functions as Minister of Defence, a title which he had assumed when he became Prime Minister. It was never his intention to create a full-blown Ministry such as has now been established. His purpose was to give definition and authority to his transactions not with the service Ministers who were members of his Government but with the Chiefs of Staff, and to this end he provided himself with a small technical staff headed by General (now Lord) Ismay.

The system which Churchill created was emphatically personal in principle and was devised to give full scope both to his military knowledge and to his vast departmental experience. It worked because he was able to handle a mass of details which would have overwhelmed any other man. It was equally personal in its method of operation. Its timetable was governed by the Prime Minister's habits. Churchill's practice was to go to bed and sleep soundly in the early afternoon. When he had dressed again he brought a refreshed mind to bear on the immediate business of the day. Exhilarated by his contact with practical difficulties, he went on to address himself to questions of policy, regularly called Cabinet meetings for 11 p.m., and, after they had ended, continued for some time to pour out comment and suggestion to those of his associates who could keep his hours. Nor was he merely equal to his self-imposed tasks; as Mr. Attlee said later, he set the pace.

The war surveys for which his return from his journeys often provided the occasion rank among the outstanding events of his parliamentary career. World-wide in range and profound in matter, they at once informed and inspired both the House and the country. The richness of their content was enhanced by a delivery characteristic of their author. Churchill's voice was not impressive in volume. But it was wide in compass. In his loftiest moments its somewhat metallic tones vibrated with passion, the more combative passages were given colour by the effective use of the rising inflexion and the frequent assertions of high resolve were made resonant by the accompaniment, felt rather than heard, of a sort of bulldog growl. Read over in the light of after events these speeches are notable for their masterly restraint. They revealed much but they concealed more; of the great plans which filled his mind and with the execution of which he must have been busy up to the moment when he rose in his place not a hint was allowed to transpire.

The Defence Committee, 1941: (seated with the Prime Minister) Lord Beaverbrook, Mr. Attlee, Mr. Eden, Mr. A. V. Alexander; (standing) Air Chief Marshal Sir Charles Portal, Admiral Sir Dudley Pound, Sir Archibald Sinclair, Captain Margesson, General Dill, General Ismay, Colonel Hollis.

At the threat of invasion, in 1940, a civilian army of volunteers was formed. *"The Home Guard overtopped the million mark, and when rifles were lacking grasped lustily the shotgun, the sporting rifle, the private pistol, or, when there was no firearm, the pike and the club."* ABOVE: The Prime Minister inspecting units of the Home Guard in Hyde Park.

Prime Minister to Secretary, War Office, 20.X.40: *"It is impossible to take away steel helmets from 'the Home Guard in Government offices.' Four were killed outside Downing Street on Thursday night."* ABOVE: Mrs. Churchill and helmeted Home Guard. TOP LEFT: Churchill at a march-past of the Women's Voluntary Services, a vital part of the civilian forces.

In September last, having been defeated in his invasion plans by the RAF, Hitler declared his intention to raze the cities of Britain to the ground, and in the early days of that month he set the whole fury of the Hun upon London. . . . We were then not prepared as we are now. Our defences had not the advantages they have since attained, and again I must admit that I greatly feared injury to our public services, I feared the ravages of fire, I feared the dislocation of life and the stoppage of work, I feared epidemics of serious disease or even pestilence among the crowds who took refuge in our by no means completely constructed or well equipped shelters.

I remember one winter evening travelling to a railway station—which still worked—on my way north to visit troops. It was cold and raining. Darkness had almost fallen on the blacked-out streets. I saw everywhere long queues of people, among them hundreds of young girls in their silk stockings and high-heeled shoes, who had worked hard all day and were waiting for bus after bus, which came by already overcrowded, in the hope of reaching their homes for the night. When at that moment the doleful wail of the siren betokened the approach of the German bombers, I confess to you that my heart bled for London and the Londoners.

All this sort of thing went on for more than four months with hardly any intermission. . . . But there was one thing about which there was never any doubt. The courage, the unconquerable grit and stamina of the Londoners showed itself from the very outset. Without that all would have failed. Upon that rock, all stood unshakable. . . .

We have to ask ourselves this question: Will the bombing attacks of last autumn and winter come again? We have proceeded on the assumption that they will. . . . We ask no favours of the enemy. We seek from them no compunction. . . . Prepare yourselves, then, my friends and comrades in the Battle of London, for this renewal of your exertions. We shall never turn from our purpose, however sombre the road, however grievous the cost, because we know that out of this time of trial and tribulation will be born a new freedom and glory for all mankind.

From the speech delivered (RIGHT and OPPOSITE PAGE) to the London County Council, July 14, 1941.

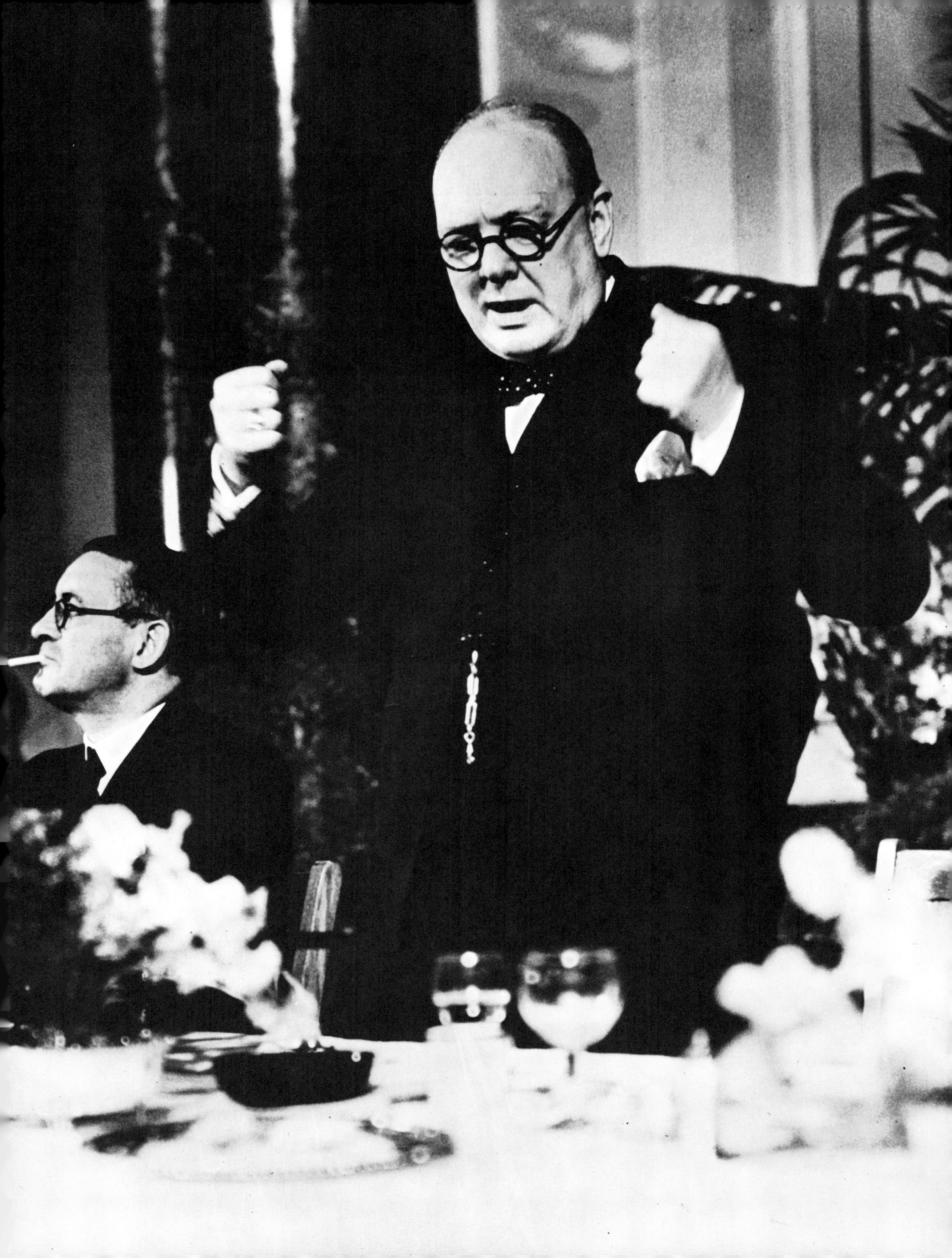

ABOVE: Fire guard on the House of Commons; Victoria Tower on the right, from the roof of Westminster Hall. *"A single bomb created ruin for years"* in the Commons, in the last—and worst—raid of the night Blitz, on May 10, 1941, in which incendiary bombs lit more than two thousand fires and killed or injured over three thousand people. RIGHT: Children evacuated from London at Wilton, with the Countess of Pembroke and her son Lord David Herbert. OPPOSITE PAGE, ABOVE: Churchill makes the V-for-victory sign as he rides through the battered port city of Hull.

Cecil Beaton

ABOVE: On a visit to Dover *"to see our heavy batteries glaring across the Channel."* OPPOSITE PAGE, RIGHT: Watching an A.A. demonstration, 1941. *"We are waiting for the long-promised invasion. So are the fishes."*

LEFT: Heinkels attacking a convoy in the Barents Sea; one is downed by a destroyer as (BELOW, CENTER) a tanker explodes.

ALLIES AGAINST THE AXIS

In the summer of 1941, Churchill triumphantly surmounted a severe test of his appreciation of the needs of war. No man had shown fiercer opposition to the Soviet Power in its revolutionary phase, and though time and the growth of the German menace had modified his judgment, he had been a party in 1939 to plans, happily found impracticable, for the dispatch of an Anglo-French expeditionary force to aid Finland in her war with Russia. Hitler's decision in June, 1941, thus confronted him with a difficult choice. He made it without hesitation, and in the most dramatic of his broadcasts announced that every possible aid would be given to the latest victim of German aggression. The declaration had prompt results. Early in July an Anglo-Soviet agreement was signed in Moscow, and in the following month the two Governments sent troops into Persia to eradicate German influence and to secure the use of the Trans-Persian railway for the conveyance of supplies to Russia. The operation led in September to the abdication of the Shah. Under his son and successor Persia signed a treaty with the allies. Meanwhile the American Government had been following these developments with sympathy; Churchill and President Roosevelt had signed the Atlantic Charter in August, and that same month the United States too signed an agreement with Russia. On the joint suggestion of the President and Churchill a three-Power conference met in Moscow at the end of September. In the following May Mr. Molotov came to London and Anglo-Russian cooperation was rounded off by the signature of a treaty of alliance. Meanwhile 26 allied nations had signed a declaration committing them to fight to a finish against the Axis. The Grand Alliance was in being.

August 12, 1941, "Somewhere in the Atlantic": *"The Atlantic Charter was not a law, but a star."*

A final salute from the "Former Naval Person," leaving the U.S.S. *Augusta* after the three-day conference with President Roosevelt that ended in the signing of the Atlantic Charter.

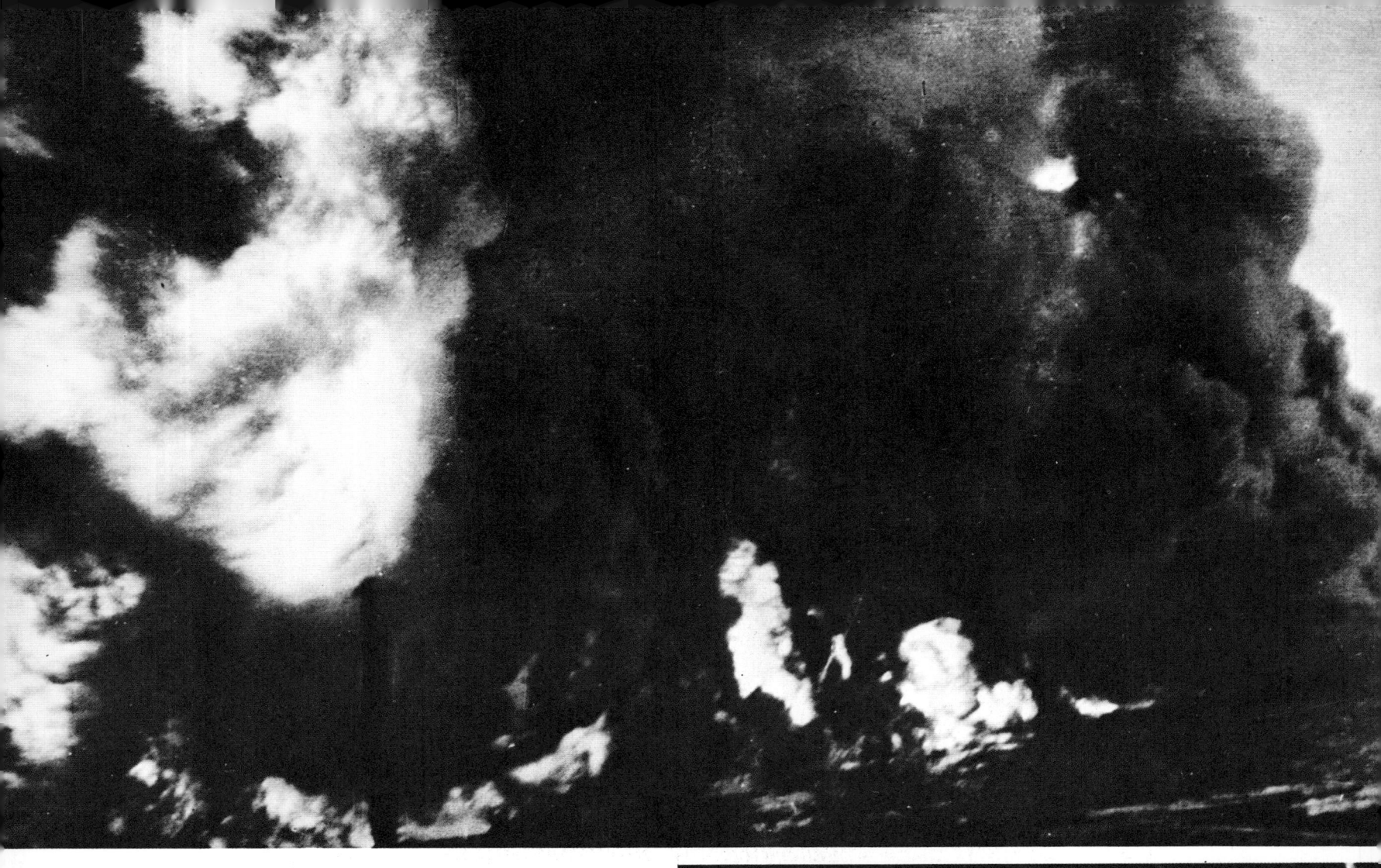

President Roosevelt before Congress, December 8, 1941, announcing the Japanese attack on Pearl Harbor (ABOVE; RIGHT).

Churchill at Downing Street with the news of Pearl Harbor; Britain declared war on Japan "within the hour."

Addressing the Congress of the United States, December 26, 1941. "*I must confess that I felt quite at home, and more sure of myself than I had sometimes been in the House of Commons. I got my laughter and applause just where I expected them. The loudest response was when, speaking of the Japanese outrage, I asked, 'What sort of people do they think we are?' The sense of the might and will-power of the American nation streamed up to me. Who could doubt that all would be well?*"

From the first Churchill had looked forward to the eventual participation of the United States in the war. Deeply appreciative of the support, material as well as moral, given by the American Government while nominally neutral and determined that friction with Britain should not obstruct the evolution of American policy, he was sympathetic towards American plans for the more effective defence of the western hemisphere and was even prepared for some small cession of territory. President Roosevelt, however, asked no more than 99-year leases of land for naval and air bases, and in September, 1940, an agreement was concluded. The bases in Newfoundland and Bermuda were leased "freely and without consideration", Britain thus aligning herself with Canada in treating the defence of North America as a matter of partnership. Six bases in the Caribbean were also leased in exchange for 50 destroyers from the United States Navy.

The Lend-Lease Act of March, 1941, and the Atlantic Charter of the following August had carried the process further, and when in December Japan attacked at Pearl

In the House of Commons, Ottawa, December 30, 1941, making his famous "Some chicken! Some neck!" speech to the Canadian Parliament. The United Nations Pact was signed in Washington three days later.

Harbor Churchill gave effect to his warning, uttered a month earlier, that a British declaration of war would follow "within the hour".

Italy's entry into the war in 1940 had exercised a decisive influence upon British strategy. Her geographical position combined with her armed strength in all three elements enabled her to close the Mediterranean to all except the most heavily convoyed traffic. The main line of Britain's Imperial communications was perforce diverted round Africa and the extension greatly added to the strain on the British mercantile marine. On all counts, therefore, it was essential to counter the Italian threat to the Suez Canal. It was with special satisfaction that Churchill had informed the Commons of the "crippling blow" struck at the Italian Fleet at Taranto in November, 1940, and he threw all his energies into the task of building up an effective striking force in the Middle East. He realized that though the war could not be won in the Mediterranean it could be lost there, and his sensitiveness to any threat in this quarter as well as his eagerness to give aid to a small and very gallant ally

THE THREAT
IN THE
MEDITERRANEAN

induced him to move troops from Africa to Greece when Germany struck her blow in the Balkans. The wisdom of this decision may be questioned. The reduction of British strength in Africa and the necessity, which Churchill immediately recognized, of returning the Australian troops when Japan declared war, opened the way to the successes of Rommel's Afrika Korps, whose formidable military quality was not, and perhaps could not have been, foreseen. There was less excuse, however, for allowing the lesson of Norway, that an army could not maintain itself against hostile air supremacy, to be repeated in the Aegean. It was widely felt that Crete should either have been evacuated earlier or more effectively held and its capture, after a tremendous German effort which came within an ace of failure, provided the one occasion in the whole war when Churchill's strategic judgment was seriously criticized by Parliament or public.

WAR IN THE DESERT

In the summer of 1942, while Churchill was in Washington, Rommel unleashed the greatest of his attacks. The British front was driven in for hundreds of miles and the crowning shock came when Tobruk, which earlier had resisted a long siege, fell almost without a fight. The blow was softened by President Roosevelt's immediate offer of American tanks to help in retrieving the position, and Westminster echoed Washington by defeating a no-confidence motion by 475 to 25. Some two months later Churchill was himself in the desert, having taken a visit to Moscow in his stride, and there effected those changes in the higher command which launched both Lord Alexander and Lord Montgomery on their great careers.

LEFT: With General Montgomery, newly in command of the Eighth Army, in the Western Desert, August, 1942. The same month, Churchill made General Alexander Commander-in-Chief in the Middle East.

"This desert warfare has to be seen to be believed." Viewing the position at El Alamein from which the Eighth Army launched its victorious attack in October, 1942.

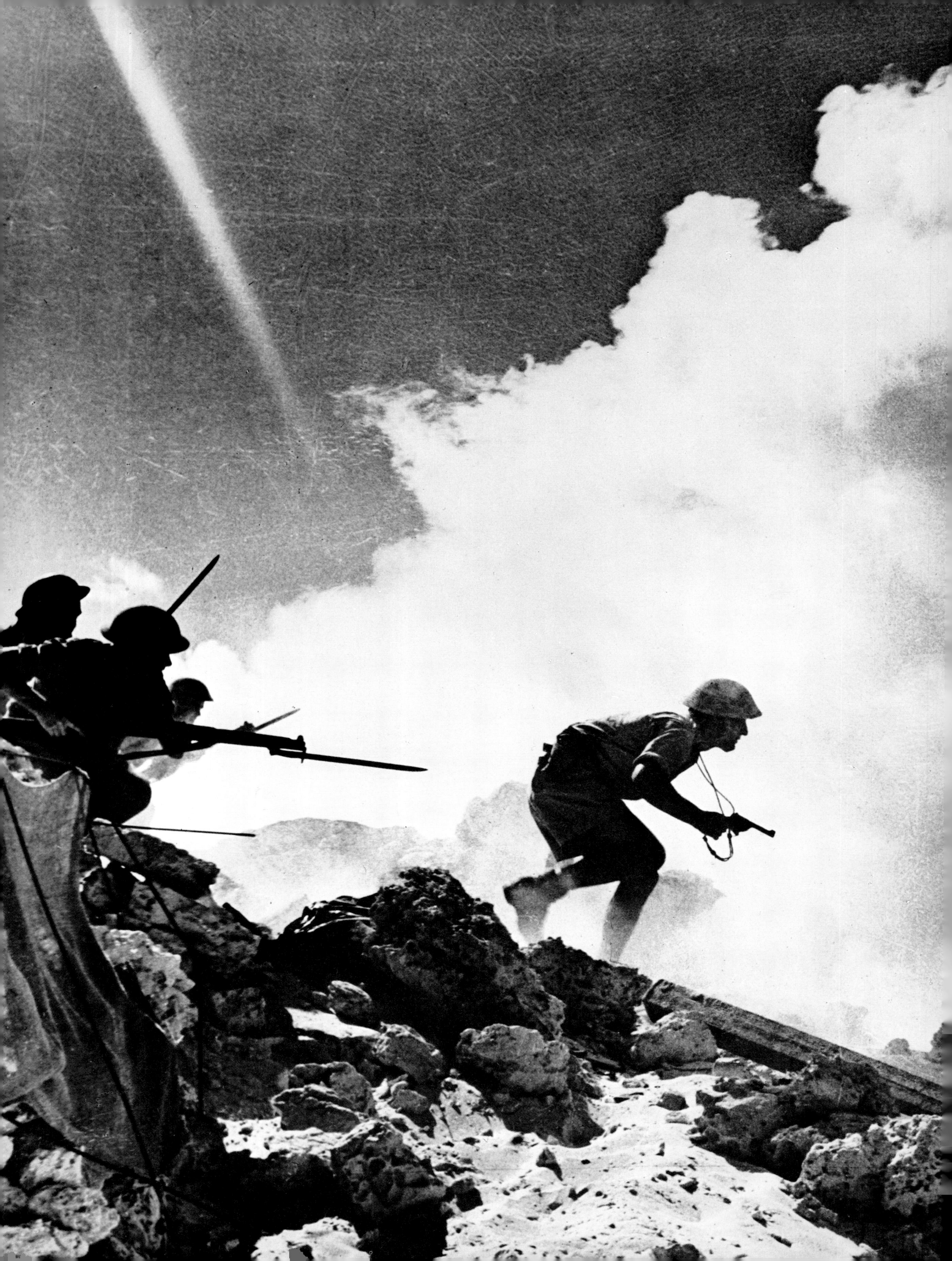

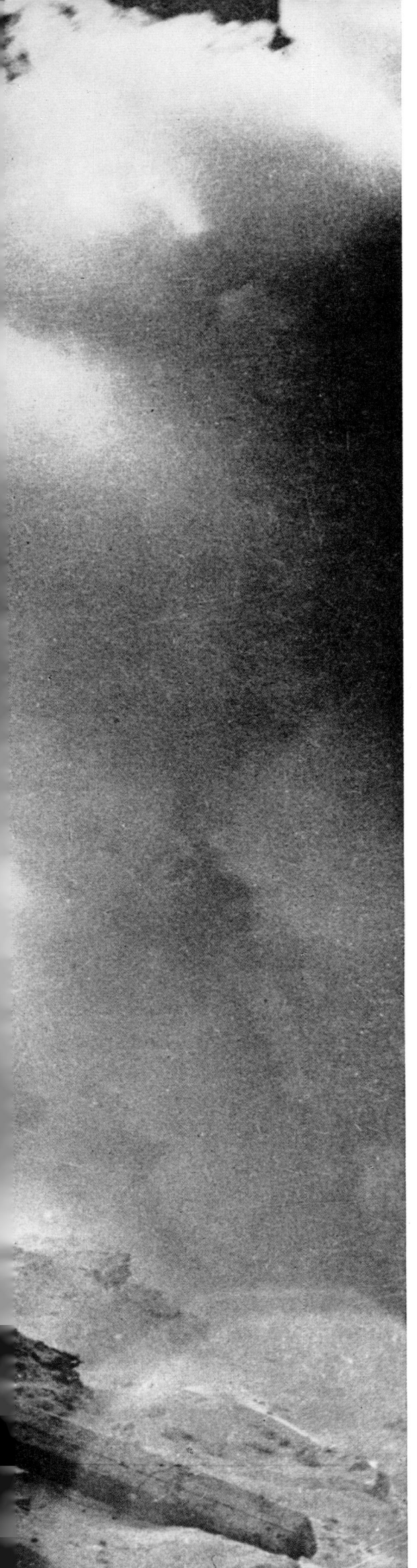

German Field Marshal Rommel with General Bayerlein during the battle of El Alamein, November, 1942.

A Victory: November, 1942

We have not so far in this war taken as many German prisoners as they have taken British, but these German prisoners will no doubt come in in droves at the end just as they did last time. I have never promised anything but blood, tears, toil, and sweat. Now, however, we have a new experience. We have victory—a remarkable and definite victory. The bright gleam has caught the helmets of our soldiers, and warmed and cheered all our hearts.

The late M. Venizelos observed that in all her wars England—he should have said Britain, of course—always wins one battle—the last. It would seem to have begun rather earlier this time. General Alexander, with his brilliant comrade and lieutenant, General Montgomery, has gained a glorious and decisive victory, in what I think should be called the Battle of Egypt. Rommel's army has been defeated. It has been routed. It has been very largely destroyed as a fighting force . . .

Now this is not the end. It is not even the beginning of the end. But it is, perhaps, the end of the beginning. . . .

Australians storming a German strong point in the Western Desert, November 3, 1942.

The British victories in the desert were followed in November, 1942, by the allied landings in North Africa. In January, 1943, Churchill and President Roosevelt met for ten days at Casablanca to plan the next steps in their joint campaign. RIGHT, BELOW RIGHT: At the press conference on January 24, at which Roosevelt first used the words "unconditional surrender," of the Allied war aim.

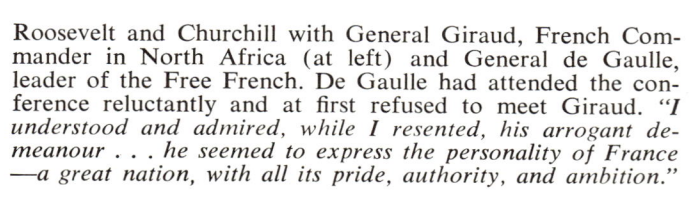

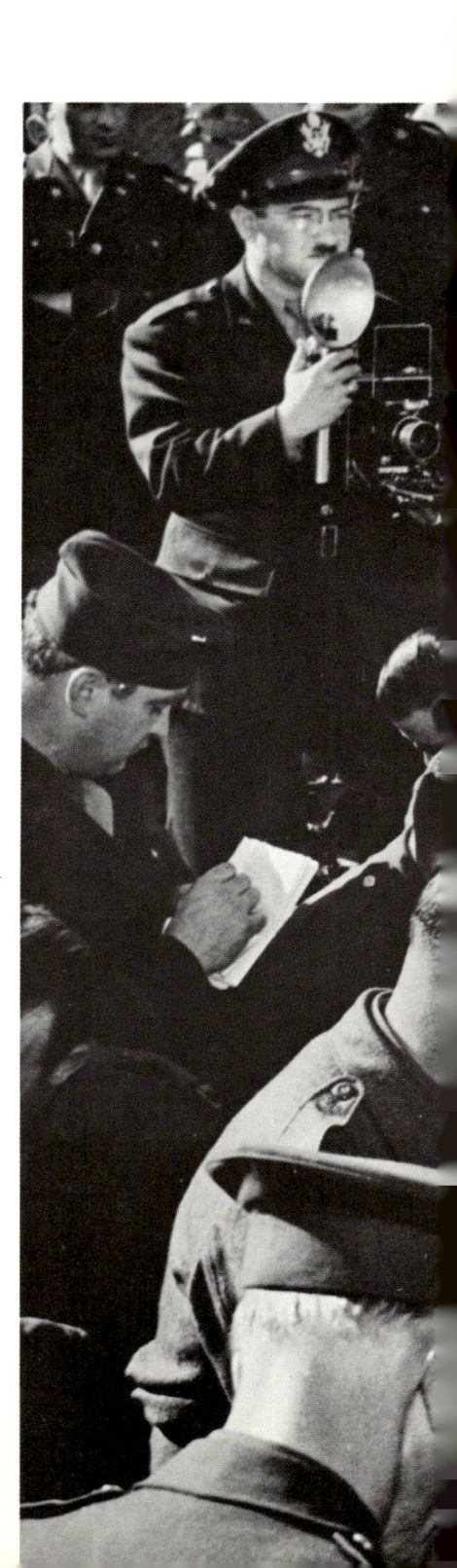

Roosevelt and Churchill with General Giraud, French Commander in North Africa (at left) and General de Gaulle, leader of the Free French. De Gaulle had attended the conference reluctantly and at first refused to meet Giraud. *"I understood and admired, while I resented, his arrogant demeanour . . . he seemed to express the personality of France — a great nation, with all its pride, authority, and ambition."*

"The President arrived on the afternoon of the 14th. We had a most warm and friendly meeting, and it gave me intense pleasure to see my great colleague here on conquered or liberated territory which he and I had secured."

THE ITALIAN SURRENDER

The decision to deploy American military strength in Africa was sufficiently in line with Churchill's strategic thought for him to describe it as "perhaps the end of the beginning", but he was also at pains to make it clear that the plan was Roosevelt's and that he had been no more than the President's lieutenant. The two met at Casablanca early in 1943 and there proclaimed "unconditional surrender" as their aim. They decided as a first step to attack what Churchill pungently described as "the soft under-belly of the Axis" and by the following September unconditional surrender had been made by such governmental authority as was left in Italy. Churchill was again in Washington when he received the news of this complete turn of fortune's wheel. But the Germans continued to turn the country into a battlefield and as "the rake of war"—the phrase is again Churchill's—was drawn throughout the length of the peninsula, he did not conceal his pity for the Italian people. Pneumonia attacked him on his return to London after the Casablanca conference and he suffered another attack towards the end of 1943, but his determined will to live pulled him through.

April 6, 1943: *"This present week the general battle in Tunisia will begin. The enemy is preparing to retire into his final bridgehead."*

OPPOSITE: In the ruins of the immense amphitheatre at Carthage, the Prime Minister addressed thousands of soldiers in June, 1943. *"The sense of victory was in the air. The whole of North Africa was cleared of the enemy.... Everyone was very proud. There is no doubt that people like winning very much."*

With Churchill's efforts from the middle of 1941 onwards to establish unity of policy and action between Britain, Russia, and the United States his war Premiership had entered upon its second phase, the first, that of preparation for insular defence, having closed when Britain ceased to fight alone. At the beginning of 1942 this second phase was overlapped by the third in which British arms suffered what Churchill himself described as "the greatest disaster which our history records". The Prime Minister was under no illusions as to the probable consequences of Japan's entry into the war. The new enemy was a first-class Power whose might the British Commonwealth, already engaged in a fight to the death with Germany and Italy, could not hope to meet on equal terms. But the Japanese pressed

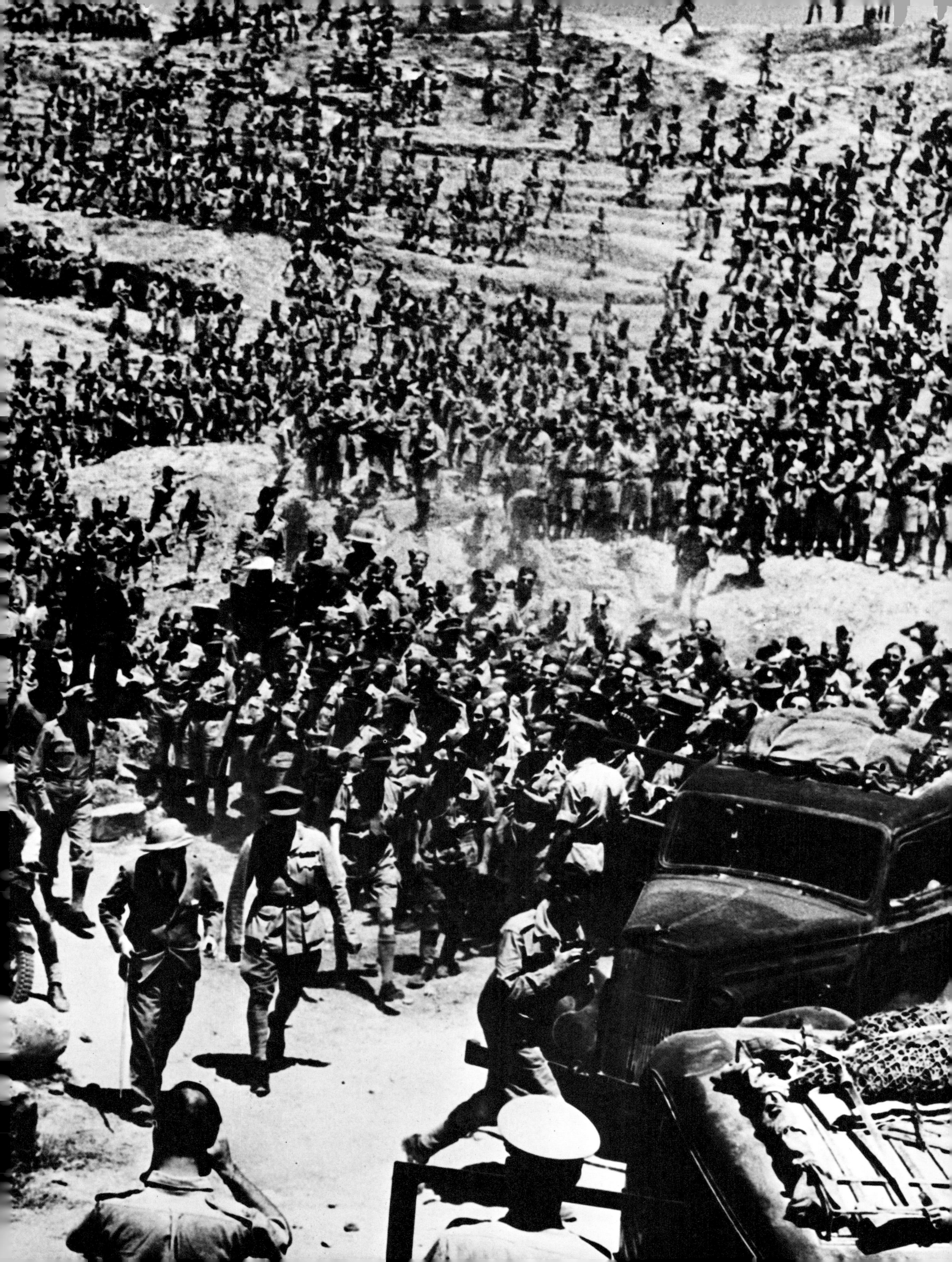

home their advantage with a success whose rapidity and extent exceeded all expectations. In December, 1941, the *Prince of Wales* and the *Repulse* were sunk in Malayan waters. Their flanks thus safeguarded, the Japanese land forces advanced and completed their conquest by the capture of Singapore at the end of February.

DISASTER IN THE FAR EAST

The tale of misfortune was not yet complete. Rangoon was occupied early in March, and with the evacuation of Mandalay the whole of Burma, which Churchill's father had added to the Empire, passed into enemy hands. Churchill firmly refused to allow any examination of the causes of these distressing events. The House of Commons endorsed this view by a vote of 464 to 1, but it is instructive for the estimate of Churchill's attitude towards public opinion to contrast his firmness in holding the veil drawn over the loss of an Empire in the Far East with his readiness to grant an inquiry into the successful escape of the *Scharnhorst, Gneisenau,* and *Prinz Eugen* from Brest into German waters, which occurred a few days before the fall of Singapore. It is equally instructive to note his disregard of the cry for "a second front now" which began to be raised in the spring and summer of 1942 as the Germans thrust ever more deeply into Russia. Dieppe was a final warning against operations on an inadequate scale and Churchill now flung himself into the elaborate preparations which occupied two full years and constitute the fourth phase of his Premiership.

Mastering an obstacle (LEFT) on a battle course.

On an inspection tour of an Armoured Division.

"War is a constant struggle and must be waged from day to day."

At a battle-course demonstration, the School of Infantry.

Watching an infantry drill with daughter Mary and Mrs. Churchill.

The Prime Minister laying bricks on a visit to an A. A. battery.

Soviet commanders at Stalingrad; Marshal Zhukov second from left.

At the airfield in Tripoli, February, 1943, the Prime Minister is greeted by General Montgomery, whose victorious Eighth Army was entering the city.

PLANNING FOR THE FUTURE

With the victories of Stalingrad and El Alamein towards the close of 1942 the "awful balance" of war began to incline towards the allies and another aspect—the fifth—of Churchill's activities became increasingly prominent. Issues of reconstruction began to thrust themselves forward, though it was not until late in 1943, the year which saw the establishment of UNRRA and the preliminaries to the creation of Food and Agriculture Organization, that vital decisions were reached. After a conference of Foreign Secretaries at Moscow in October had cleared the ground and itself reached important conclusions as to the future organization of Europe, Churchill and Roosevelt met General Chiang Kai-shek at Cairo in November and there agreed to strip Japan of all her conquest during the past 50 years. President and Prime Minister then flew to Teheran, where they met Stalin. The three statesmen declared their resolve to conclude a peace which would "banish the scourge and terror of war for many generations" and their readiness to welcome all freedom-loving peoples "into a world family of democratic nations".

At the Quebec Conference, August, 1943, with Prime Minister Mackenzie King, the Earl of Athlone (seated), and President Roosevelt.

RIGHT: The last in a series of five postcards given Roosevelt by Churchill at the Teheran Conference, November, 1943. The Persian legend concerns a cruel king named Zohak, but riding triumphant at the head of the avenging armies are the real-life leaders Churchill, Stalin, and Roosevelt.

Planning the invasion of Italy, at Allied Headquarters in Algiers, June, 1943, with (from left) Eden, Brooke, Tedder, Cunningham, Alexander, Marshall, Eisenhower, Montgomery.

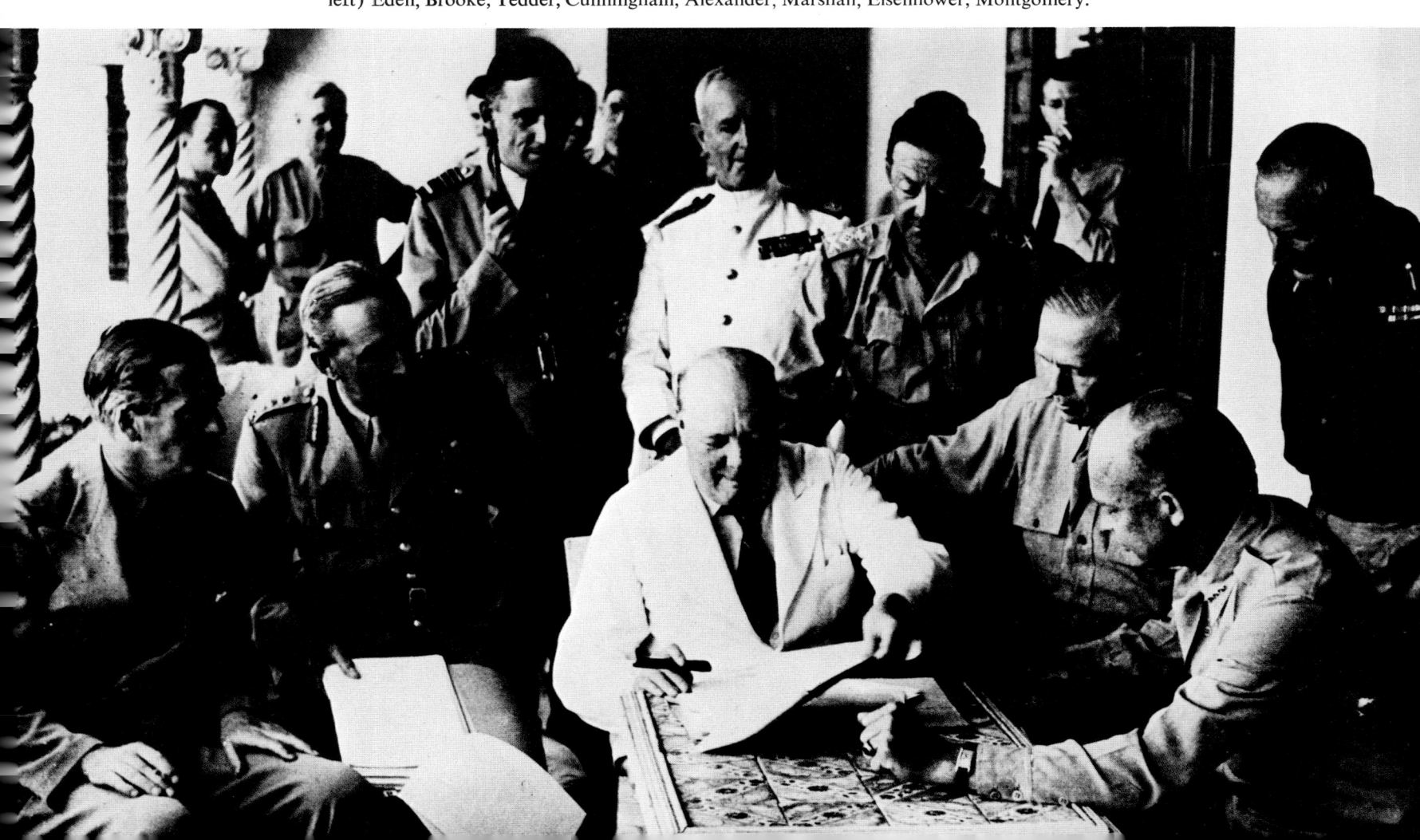

"The battle in Italy will be hard and long." BELOW: Paratroopers (LEFT) and U.S. Rangers advancing above Anzio.

Monte Cassino (ABOVE), captured in May, 1944, after five months' fighting (BELOW) and 13,000 casualties.

At a forward observation post in the XIIIth Corps area in Italy, watching the result of an artillery barrage, 1944. "This," Churchill commented, "is rather like sending a rude letter and being there when it arrives."

146

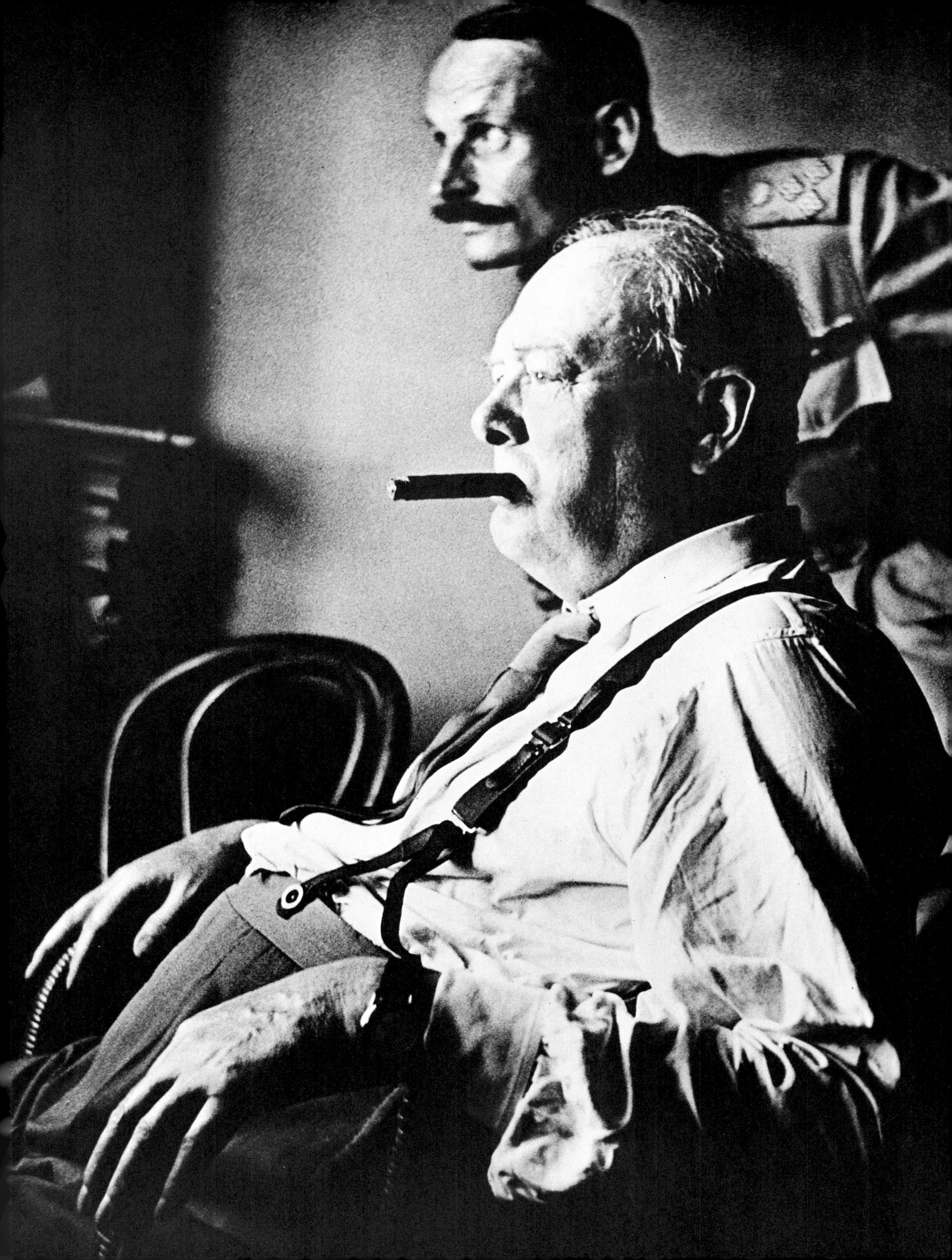

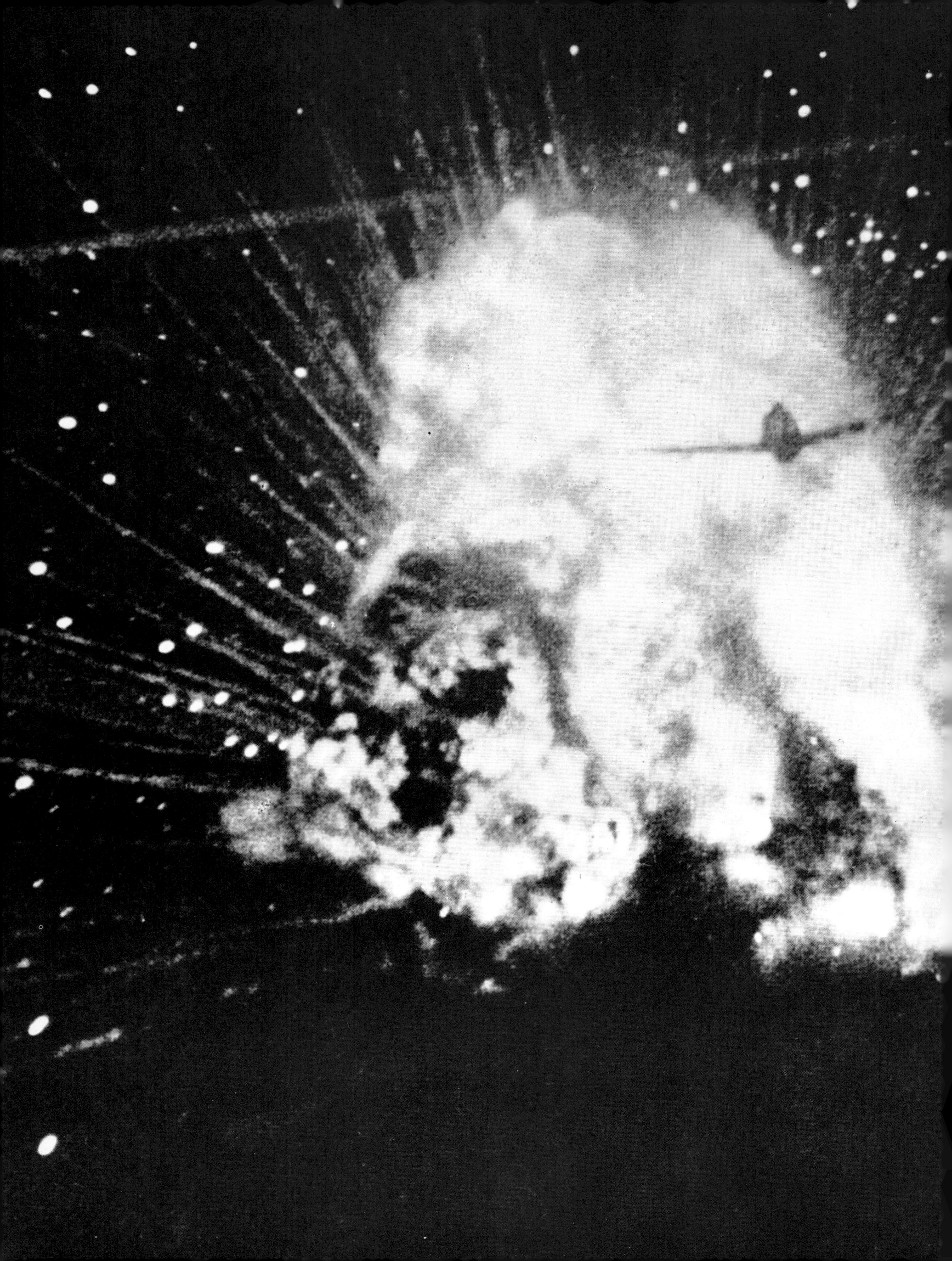

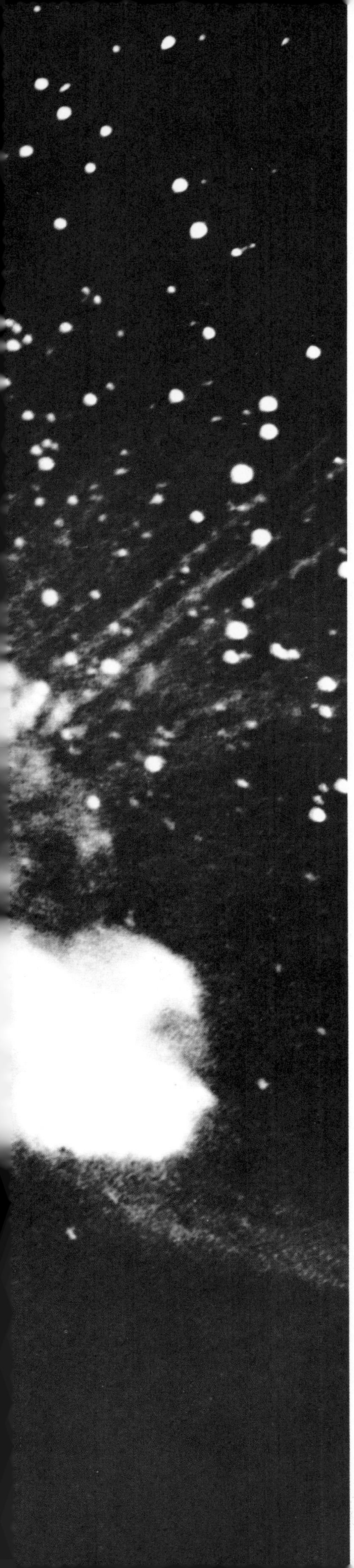

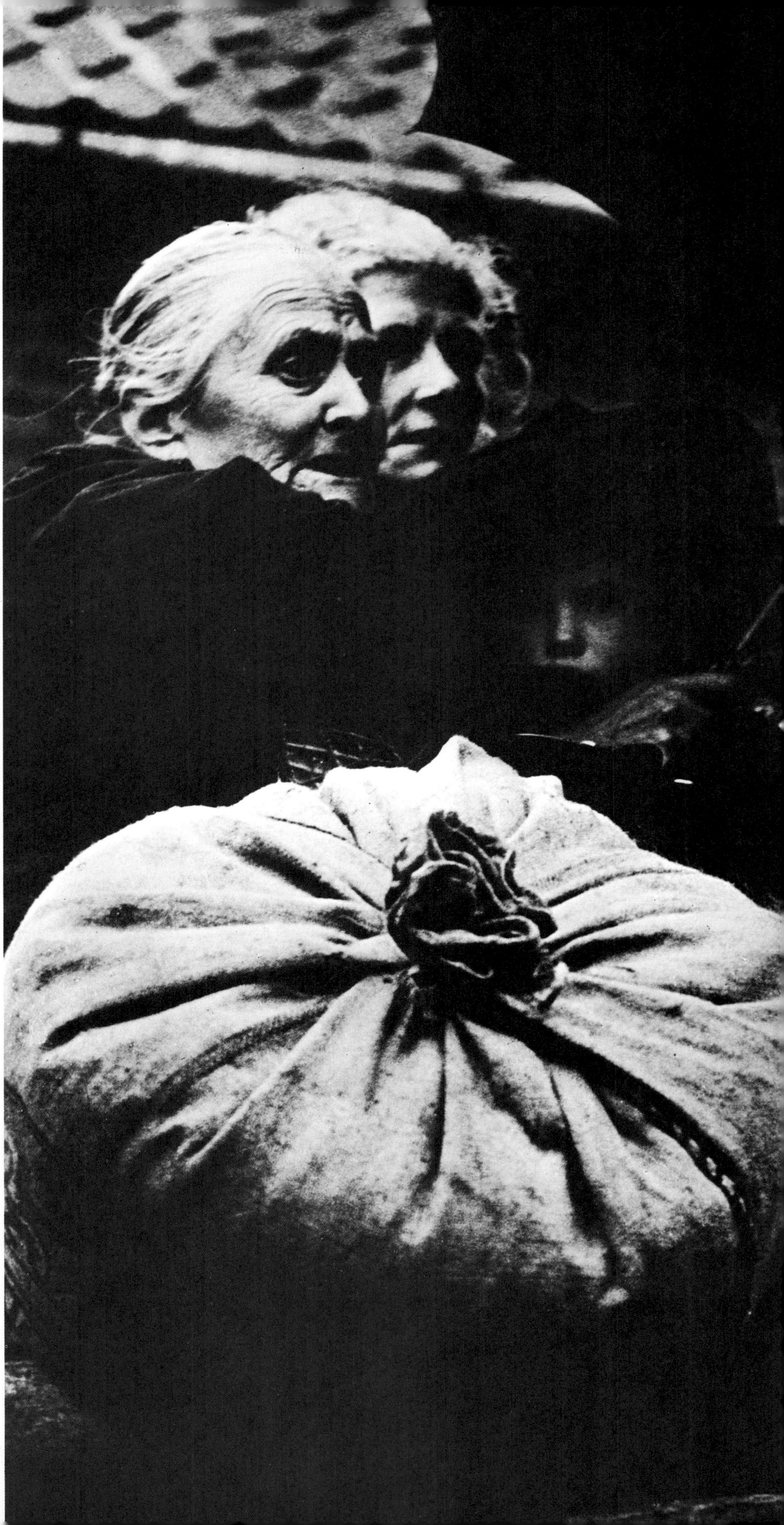

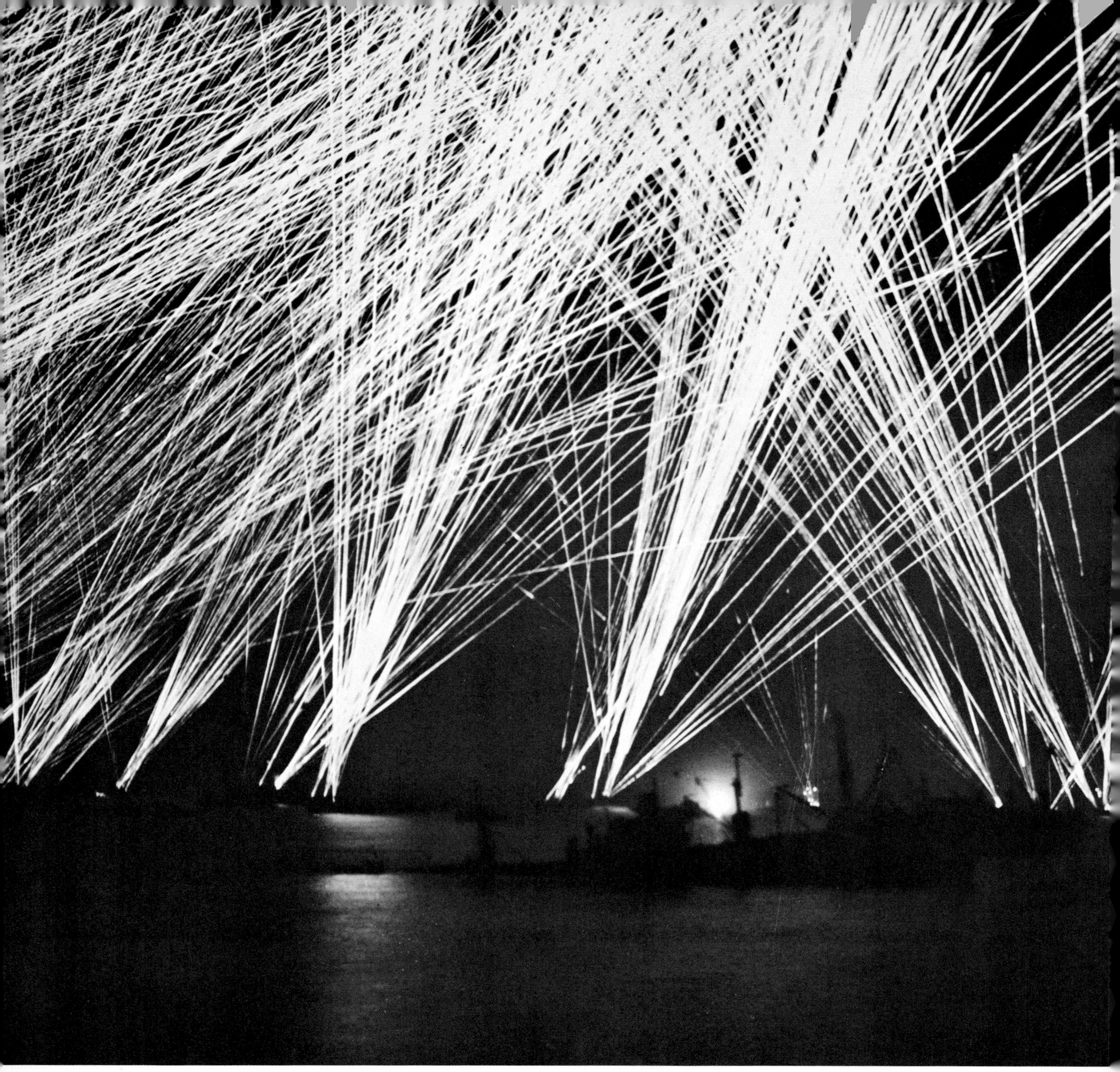

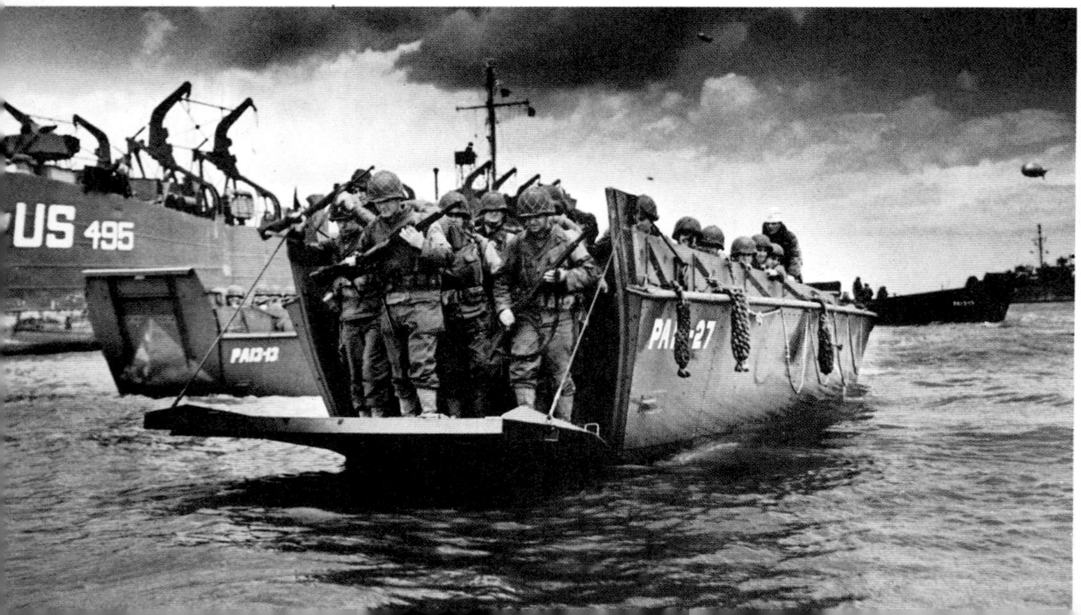
US 495
PA13-13
PA13-27

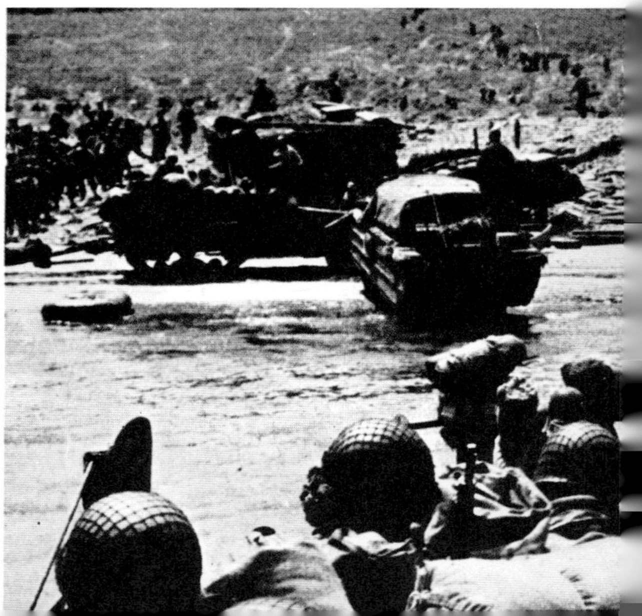

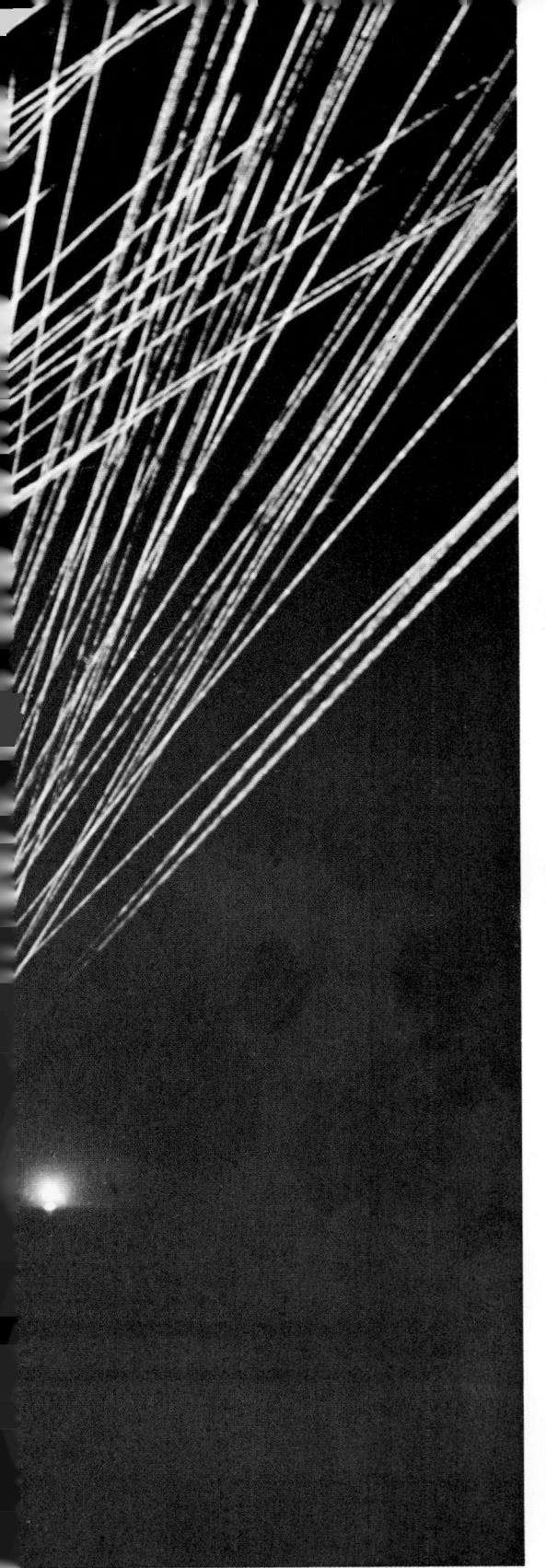

"The hour of our greatest effort and action is approaching." As the allies stepped up the pace of their preparations for D-Day, massive air attacks on railway and munitions centres in France, Belgium, and Western Germany left many civilians homeless. (PRECEDING PAGES: A Nazi ammunition truck is destroyed by a U.S. Thunderbolt fighter plane; evacuees flee a bombed town with all their possessions on a horse-drawn cart.) LEFT: A night raid on Cherbourg.

June 6, 1944: The first wave of troops landing (LEFT) on Omaha Beach in Normandy, as the Prime Minister told the House of Commons, *"So far the commanders who are engaged report that everything is proceeding according to plan. And what a plan! This vast operation is undoubtedly the most complicated and difficult that has ever taken place."* When the beachhead was established, Churchill toured the battle area (ABOVE) in a captured two-seater observation plane.

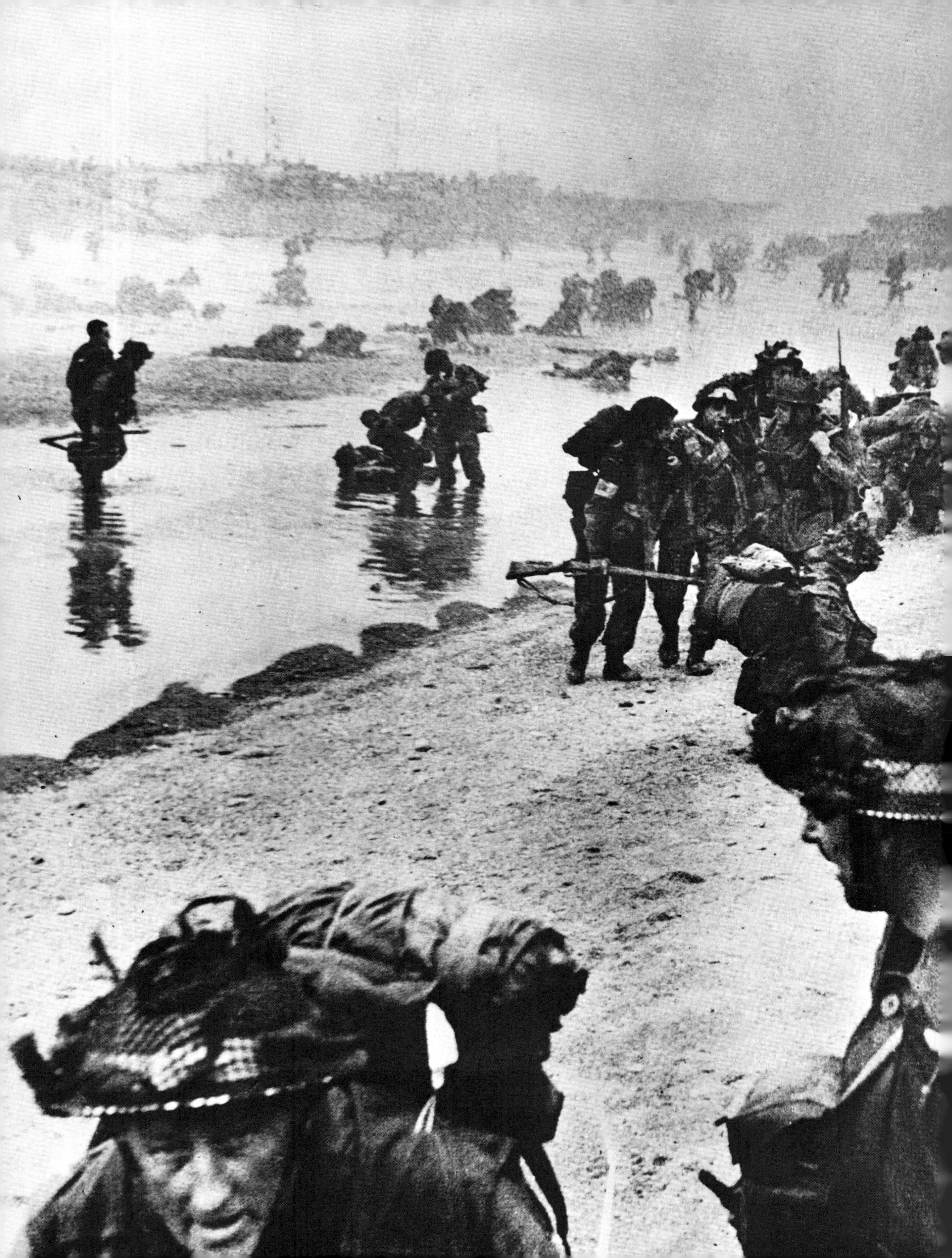

"An immense armada of upwards of 4000 ships, together with several thousand smaller craft, crossed the Channel. . . . The battle that has now begun will grow constantly in scale and in intensity." LEFT: Troops assembling under fire on a Normandy beach, as Red Cross men bring up the wounded.

Grave of an "unknown British soldier" killed in the advance after D-Day.

"*On June 10 [1944] General Montgomery reported that he was sufficiently established ashore to receive a visit.*" Churchill set off from Portsmouth on a destroyer. "*Montgomery, smiling and confident, met me at the beach as we scrambled out of our landing-craft* (ABOVE). *There was very little firing or activity. The weather was brilliant. We drove through our limited but fertile domain in Normandy* (RIGHT). *The General was in the highest spirits. I asked him how far away was the actual front. He said about three miles.*" On his return to London, Churchill wrote to President Roosevelt: "*I had a jolly day on Monday on the beaches and inland. You used the word 'stupendous' in one of your early telegrams to me. I must admit that what I saw could only be described by that word. How I wish you were here!*"

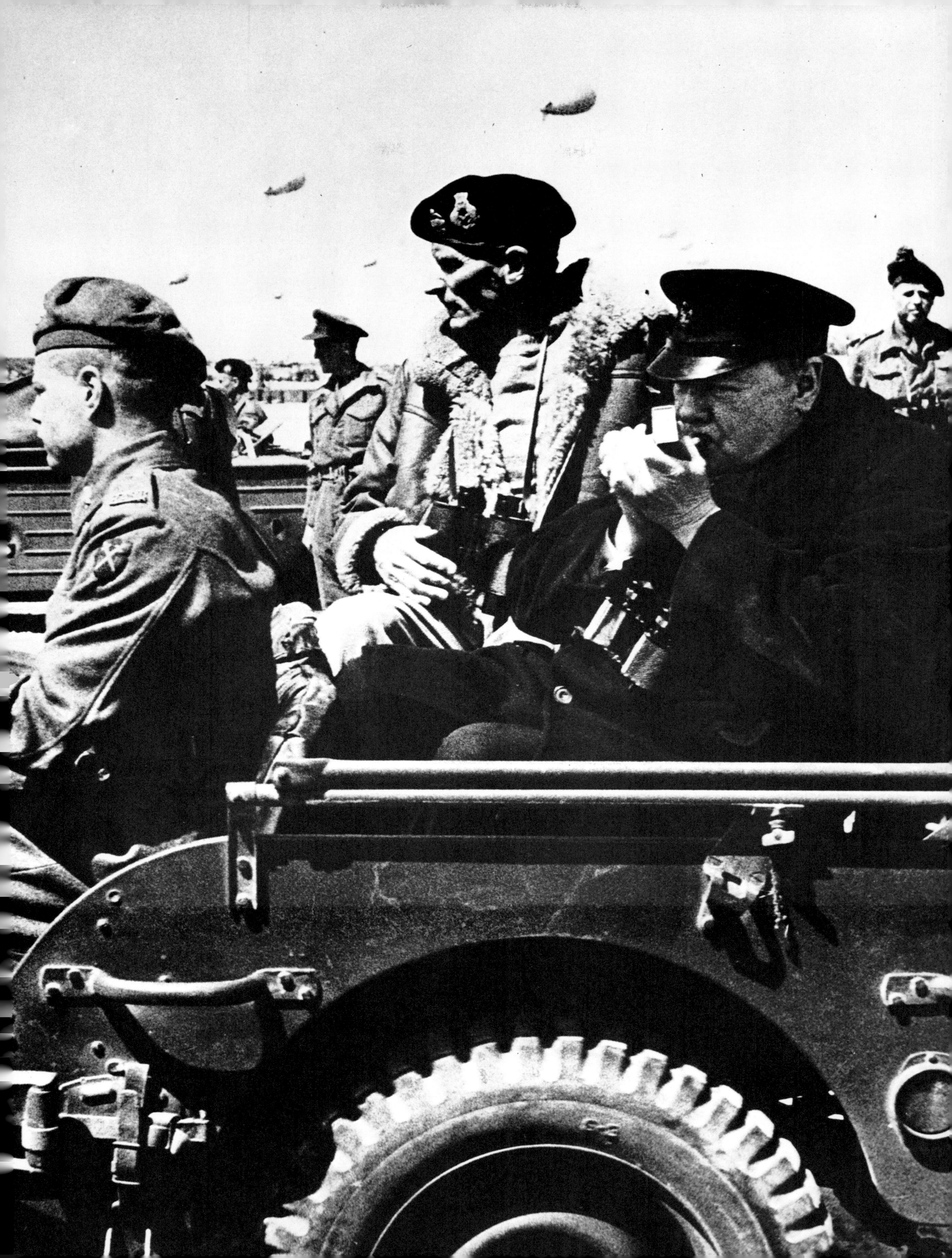

"Always remember, however sure you are that you can easily win, there would not be a war if the other man did not think he also had a chance." As the allied armies drove northward and eastward from Normandy towards the German frontier, enemy resistance (BELOW) stiffened. RIGHT: An airborne infantryman on a one-man sortie in Belgium, 1944.

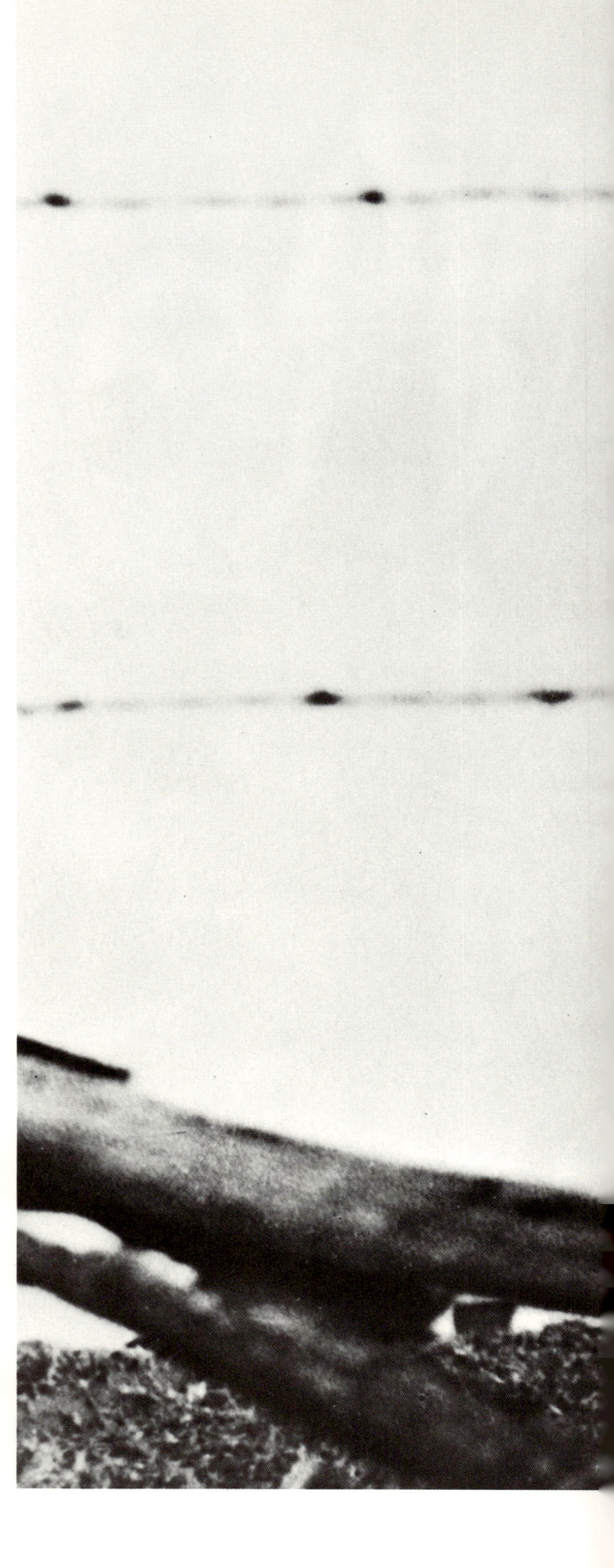

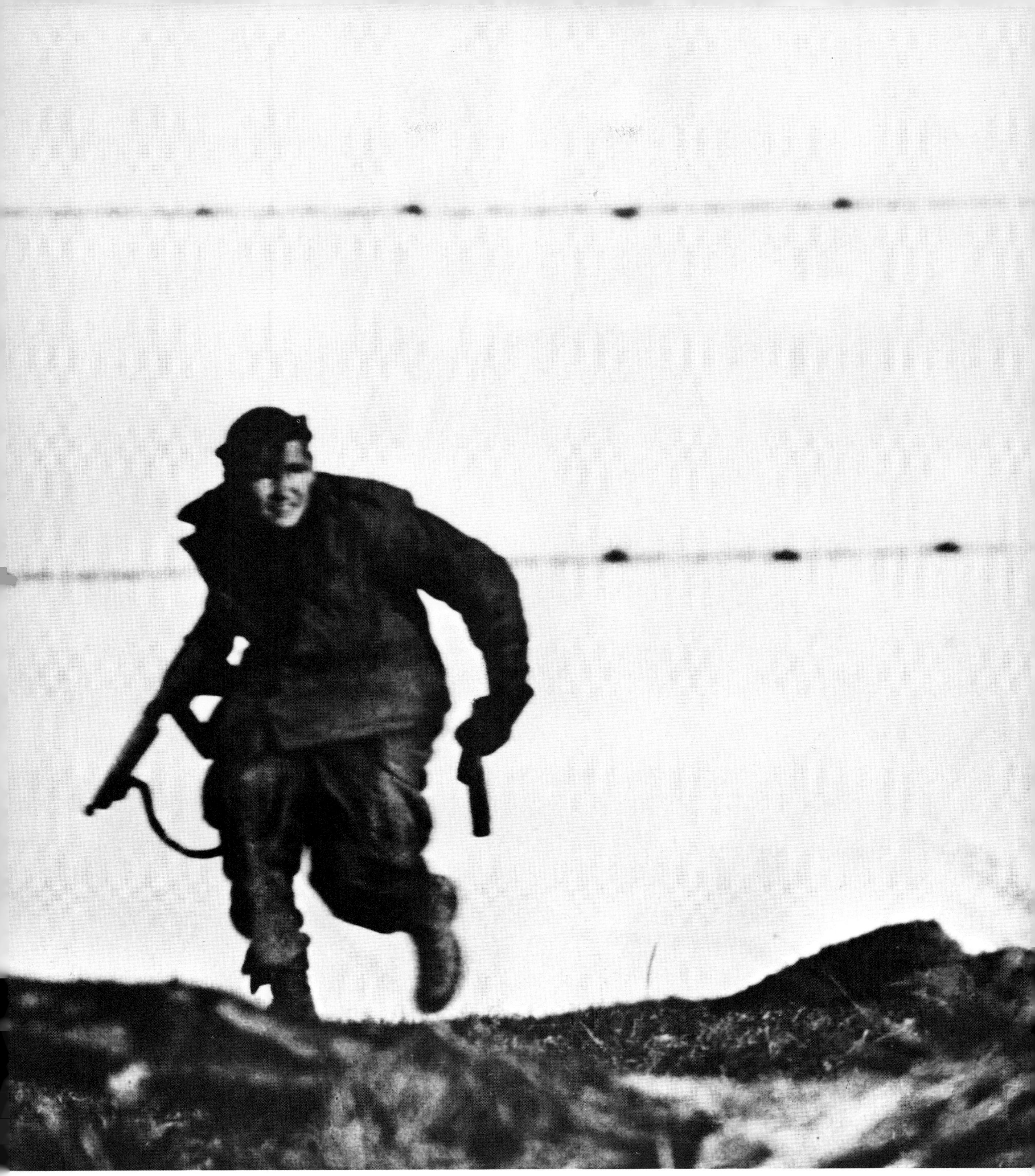

LEFT: At the Second Quebec Conference, September, 1944, with President Roosevelt, General Marshall (far left), and Admiral Leahy.

Mrs. Churchill greeting her husband (RIGHT) on his return from a *"profoundly interesting fortnight"* in Moscow, October, 1944.

JOURNEYINGS
FOR A PURPOSE

There was no meeting of the Big Three in 1944. But Churchill's many journeys, apart from visits to the front, took him to Quebec in September to concert plans with Roosevelt, to Moscow in October to seek a solution of the Polish difficulty, and to Athens at Christmas in an effort to bring toleration and decency back into Greek public life. Churchill's ceaseless journeyings between 1941 and 1945 serve to emphasize that if the war was won by the collaboration of the three great Powers, he was the architect of their cooperation. He built the Grand Alliance and held it together.

November 11, 1944: With de Gaulle on the Champs Elysées (BELOW). *"The General and I walked together, followed by a concourse of the leading figures of French public life, for half a mile down the highway I knew so well."* The Armistice Day parade ended with a march-past of troops.

158

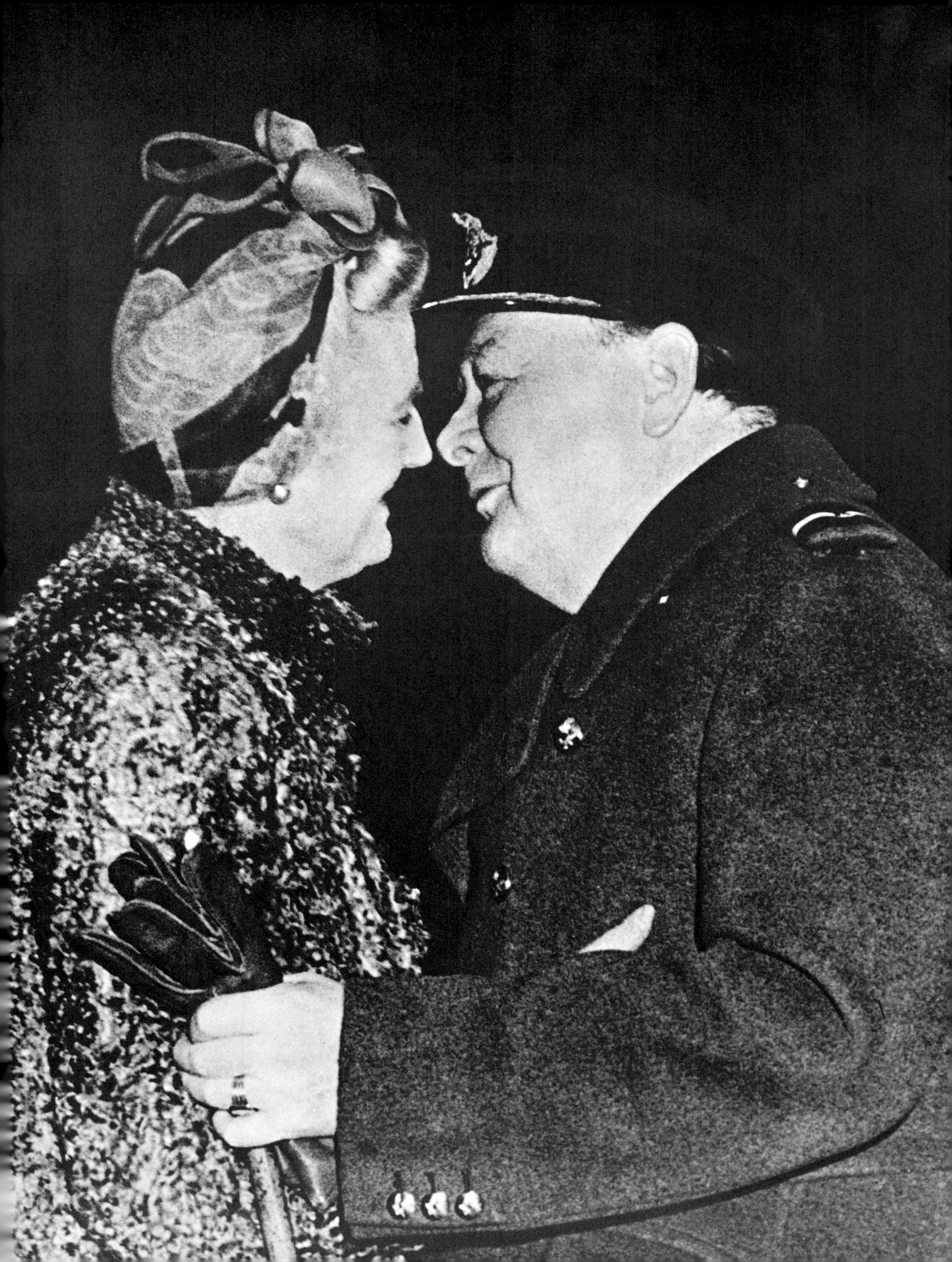

The most vital of all the great Power meetings came in February, 1945, at Yalta. At that conference the Allies concerted their plans for the final assault on Germany, settled the terms on which Russia should enter the war against Japan, and sought agreement about a defeated Germany and about the future of the United Nations Organization. Many of the problems which later beset the world have been traced in their origins to Yalta. But references in published memoirs and the American version of the proceedings published 10 years later all bear witness to the prescience and grasp of realities Churchill brought to the conference table. Roosevelt, enfeebled by the great strain of his office and within two months of his death, believed that he could "handle" Stalin and took an optimistic view of his trustworthiness. Churchill had a juster appreciation of the uses Russia would make of the great power and opportunities she possessed. His ideas on the settlement of Europe displayed an altogether deeper sense of history. Deprived this time of the President's solid support in negotiation, and placing allied unity first among the objects to be achieved, he was obliged to acquiesce in decisions about which he expressed deep misgivings.

Marshal Stalin

After their conference with Stalin at Yalta, in the Crimea, Churchill and Roosevelt met again, briefly, in Egypt. The President entertained King Ibn Saud of Saudi Arabia (BELOW) on February 14, 1945, aboard the U.S.S. *Quincy,* anchored in the Bitter Lake; the following day Churchill boarded the cruiser in Alexandria harbour for what was to be his last encounter with Roosevelt.

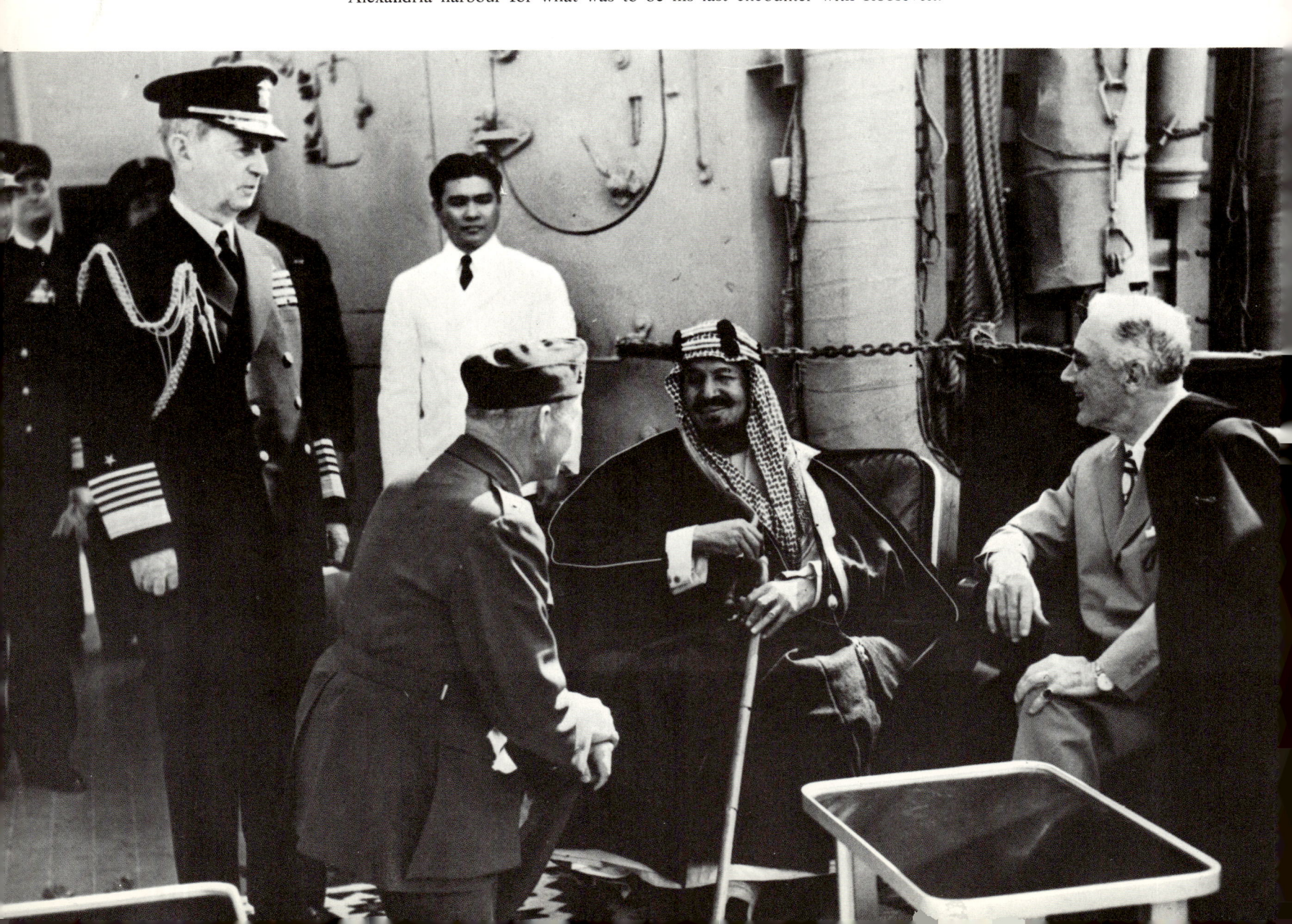

Roosevelt and Churchill at Yalta: *"This comradeship in great affairs was founded upon friendship."*

April 13, 1945: When the news of President Roosevelt's death reached him, Churchill went down to the House of Commons (RIGHT) and proposed it pay its respects to *"the greatest American friend we have ever known"* by adjourning immediately.

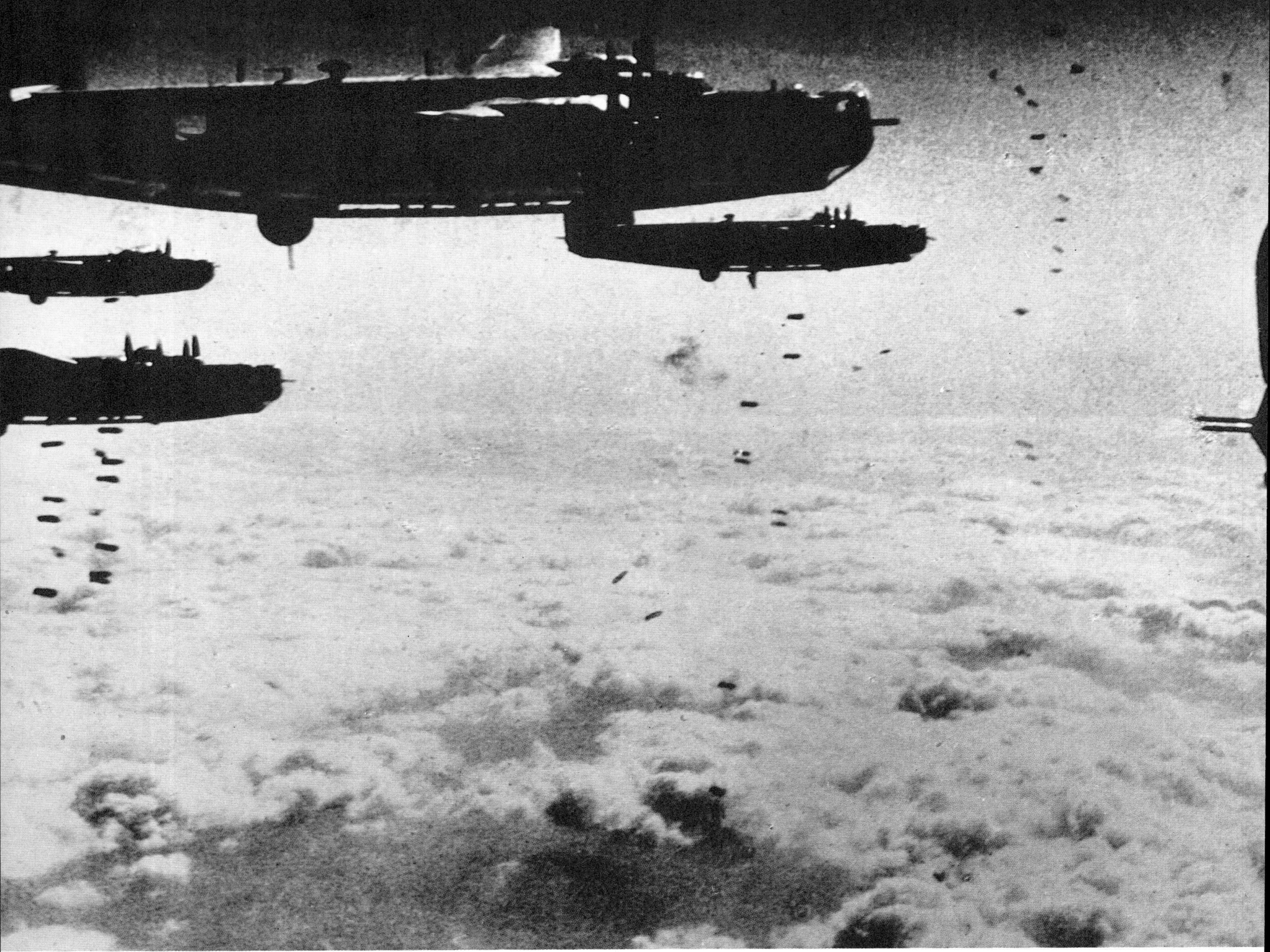

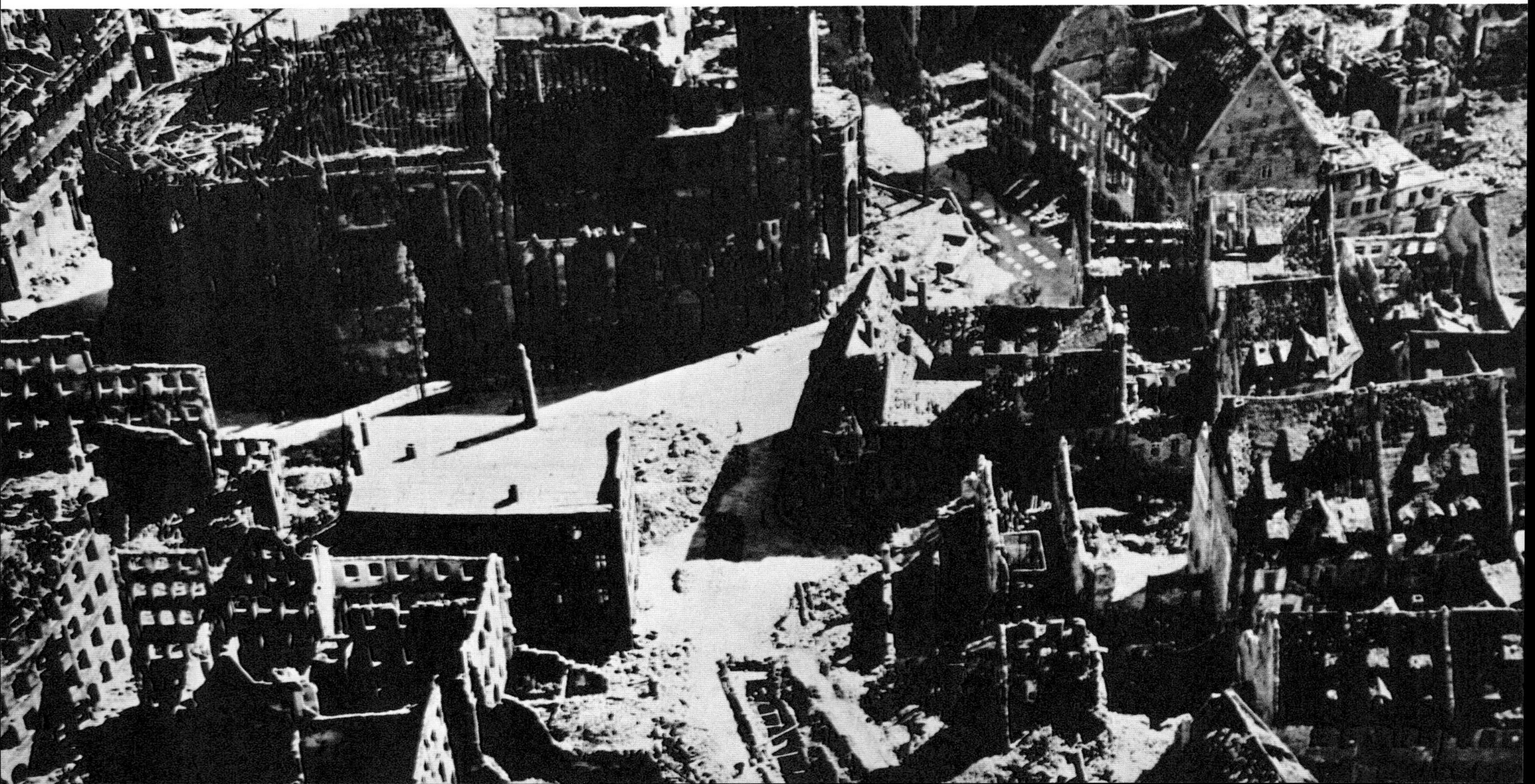

The final assault on Germany: Liberator bombers leave the cathedral city of Cologne in ruins.

Hitler surveys bitterly the rubble left by allied bombing raids. RIGHT: Wrecked vehicles before the shattered Reichstag building, Berlin. On April 22, 1945, Hitler announced he would stay to the end in the capital. *"It remained for him to organize his own death amid the ruins of the city."*

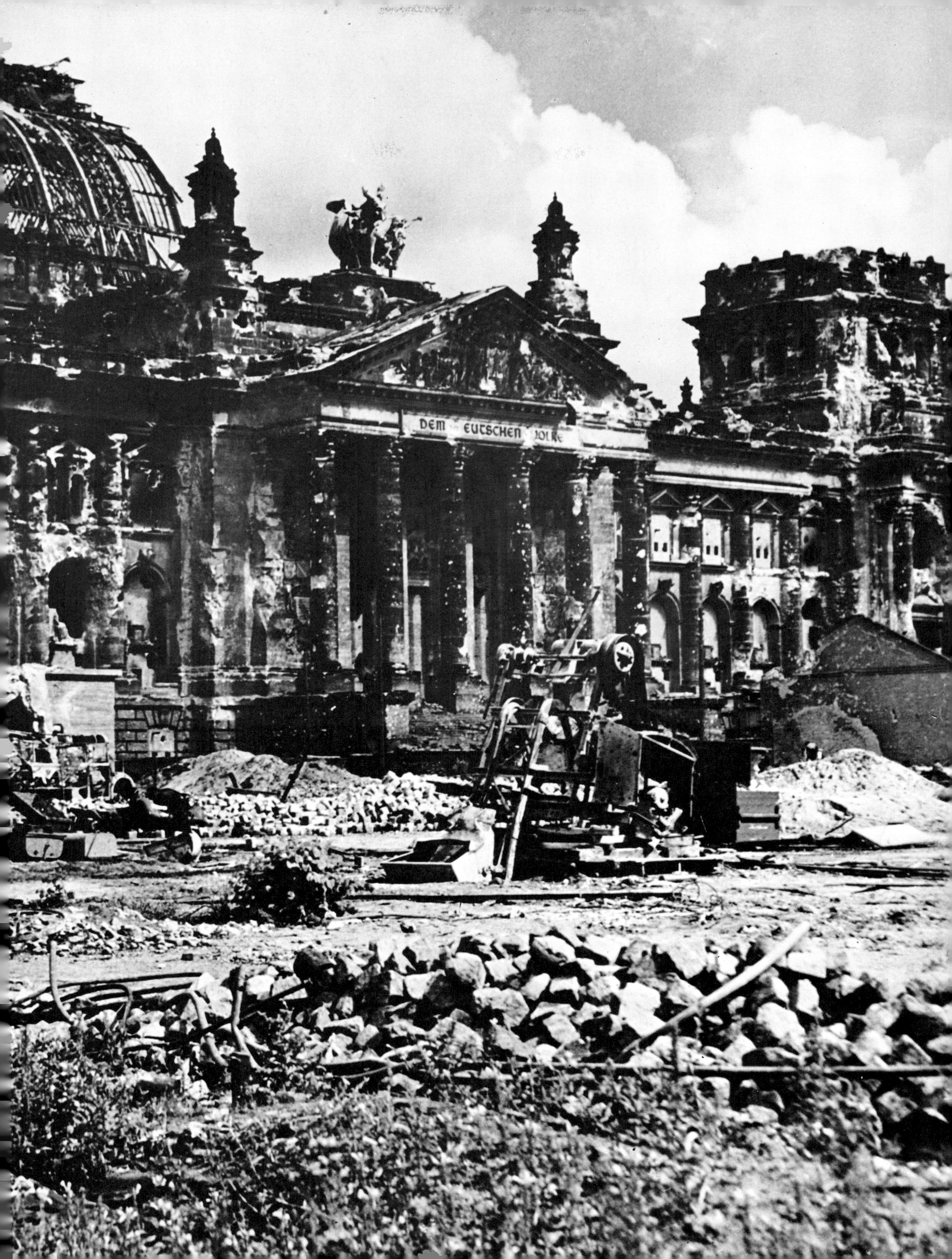
DEM EUTSCHEN OLKE

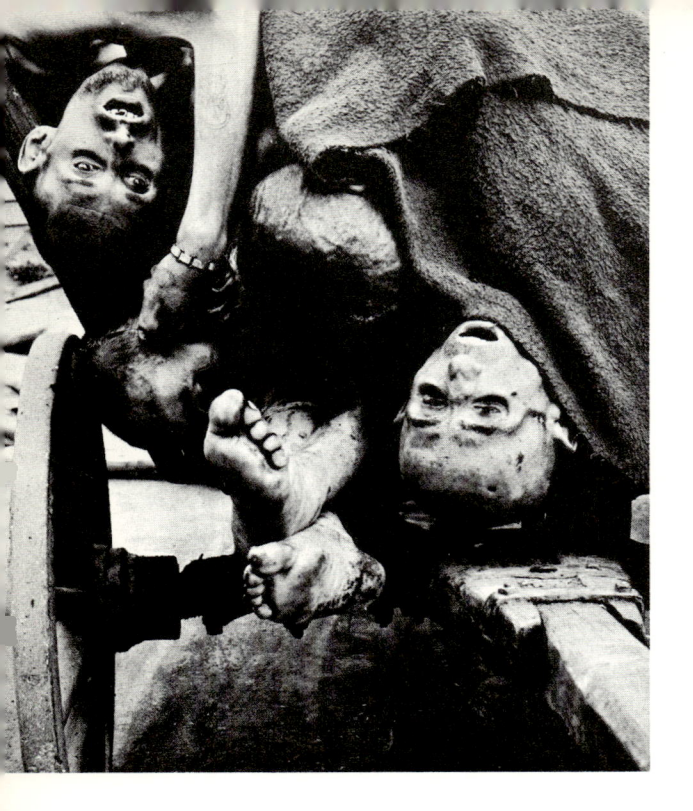

"A river of blood has flowed . . . between the German race and the peoples of nearly all Europe. It is not the hot blood of battle, where good blows are given and returned. It is the cold blood of the execution yard and the scaffold, which leaves a stain indelible for generations and for centuries."

Bodies of concentration camp victims (ABOVE) near Linz, Austria. RIGHT: German civilians are forced to walk past the bodies of thirty Jewish women, starved by SS troops on a forced march of 300 miles across Czechoslovakia.

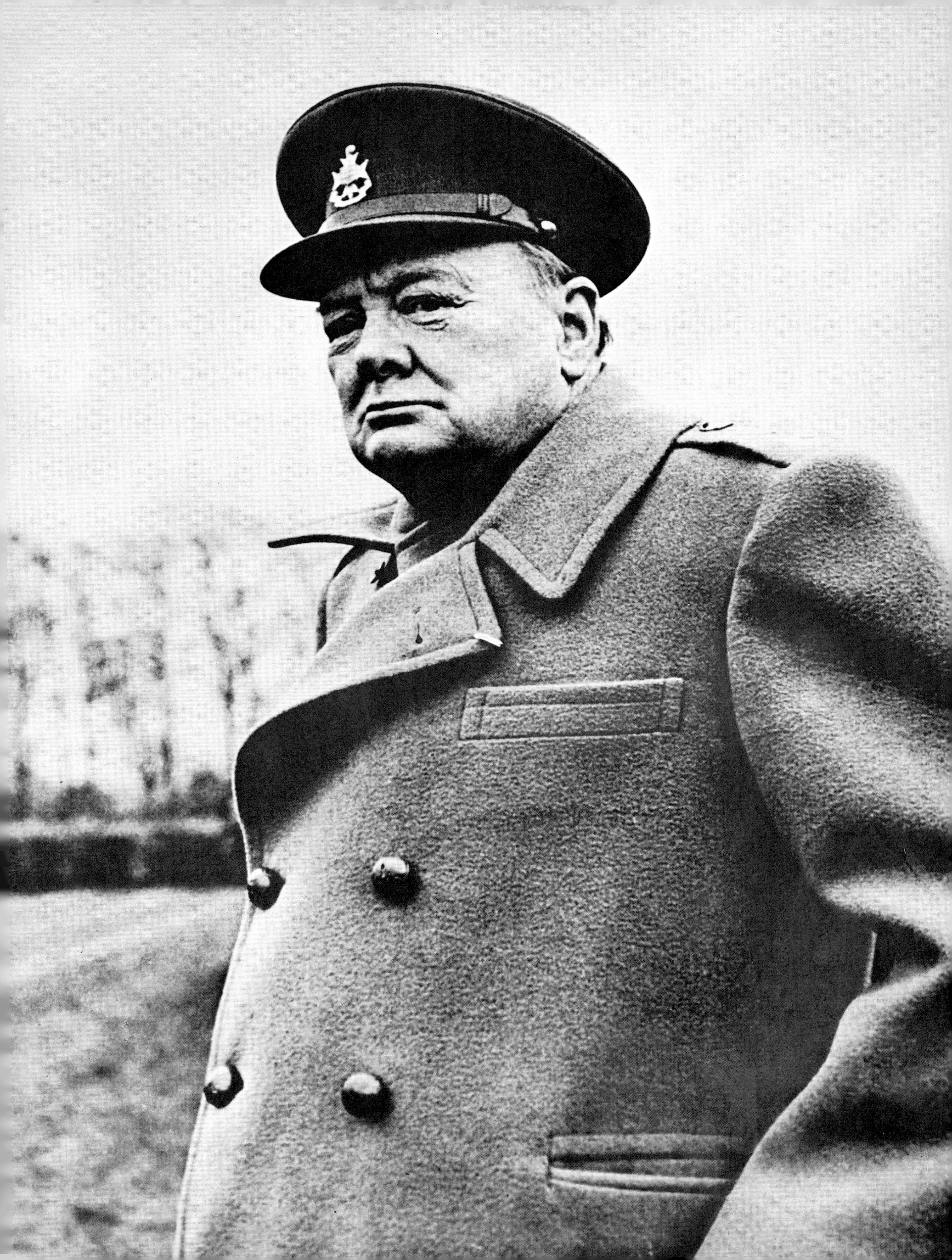

"The Rhine—here about four hundred yards broad—flowed at our feet. I saw a small launch come close by to moor. So I said to Montgomery, 'Why don't we go across and have a look at the other side?' Somewhat to my surprise he answered, 'Why not?' We landed (LEFT) in brilliant sunshine and perfect peace on the German shore."

Prime Minister to Marshal Stalin, 23 Mar. 45: "I am with Field Marshal Montgomery at his H.Q. He has just ordered the launching of the main battle to force the Rhine on a broad front. . . . It is hoped to pass the river tonight and tomorrow and to establish bridgeheads. Once the river has been crossed a very large reserve of armour is ready to exploit the assault." OPPOSITE: With General Eisenhower, Supreme Commander of the allied forces in Europe, as the gigantic attack was launched, March 25, 1945.

May 4, 1945, saw the surrender of all the German forces facing the British, in northwest Germany, Holland, and Denmark. ABOVE: Field Marshal Montgomery reads the terms of surrender to the German Admiral Friedeburg (centre) at British headquarters.

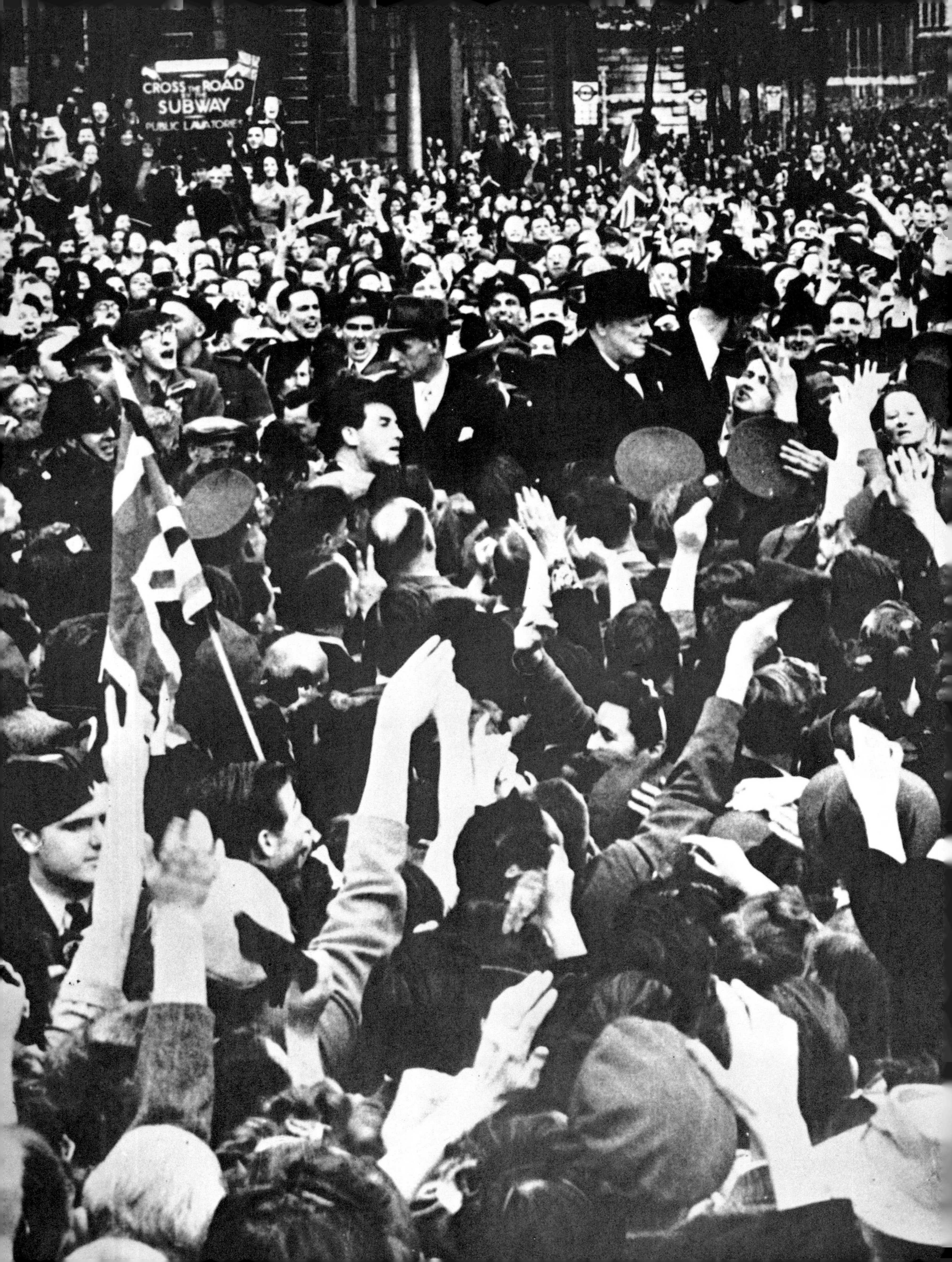
CROSS ROAD
SUBWAY

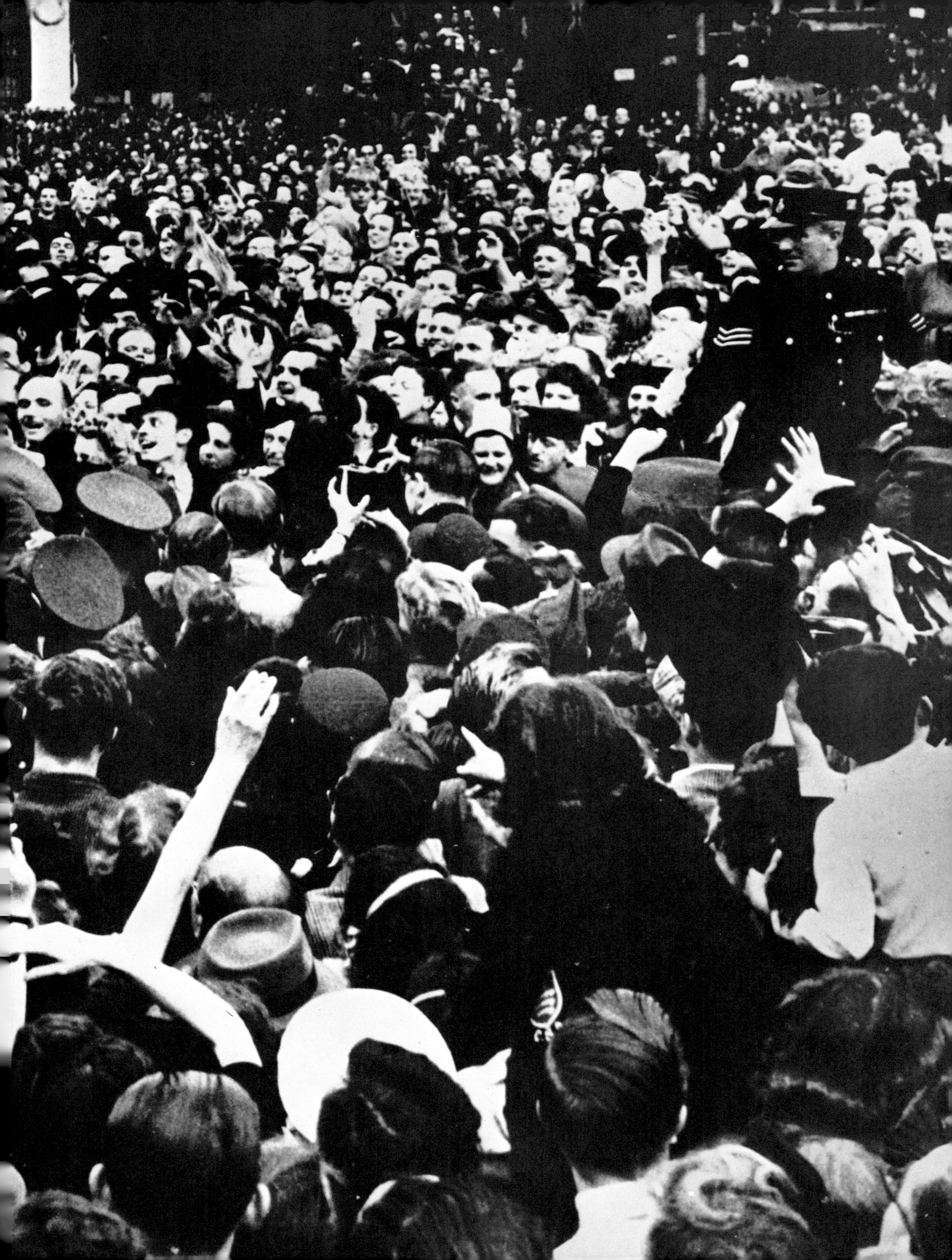

May 8, 1945: Jubilant Londoners surround the Prime Minister (PRECEDING PAGE) as he leaves No. 10 Downing Street for the House of Commons to announce the unconditional surrender of all the German forces in Europe. ABOVE: With the Royal Family on the balcony at Buckingham Palace; and speaking (BELOW) from the Ministry of Health building to the crowds in Whitehall.

"God bless you all. This is your victory! It is the victory of the cause of freedom in every land. In all our long history we have never seen a greater day than this. Everyone, man and woman, has done their best. Everyone has tried. Neither the long years, nor the dangers, nor the fierce attacks of the enemy, have in any way weakened the independent resolve of the British nation. God bless you all."

Making his broadcast announcement of the German surrender on V-E Day.

Churchill in 1946: a portrait by Oswald Birley.

IV

The Shaping of the Future: 1945-1965

Perhaps the best account of Churchill's part in the war was given in 1957 by Lord Alanbrooke, who was Chief of the Imperial General Staff and chairman of the Chiefs of Staff committee from 1941 until the end of the war, in *The Turn of the Tide,* written by Sir Arthur Bryant and based on Alanbrooke's war diaries. Irritation at Churchill's incorrigible desire for action, which was seldom related to the resources available, is frequently expressed, and at his perpetual goadings of his staff—"I sometimes think some of my Generals don't want to fight the Germans", Churchill once remarked when his plans for a landing at Trondheim were being opposed. This was taken by some at the time to be a denigration of the great man, but the book was in fact a truthful panegyric. Churchill's greatest single contribution in Alanbrooke's view was that he carried the Americans with him—he kept together the alliance that won the war.

In the final throes of Germany's defeat Churchill had seen more clearly than ever the importance of thrusting as far eastwards as possible before the Russian armies should be drawn into the vacuum of central Europe. He pressed this view upon Roosevelt, Mr. Truman, who succeeded him as President in April, 1945, and General Eisenhower.

"I do not underrate the difficult and intricate complications of the task which lies before us; I know too much about it to cherish vain illusions; but the morrow of such a victory as we have gained is a splendid moment both in our small lives and in our great history."

July 16, 1945: Arriving in Berlin for the Potsdam Conference, Churchill toured the city (BELOW), finding *"nothing but a chaos of ruins."* A crowd that had gathered outside the shell of Hitler's Chancellery (OPPOSITE PAGE, BELOW) began to cheer. *"I was much moved by their demonstrations, and also by their haggard looks and threadbare clothes. My hate had died with their surrender."*

"I have always laid down the doctrine that the redress of the grievances of the vanquished should precede the disarmament of the victors." ABOVE: Reviewing a victory parade in Berlin, with Field Marshal Montgomery, Attlee, Eden, and others.

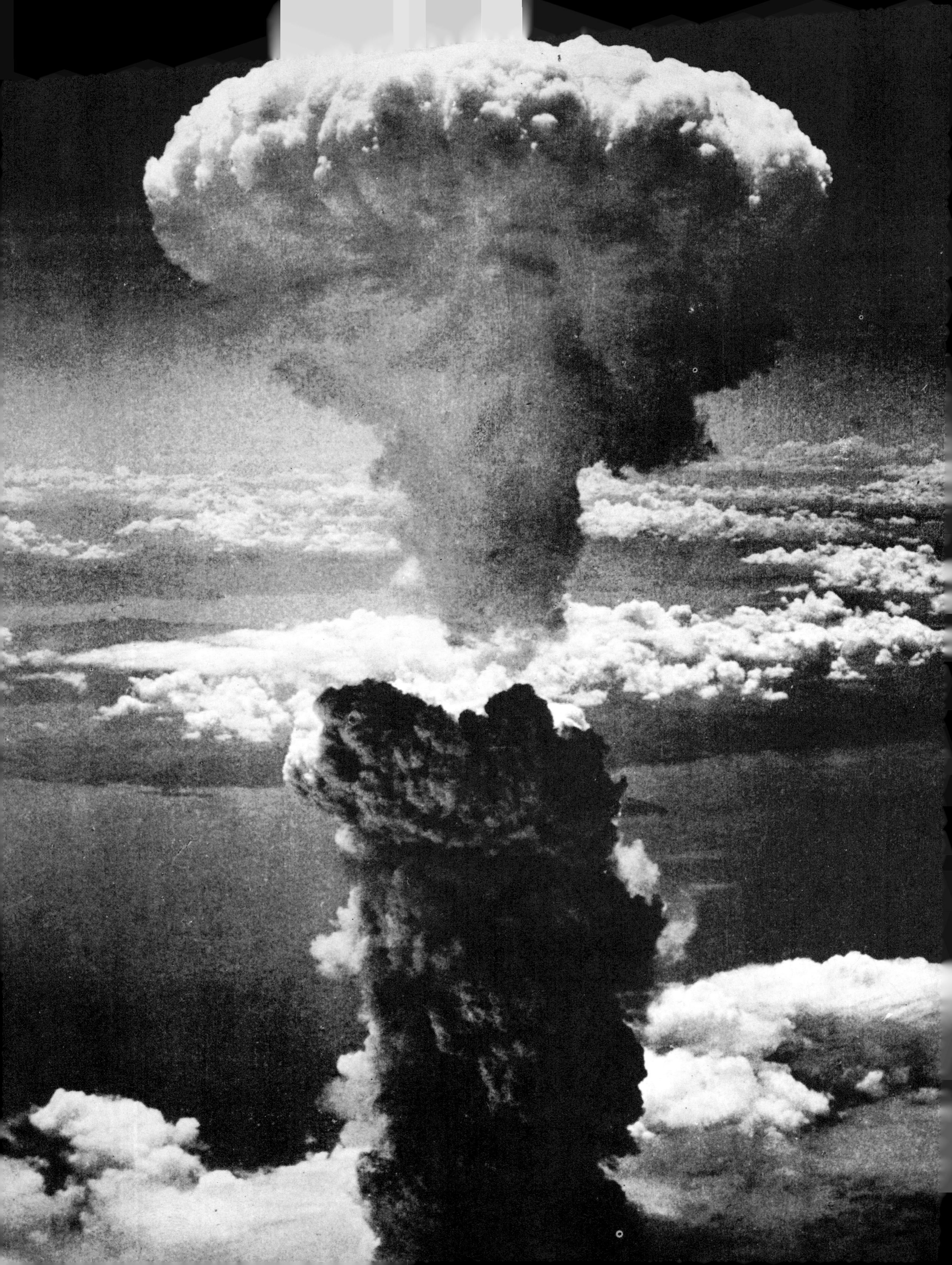

A three-way handshake (RIGHT) as the Potsdam Conference drew to a close, July 23, 1945. The following day, President Truman told Premier Stalin the news Churchill had already received: that an atomic bomb had been successfully detonated in the New Mexico desert. The bomb (OPPOSITE, as it was dropped on Nagasaki) brought the war with Japan to an end within weeks.

Churchill had particularly urged that the allied armies should advance to Berlin and Prague when these capitals came within their grasp. As early as April 5 he warned Roosevelt that "we should join hands with the Russian armies as far to the east as possible, and, if circumstances allow, enter Berlin". But another policy prevailed in Washington.

Soon after the German surrender the Coalition Government broke up. Churchill, after forming a "caretaker" Government, was preoccupied for a while with final plans for the defeat of Japan. In June, accompanied by Mr. Attlee as his "friend and counsellor", he went to Potsdam to settle with Stalin the many matters which the end of the war had made ripe for decision and join with President Truman in a final warning to Japan. Then he returned to London to receive the election results which dismissed him from office.

THE POTSDAM CONFERENCE

September 2, 1945: Japanese envoys signing the surrender document aboard the U.S.S. *Missouri* in Tokyo Bay.

The conduct of Churchill during the campaign of the 1945 election will always seem one of the strangest episodes of his career. The swing against the Conservative Party, which had started before the war, was so strong that even his reputation as a national leader could be of no avail. But he could have emerged from the election with that reputation untarnished. Instead he indulged in accusations, imputations and even personal abuse against his wartime colleagues which shocked his hearers—even his friends—and embittered his opponents.

With Prime Minister Attlee (on his right), Canadian Prime Minister Mackenzie King, and Field Marshal Smuts, Prime Minister of the Union of South Africa, at a Victory Parade in London, June, 1946.

LEADER OF THE OPPOSITION

Churchill was undoubtedly dismayed and unsettled by the verdict of the election—and he had to lead a party which was just as disheartened and just as unsure of itself. In the House of Commons he was less assured than ever before, and his weekly brushes with the Leader of the House, Mr. Herbert Morrison, which came to be known as "Children's Hour", saddened many of his admirers. In his criticisms of the Labour Government's social and economic policies he never seemed able to strike the right note. He did strike some of his old notes in his speeches opposing the Government's Indian policy. He was bitterly critical of the proposal to give independence to India, and when, towards the end of 1946, the Government announced their intention of granting self-government to Burma he denounced it fiercely as a policy of scuttle. In 1947 the Government fixed a date for the handing over of power to the Indians, and Churchill's opposition was even more violent.

However, he welcomed as a statesmanlike means of averting civil war the intention to confer immediate Dominion status on the two succession states likely to emerge in India and promised to facilitate the passage of the necessary legislation. For a man whose vision could be so wide Churchill appeared sometimes to close his eyes to the nature of the problems facing Britain in India. He had inherited from his father a romantic—Disraelian—attitude to India which warped his judgment. The story, nevertheless, ended on a happier note. When he again returned to office, his own and his Government's relations with India were cordial, and it was his Government which supported Indian initiative on the Korean question at the United Nations.

He used the years out of office to make headway with his history of *The Second World War*. The first volume was published in 1948 and the sixth and last six years later. "In War: Resolution. In Defeat: Defiance. In Victory: Magnanimity. In Peace: Goodwill", was the motto of the work; the greatest of the war leaders, he chose with perfect aptness these ancient, simple, and resonant virtues. The work, which puts forward his personal interpretation of events, varies considerably in quality, but at its best it matches the magnificence of its theme. Churchill had moved far from his early models, Macaulay and Gibbon, and had fashioned a less studied manner of his own. His account of the battle for Crete stands comparison with the finest passages of narrative prose, and the closing chapters of the work are charged with a tragic irony that Aeschylus would have acknowledged with applause.

"For my part, I consider that it will be found much better by all parties to leave the past to history, especially as I propose to write that history myself."
RIGHT· At Guildhall for a Freedom Ceremony, 1946.

Addressing the Grand Court of Shepway, August 15, 1946, after his installation at Dover as Lord Warden of the Cinque Ports; he was the first commoner to receive that honour.

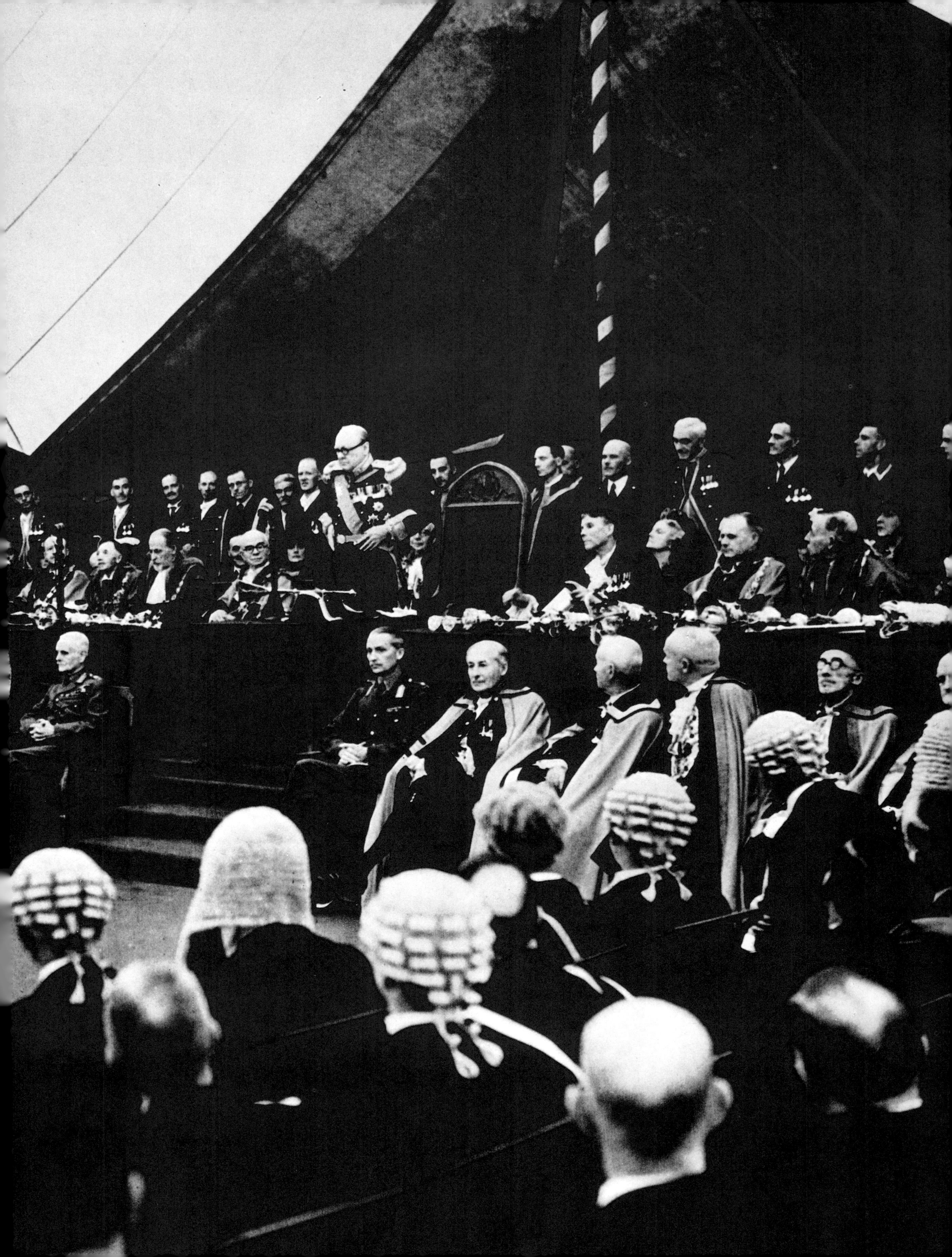

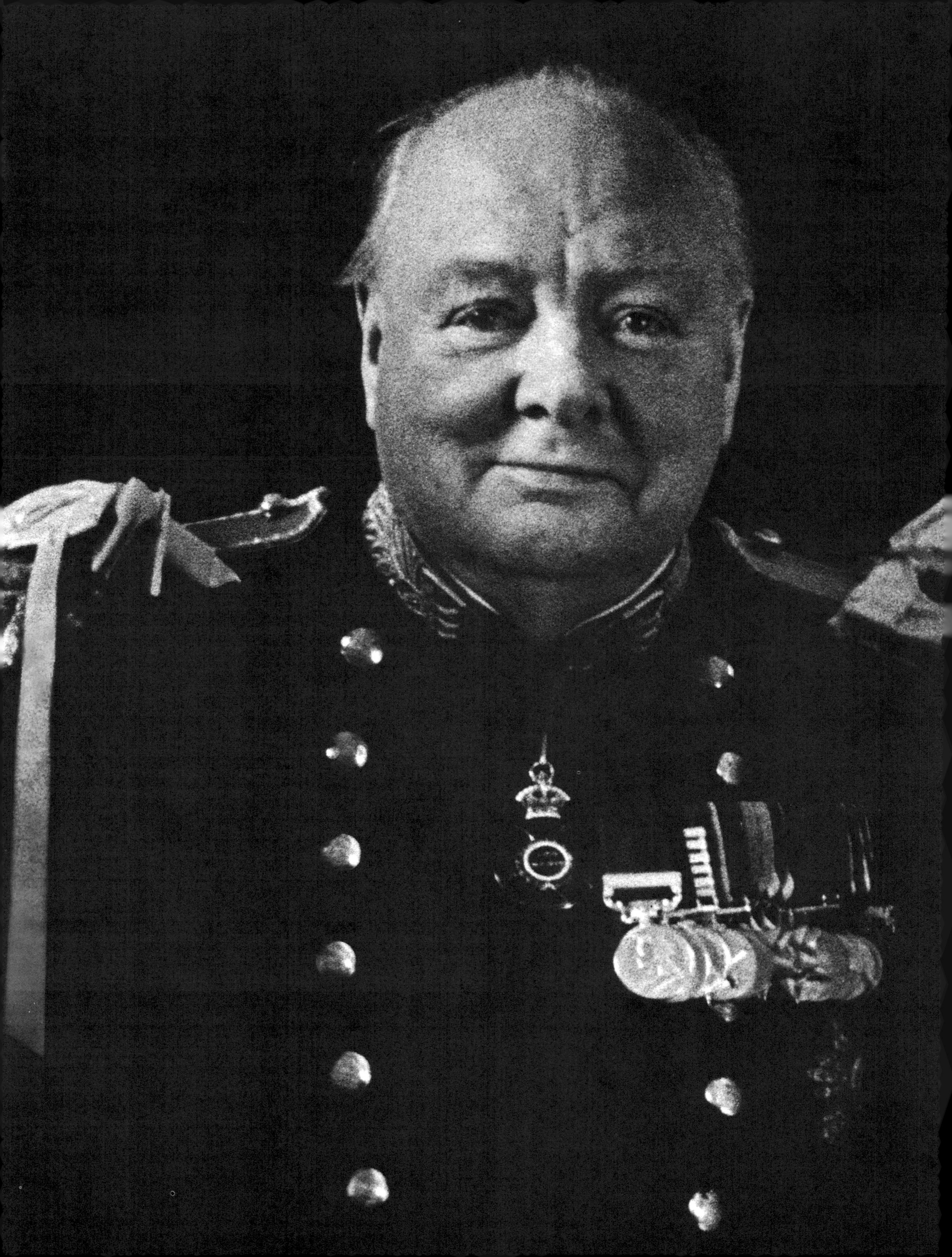

Mrs. Churchill, with her daughters Mary (left) and Sarah, after she was honoured by the King with the Dame Grand Cross of the Order of the British Empire, July, 1946.

His vision did not desert him in the postwar years when he addressed himself to the problems of foreign policy. Churchill's ideas on foreign policy developed so consistently after 1945 that it is impossible to draw a line at the point in 1951 when he was again returned to power, the Conservatives under his leadership winning a parliamentary majority of 17. But it is worth noticing the precise nature of his achievement while he was in Opposition. He made a series of speeches which were as important as statements by a sovereign Government. They had a world-wide influence. They were creative. They helped to form the policies, not only of Britain, but of the whole free world. Yet when he made them he was out of office and speaking only for himself.

It was in March, 1946, when he visited the United States at the invitation of Mr. Truman and was accompanied by the President to the town of Fulton, Missouri, that he first addressed the world as its seer. The occasion, with the President of the United States present, was clearly chosen to give the speech the widest prominence—and Churchill began by offering openly his "true and faithful counsel in these anxious and baffling times". The first purpose of the speech was to present a clear picture of the change which had been wrought in the world since the end of the war. The "splendid comradeship in arms" had not continued. Instead, "from Stettin in the Baltic to Trieste in the Adriatic, an iron curtain" had "descended across the Continent".

THE "IRON CURTAIN" SPEECH

Here, in two words, was the crystallization. The phrase, the "iron curtain", only summarized a cogent argument, but it vividly painted the background against which all thinking about foreign policy had to be done. From this followed Churchill's three important conclusions: that there should be a close association between Britain and the United States —providing "no quivering, precarious balance of power to offer its temptation to ambition or adventure"; that "the secret knowledge or experience of the atomic bomb" should remain largely in American hands; and that "the safety of the world requires a new unity in Europe from which no nation should be permanently outcast".

OPPOSITE: Churchill at a later date, in the uniform of Lord Warden of the Cinque Ports.

At Chartwell, correcting the galley proofs of his war memoirs, which later helped to earn him the Nobel prize for literature.

Hat in the air, a smiling daughter Mary at his side, before a cheering crowd at the Zürich Town Hall.

This last point was elaborated in a speech which he delivered at Zürich University on September 19, 1946. "What is the sovereign remedy", he asked, "for the tragedy of Europe? It is to re-create the European family, or as much of it as we can. . . . We must build a kind of United States of Europe." There followed another forward-looking proposal. "I am now going to say something that will astonish you. The first step in the re-creation of the European family must be a partnership between France and Germany. In this way only can France recover the moral leadership of Europe. . . . The structure of the United States of Europe, if well and truly built, will be such as to make the material strength of a single State less important." A United States of Europe—"or whatever name or form it may take" —to include "a spiritually great Germany"; the seeds of future policy were being sown. The next time Churchill spoke in a foreign affairs debate in the House of Commons (October, 1946) he was able to say, with perfect truth, that "what I said at Fulton has been outpaced and overpassed by the movement of events and by the movements of American opinion. If I were to make that speech at the present time and in the same place, it would attract no particular attention".

Throughout 1947 and 1948 Churchill devoted much of his energy to the concept of a United Europe. He had no very clear idea of what he meant or intended. The differences between federation and confederation baffled and did not particularly interest him. But much of the criticism of his role in these years was misplaced. Churchill was not primarily concerned with building a political structure. He himself said at a United Europe meeting at the Albert Hall on May 14, 1947, "We are not acting in the field of force, but in the domain of opinion". And he went on: "It is not for us at this stage to attempt to define or prescribe the structure of constitutions. We ourselves are content, in the first instance, to present the idea of United Europe . . . as a moral, cultural and spiritual conception to which all can rally. . . . It is for us to lay the foundation, to create the atmosphere and give the driving impulsion."

Receiving the Médaille Militaire from Premier of France Paul Ramadier in Paris, 1947.

When, at the Congress of Europe in May, 1948, he noticed that "16 European States are now associated for economic purposes; five have entered into close economic and military relationship", he could not hide the implication that these achievements owed something to the concept of a United Europe. They certainly owed much to his own initiative.

Churchill shows emotion (ABOVE) at the ovation which greeted his speech at the Congress of Europe, The Hague, May, 1948. Applauding him are (from left) Dr. Kerstens of Holland, organizer of the Congress; Premier Ramadier of France; Dr. Retinger, Secretary General of the Congress; and Denis de Rougemont.

"For us and for all who share our civilization and our desire for peace and world government, there is only one duty and watchword: Persevere."

"Here I say to parents, 'Don't give your son money. As far as you can afford it, give him horses.' No one ever came to grief—except honourable grief—through riding horses. Young men have often been ruined through backing horses, but never through riding them; unless of course, they break their necks, which, taken at a gallop, is a very good death to die." At 74, he still could ride, and (OPPOSITE) did. LEFT: With his grandson Winston, watching his horse Colonist II win the Lime Tree Stakes, 1949. BELOW: On a visit to Harrow School, whose boys he had urged in 1941, at the height of the war: *"Never give in, NEVER, NEVER, NEVER, NEVER—never give in except to convictions of honour and good sense."*

At the back of Churchill's ideas from the Fulton speech on was the belief in negotiation from a position of strength. It was possible to deal with the Russians, he said in March of 1949, "only by having superior force on your side on the matter in question: and they must be convinced that you will use—you will not hesitate to use—these forces, if necessary, in the most ruthless manner". He found encouragement in the fact that "our forces are getting stronger, actually and relatively, than they were a year ago".

PROPOSAL FOR A SUMMIT MEETING

It was because of this slowly changing balance of power that in February, 1950, he threw out "the idea of another talk with Soviet Russia upon the highest level". The suggestion was made at the end of an election speech at Edinburgh and was immediately dismissed as a "stunt". At the time it seemed, even to the non-partisan, to offer few real hopes.

But the idea was a natural development of Churchill's Fulton argument and not a contradiction of it. The idea of "talks at the summit" recurred at intervals throughout the next five years in his foreign policy speeches. It was taken up by the Opposition, and he was increasingly criticized for delay in bringing a meeting about. His explanation came unexpectedly, in 1955, in the course of a debate on the White Paper on Defence.

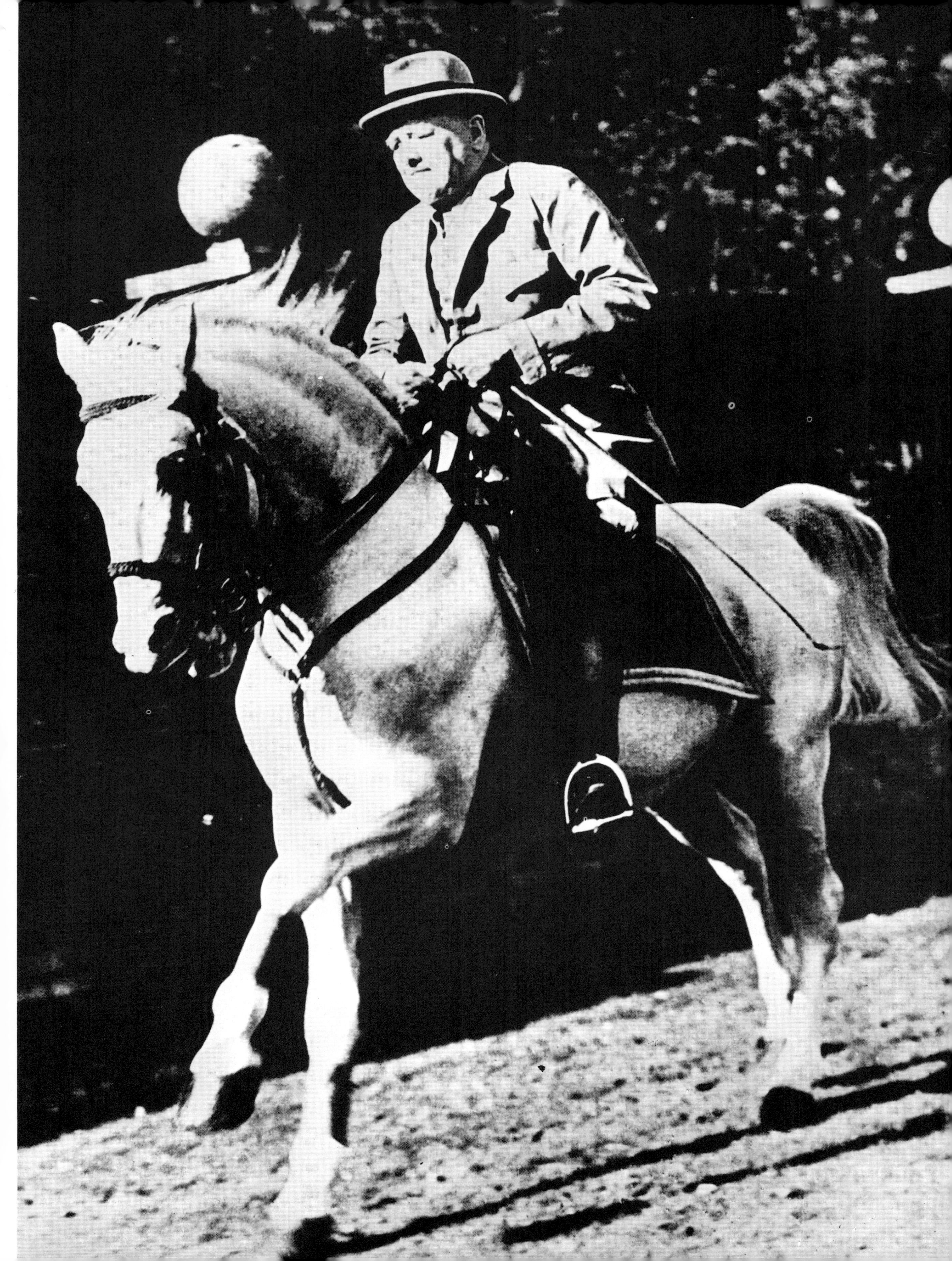

© 1950 Toni Frissell

Mrs. Churchill with her granddaughter Edwina Sandys, 1950.

One of Mrs. Churchill's favourite pictures of her husband.

© 1959 Toni Frissell

The speech with which Churchill opened the debate on defence in March, 1955, can be rated among his great orations. He held a packed House in silence while he expounded his appreciation of the world situation which had determined the Government to press forward with the manufacture of the hydrogen bomb and the means of its delivery. On its deterrent power he founded his hopes for peace. If the ability and determination to use the weapon in self-defence were well understood on both sides war might be averted. "That is why", he said, "I have hoped for a long time for a top-level conference where these matters can be put plainly and bluntly. . . . Then it might well be that, by a process of sublime irony, we shall have reached a stage in this story where safety will be the sturdy child of terror and survival the twin brother of annihilation."

But later in the debate when Mr. Bevan taunted him with being prevented from holding such a conference by the United States, Churchill rose to explain the reasons for delay. He would have liked, he said, to have seen a conference shortly after Malenkov took power and he had prepared to go over to see President Eisenhower to arrange for the invitation. "However, I was struck down by a very sudden illness which paralysed me completely physically, and I had to put it all off, and it was not found possible to persuade President Eisenhower to join in that process." He went on to speak of the hopes he had entertained of a dual meeting at Stockholm or some like neutral place. "But then the Soviet Government began a very elaborate process of trying to stop the ratification of E.D.C., which I thought had been more or less accepted . . . and so all this other matter has come up now and stood in the way of further general talks."

"I have never accepted what many people have kindly said, namely that I inspired the nation. It was the nation and the race dwelling round the globe that had the lion's heart. I had the luck to be called upon to give the roar. I also hope that I sometimes suggested to the lion the right place to use his claws." BELOW: At the London Zoo in Regent's Park feeding Rota, a lion presented to him as a cub.

Through all the diplomatic activity of the autumn of 1954 which followed the French Assembly's rejection of the European Defence Community treaty, Churchill had remained in the background. It was his Foreign Secretary who described and executed British policy and who announced the Government's historic decision, reversing the policy of ages, to commit troops to the Continent for a period of some fifty years. And it was Sir Anthony Eden who went to Geneva the following summer for the long-awaited conference of heads of state.

Churchill's record during the Parliament of 1951 is less impressive in domestic affairs than in foreign. This is partly due to the policy of his Government, which was to repair the national economy and grant a respite from major legislation, and partly to his preoccupation with the great questions that lay unsettled between the nations. In the more controversial domestic debates it was not he but his subordinate Ministers who appeared in the front line. Churchill himself, in contrast to his tactics while in opposition after 1945, exerted his parliamentary talents in the mitigation of party strife. Yet it was while under his leadership that the Conservative Party revolutionized its policy, became a guarantor of the welfare state, and stole so many of its opponents' clothes; and it was while he was Prime Minister that the party gave proof of its new convictions in office. It was not too difficult a transformation for one who had been a member of the Liberal Government of 1906. After his illness in 1953, his movements it was noticed were less vigorous, his uptake in the Commons less quick, but again and again he came to the dispatch box and reasserted his mastery.

CONSERVATIVE POLICY AND DOMESTIC AFFAIRS

BELOW RIGHT: Wearing his party colours and leading a bulldog—symbol of both the British nation and his own tenacious courage—the Member for Woodford makes a last-minute visit to his constituency before the February, 1950, election that returned him to Parliament. The Labour Party remained in power, but before the next year was out another general election was to give the Conservatives a majority.

Churchill arriving (BELOW) at St. Stephen's Hall, South Kensington, to record his vote in the general election, October 25, 1951. Outside the polling station, actor John Forrest's dog Beary (RIGHT) looks on from a shopping cart, suitably inscribed. The next day (OPPOSITE PAGE, with his wife as news of the victory reached him) Churchill again became Prime Minister.

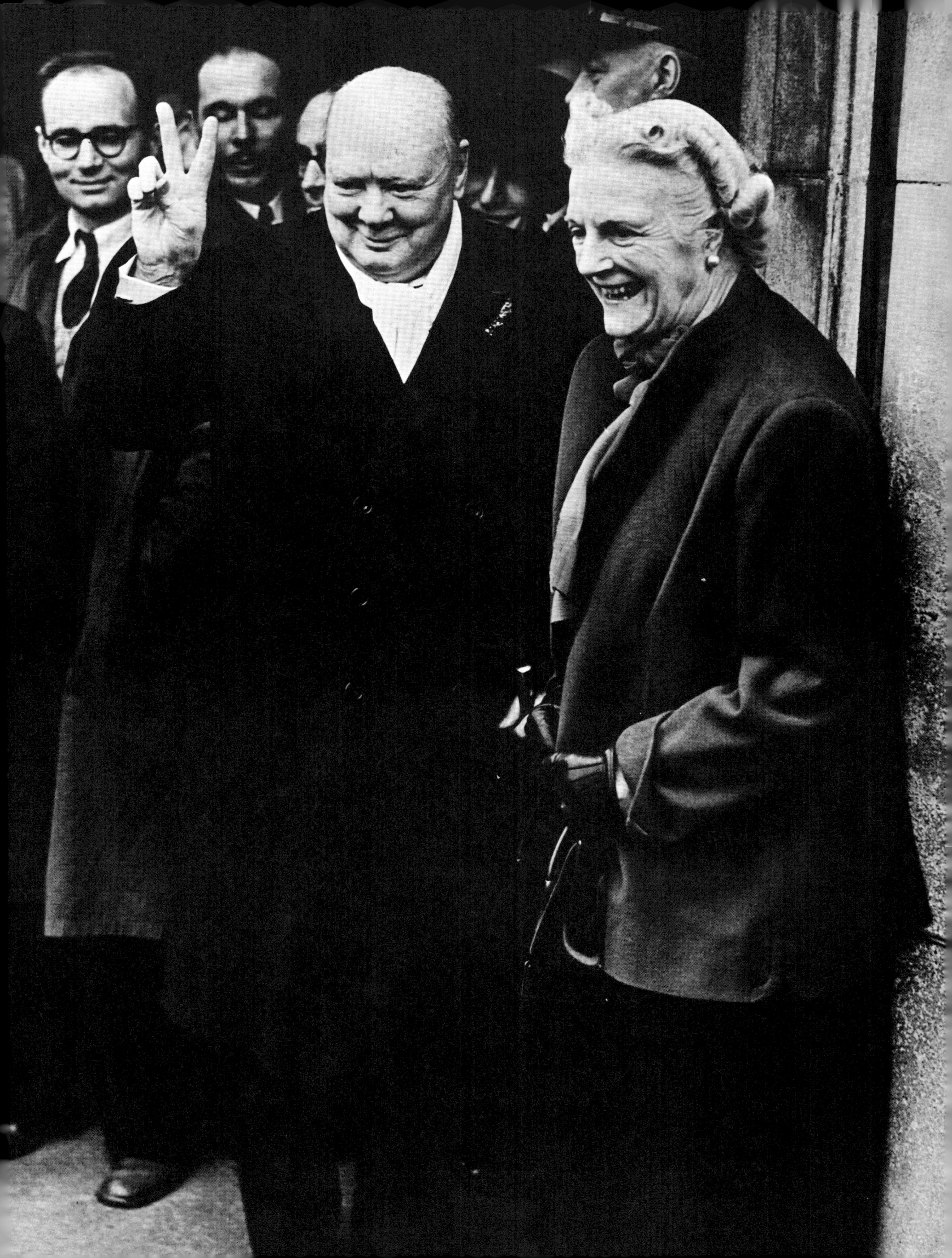

Members of the Royal Family watch from the roof, and the Prime Minister from inside (ABOVE), as Princess Elizabeth and her husband, the Duke of Edinburgh, take off for Nairobi on January 31, 1952, on the first lap of a journey to Australia. The King died on February 6, and Elizabeth, now Queen, flew home the next day. At the airport to greet his new Sovereign, the sixth he had served in his long public life, was Winston Churchill (OPPOSITE PAGE, with Leader of the Opposition Clement Attlee and Foreign Secretary Anthony Eden [left], as the Queen descends from her plane).

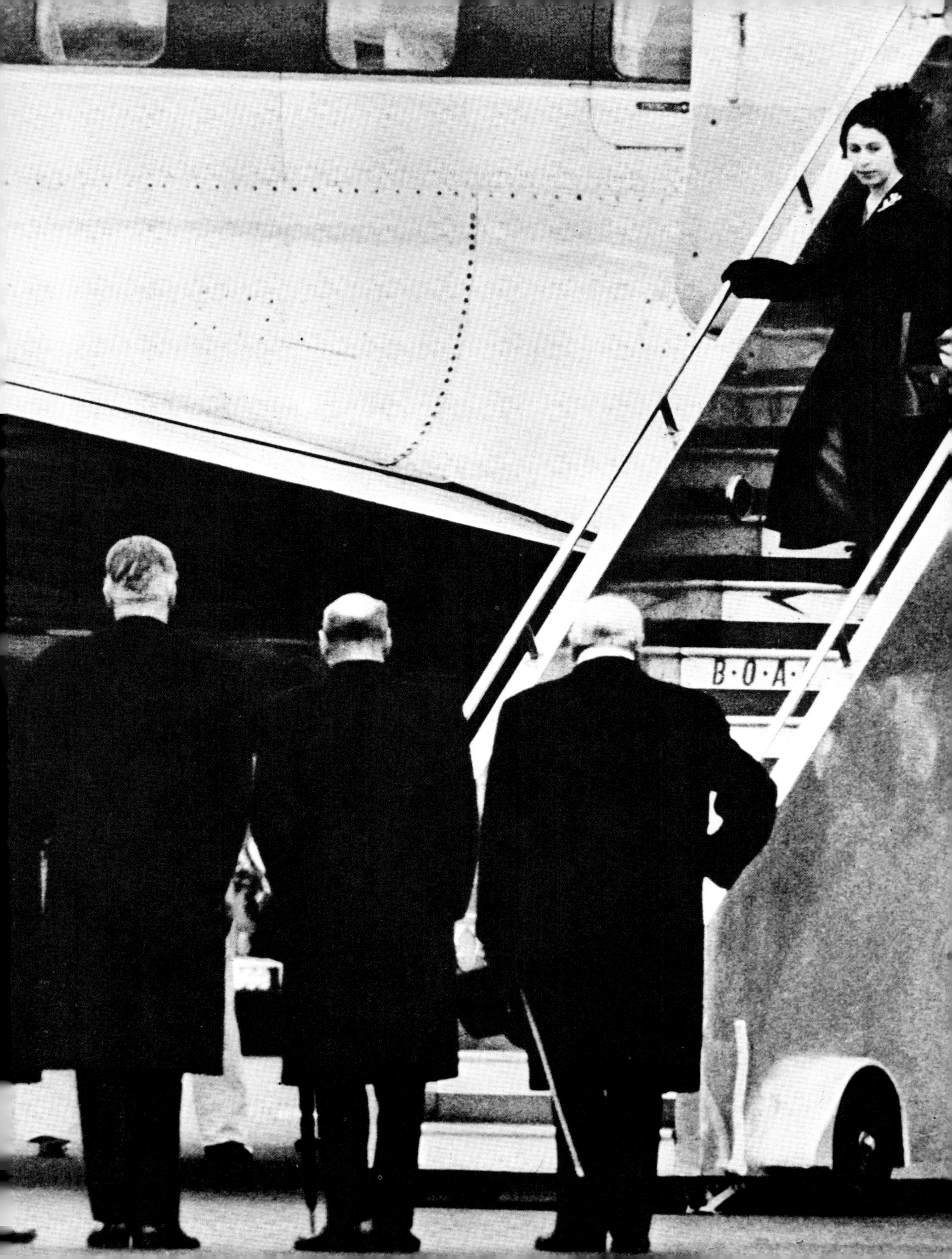
B·O·A

The Coronation of Elizabeth II, Westminster Abbey, June 2, 1953. BELOW, RIGHT: Sir Winston and Lady Churchill at the Abbey.

The Queen, bearing the Orb and Sceptre, leaves the Abbey after her Coronation. BELOW: With Prince Philip at Buckingham Palace.

Lady Churchill with her granddaughter Emma Soames, after the Coronation, June, 1953.

© 1959 Toni Frissell

© 1959 Toni Frissell

Sir Winston at Downing Street after the Coronation. He had been knighted by the Queen on April 24, 1953, and invested with the Insignia of a Knight Companion of the Most Noble Order of the Garter.

"There is no doubt that of all the institutions which have grown up among us over the centuries, or sprung into being in our lifetime, the constitutional monarchy is the most deeply founded and dearly cherished by the whole association of our peoples. In the present generation it has acquired a meaning incomparably more powerful than anyone had dreamed possible in former times. The Crown has become the mysterious link—indeed, I may say, the magic link—which unites our loosely bound but strongly interwoven Commonwealth of nations, states, and races...."

At Waterloo Station with the Queen, Prince Charles, and Princess Anne. *"Here at the summit of our world-wide Commonwealth is a lady whom we respect because she is our Queen and whom we love because she is herself."*

Leaving St. Paul's with Lady Churchill (OPPOSITE) after a service of thanksgiving for the Coronation of Elizabeth II, June, 1953.

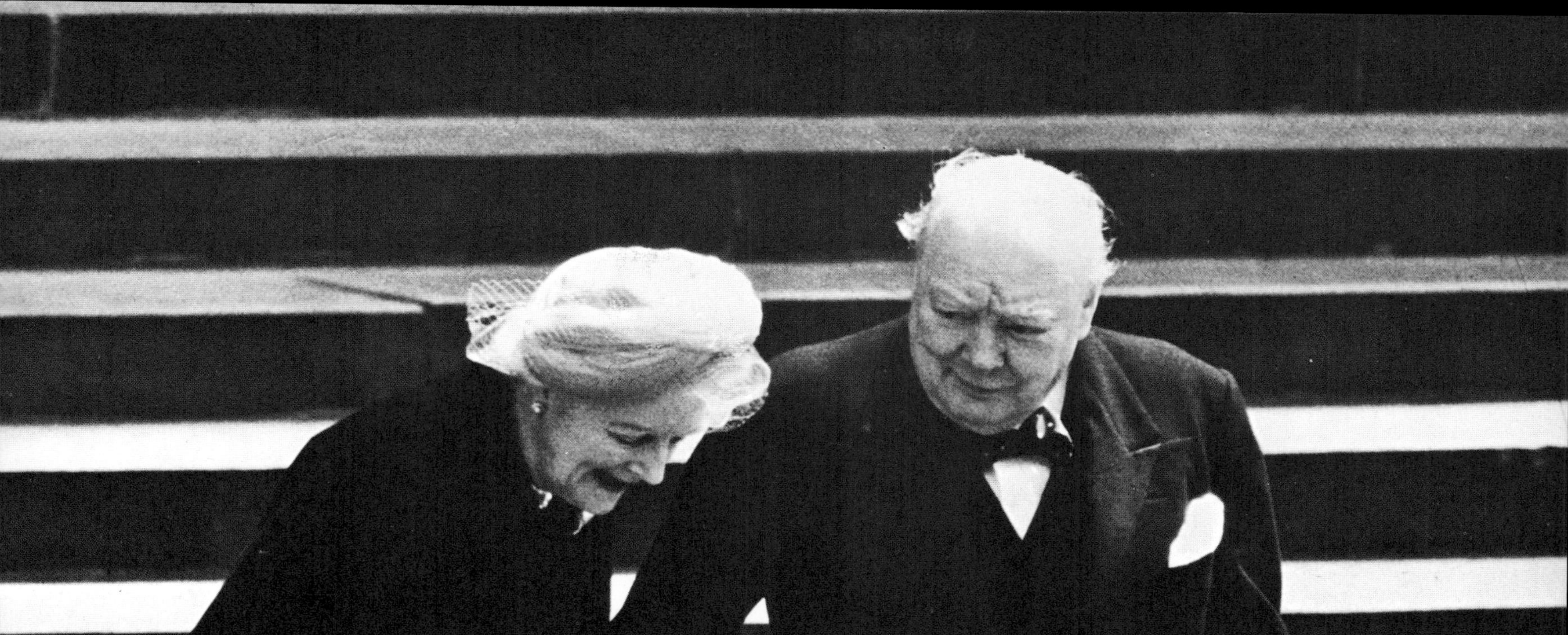

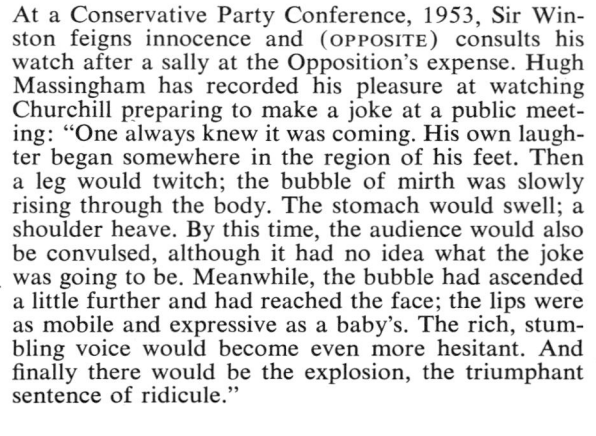

At a Conservative Party Conference, 1953, Sir Winston feigns innocence and (OPPOSITE) consults his watch after a sally at the Opposition's expense. Hugh Massingham has recorded his pleasure at watching Churchill preparing to make a joke at a public meeting: "One always knew it was coming. His own laughter began somewhere in the region of his feet. Then a leg would twitch; the bubble of mirth was slowly rising through the body. The stomach would swell; a shoulder heave. By this time, the audience would also be convulsed, although it had no idea what the joke was going to be. Meanwhile, the bubble had ascended a little further and had reached the face; the lips were as mobile and expressive as a baby's. The rich, stumbling voice would become even more hesitant. And finally there would be the explosion, the triumphant sentence of ridicule."

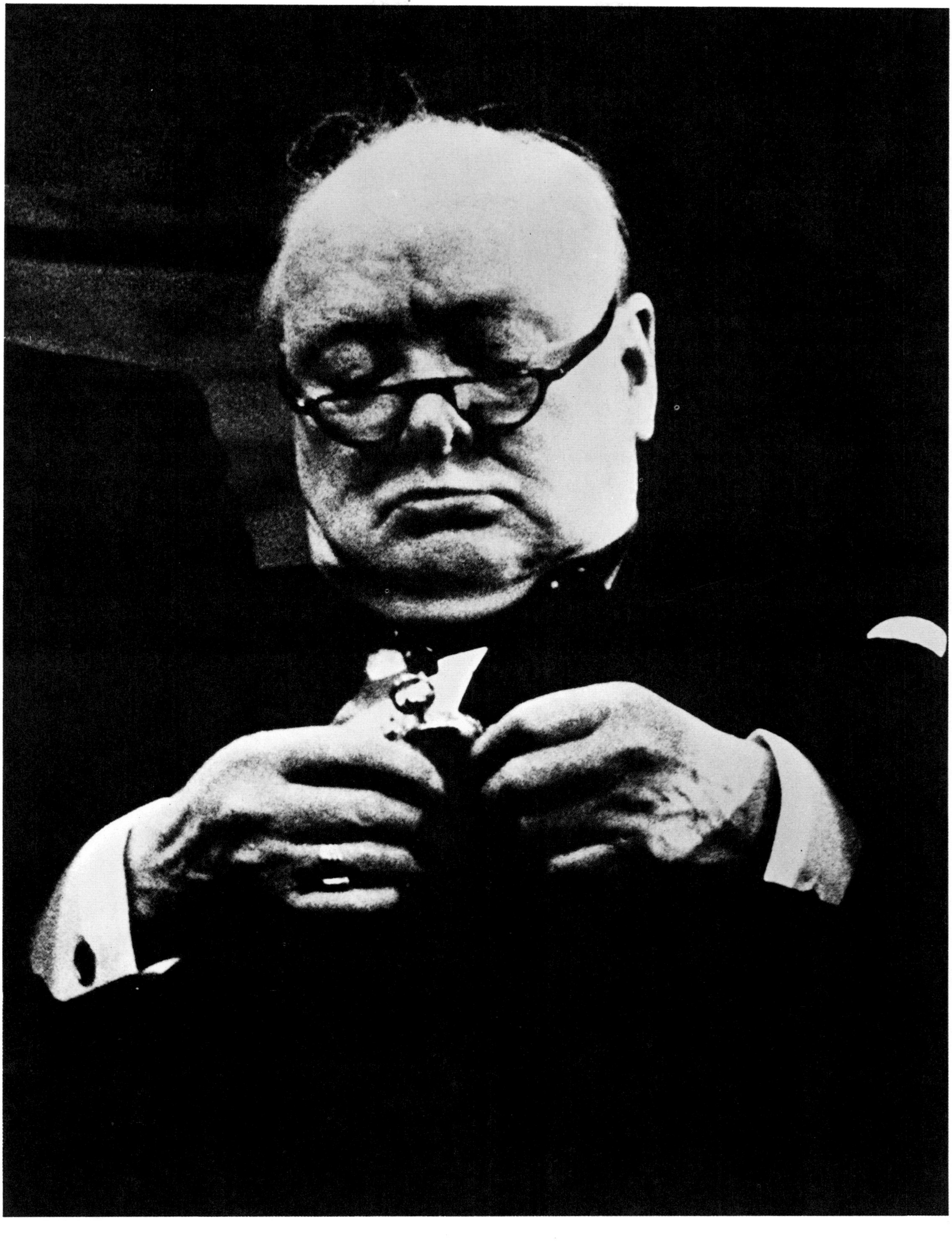

June 14, 1954: At Windsor Castle (OPPOSITE), following the Guard of Honour in a procession to St. George's Chapel, to be installed as a Knight Companion of the Order of the Garter, the highest order of chivalry a British citizen can attain and still be eligible to sit in the House of Commons. ABOVE: Leaving the Chapel with Lady Churchill after the installation ceremony.

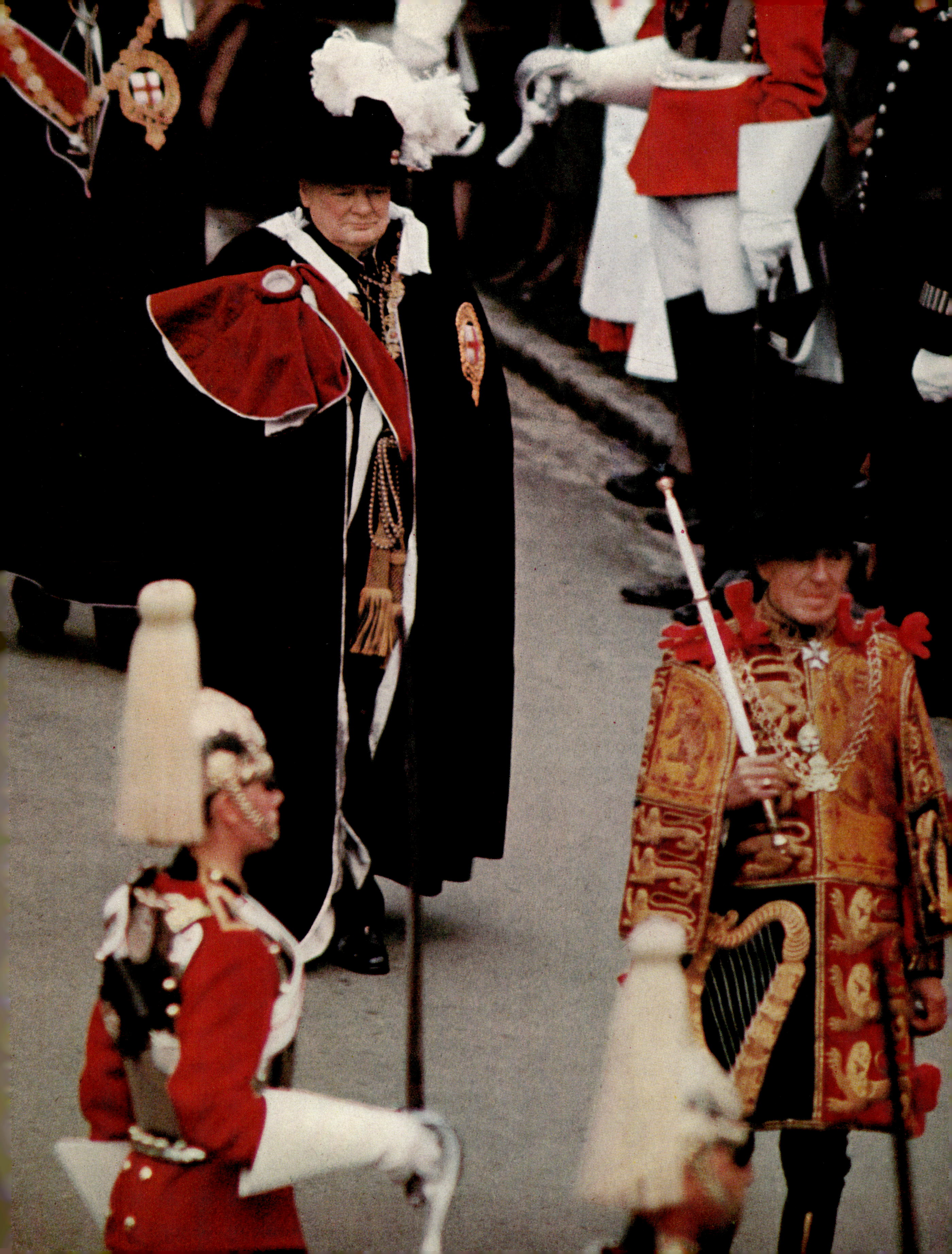

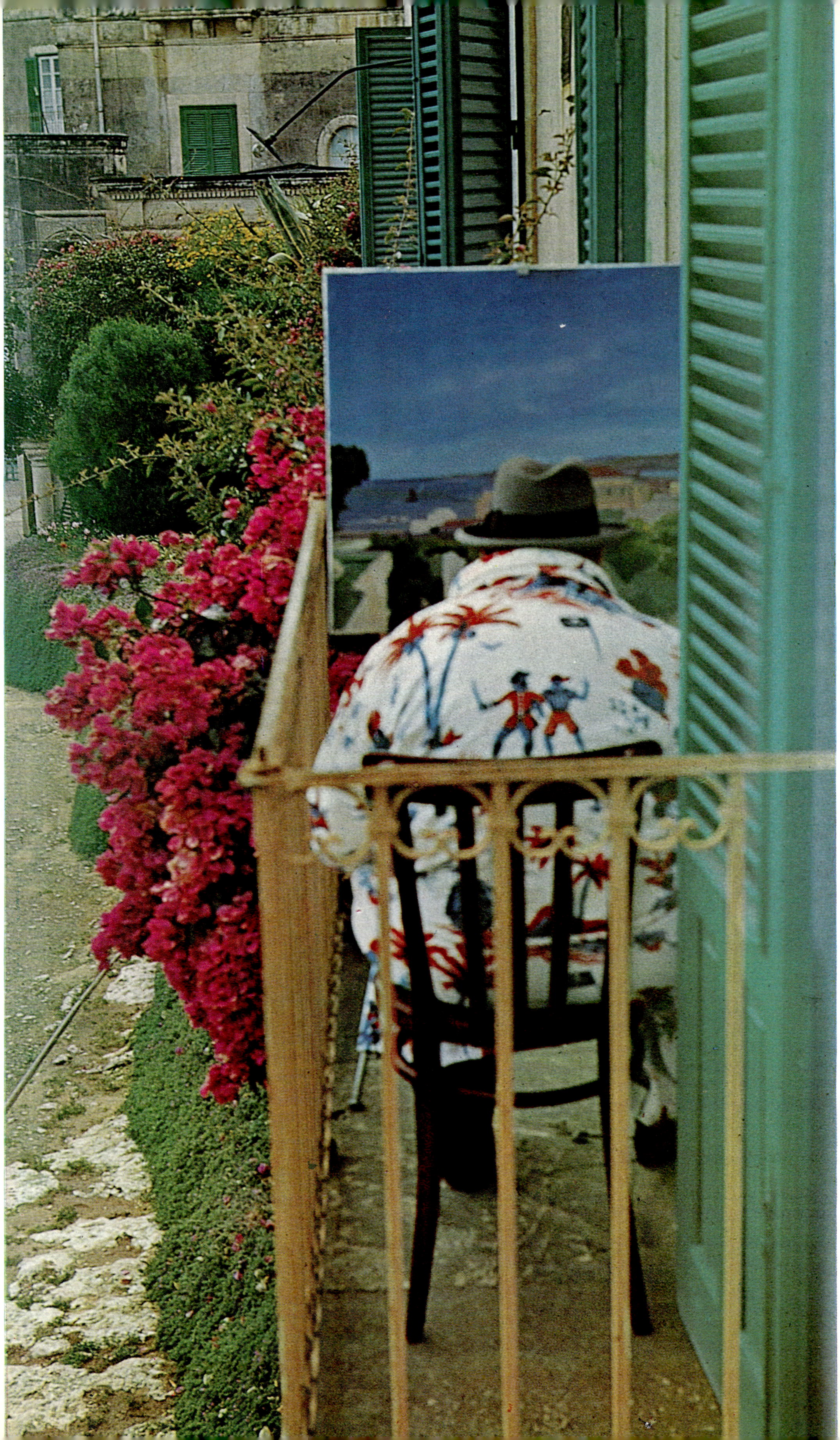

A glowing loyalty to the Monarchy, which was fed by the romantic strain in Churchill's nature, was matched by a warm personal regard for the Sovereigns whom he served. His attachment to George VI was especially marked, and can be measured by the fact that he deferred to the King's wish that he should not, as he had planned and as he dearly wanted to, embark in a warship on D-Day to observe the bombardment of the Normandy coast. The panegyric which he broadcast the night after King George's death was deeply moving in its sincerity. For similar reasons the Knighthood of the Garter, conferred on him by Queen Elizabeth just before her coronation, was a source of particular gratification to him. He had declined the same honour at the hands of her father in 1945, before the restoration of the practice by which conferment of the Order is the sole prerogative of the Sovereign, who does not act on the recommendation of the Prime Minister.

His eightieth birthday on November 30, 1954, found him still in office and in full control. The occasion drew forth tributes from his countrymen and from abroad of such number and warmth as have never been accorded to any English statesman before. Both Houses of Parliament met in Westminster Hall to present him with gifts. It was an occasion with no parallel, perhaps the climax of the public honour paid him during his life-time.

His resignation as Prime Minister had long been rumoured, and when it came on April 5, 1955, it unhappily coincided with a strike in offices of the London national newspapers which prevented their publication. Yet the public did not need to be reminded in order to be aware that the last page was turned of one of the greatest chapters of British statesmanship. Preferring to the highest honours which might have been bestowed upon him to remain a private member of the House of Commons, he presented himself again to the electors of Woodford, as he did once more in 1959. Though he was often in the Chamber of the House during these last years, he took no further part in its debates.

He used his leisure to work at the long-projected *History of the English Speaking Peoples* in four volumes. Professional historians found much to cavil at, in spite of the assistance Churchill had from some of their number. But the public recognized in it a master hand of historical narrative, a shrewd and appreciative judgment of magnanimity, and an endearing preference for the good old stories, however "tiresome investigators" might have undermined them.

Two of his private pursuits in particular excited public interest—his horse-racing and his painting. He became a racehorse owner late in life. His racing colours were registered in 1949 and two months later he won his first race with Colonist II. It was a popular victory.

His taste for painting was of much longer standing. He began during enforced inactivity after his removal from the Admiralty in 1915. Four years later he exhibited a portrait at an exhibition of the Royal Society of Portrait Painters. But it was landscapes that he grew to prefer. "Audacity", he wrote, "is a very great part of the art of painting." And his decisive, boldly coloured, impressionistic works became familiar at the Royal Academy. His election to that body as Royal Academician Extraordinary was an honour he particularly relished, and his speeches at the annual banquets added much to the gaiety of the occasion. An exhibition of 62 of his paintings held at Burlington House in the summer of 1959 brought more than 140,000 visitors.

In his Chancellor's robes, speaking at Bristol University, 1954.

"When I get to heaven I mean to spend a considerable portion of my first million years in painting, and so get to the bottom of the subject. But then I shall require a still gayer palette than I get here below. . . . There will be a whole range of wonderful new colours which will delight the celestial eye." OPPOSITE: Painting in Sicily.

November 30, 1954: The Prime Minister speaking in Westminster Hall to both Houses of Parliament, assembled to honour him on his eightieth birthday. One of their gifts was the portrait behind him, by Graham Sutherland. BELOW: The dedication page and binding of the commemorative book, signed by members of the House of Commons, also presented to Churchill on this occasion.

To
Sir WINSTON LEONARD SPENCER-CHURCHILL
KNIGHT OF THE MOST NOBLE ORDER OF THE GARTER,
MEMBER OF THE ORDER OF MERIT, MEMBER OF
THE ORDER OF THE COMPANIONS OF HONOUR
Prime Minister of the United Kingdom, First Lord of the Treasury and One of Her Majesty's Most Honourable Privy Council, a Tribute of Devotion and Regard from the Commons of Her Majesty's Parliament on the Occasion of the Eightieth Anniversary of his Birthday on the Thirtieth day of November in the year One thousand nine hundred and fifty-four.

WE,
The ELECTED MEMBERS of the HOUSE of COMMONS representing all political parties and all the peoples within Her Gracious Majesty's Realm of the United Kingdom of Great Britain and Northern Ireland, do hereby join in one accord to show our deep affection to your person and our abiding gratitude for your incomparable service to the Parliament and Peoples of this Realm and to the causes of Justice, Freedom and Peace during more than Fifty years

YOU HAVE BEEN SO FAITHFUL AND SO LOVING TO US, YOU HAVE FOUGHT SO STOUTLY FOR US, YOU HAVE BEEN SO HEARTY IN COUNSELLING OF US THAT WE SHALL NEVER FORGET YOUR FAVOUR TOWARDS US

Last Speech to the House of Commons as Prime Minister, 1955

I beg to move,

That this House will, Tomorrow, resolve itself into a Committee to consider an humble Address to Her Majesty praying that Her Majesty will give directions that a Monument be erected at the public charge to the memory of the late Right Honourable the Earl Lloyd-George of Dwyfor, O.M., with an inscription expressive of the high sense entertained by this House of the eminent services rendered by him to the Country and to the Commonwealth and Empire in Parliament, and in great Offices of State. . . .

David Lloyd George was a House of Commons man. He sat here for one constituency for fifty-five years. He gave sparkle to our debates. He guided the House through some of its most critical years, and without the fame and authority of the Mother of Parliaments he could never have rendered his services to the nation.

The Committee which this Motion will set up will no doubt wish those who were nearest him to express their opinion as to where he would have chosen his monument to be. He might have liked it to be as near this Chamber as possible.

The duty that falls to me this afternoon strikes a curious coincidence. It is exactly ten years ago to the day, 28th March, since I stood at this Box, in my present office, and, at the first opportunity after Lloyd George's death, addressed the House on his career. The discussion that followed is well worth re-reading. There will be seen the unanimity and the fervour of the testimony given to his work from all parts of the House.

I was perplexed, I admit, when I was thinking of how to commend this Motion to you, Mr. Speaker, to find, on looking back, that I had already said much that I now wish to say. My friendship for this remarkable man covered more than forty years of House of Commons life, including long periods during which I served with and under him as his Cabinet colleague. Whether in or out of office, our intimate and agreeable

(Continued on page 216)

In the Cabinet Room at No. 10 Downing Street a few days before his birthday in 1954.

The Queen and (RIGHT) the Duke of Edinburgh were among the guests at a dinner party given by the Churchills at No. 10 Downing Street on April 4, 1955.

Sir Winston sees the Queen to her car, then watches with Lady Churchill (BELOW) as the Royal guests depart. The next day he visited the Queen to announce his retirement as Prime Minister.

(Continued from page 213)

companionship was never darkened, so far as I can recall, by any serious spell of even political hostility.

As a first-hand witness, as I may claim to be, I wish to reaffirm the tribute I paid to his memory on his death. I feel that what was said then has only grown and strengthened and mellowed in the intervening decade. There were two great spheres of his activity and achievements. He launched the Liberal and Radical forces of this country effectively into the broad stream of social betterment and social security along which all modern parties now steer.

His warm heart was stirred by the many perils which beset the cottage homes, the health of the bread winner, the fate of his widow, the nourishment and upbringing of his children, the meagre and haphazard provision of medical treatment and sanatoria, and the lack of any organized accessible medical service from which the mass of the wage earners and the poor in those days suffered so severely. All this excited his wrath. Pity and compassion lent their powerful wings. He knew the terror with which old age threatened the toiler—that after a life of exertion he could be no more than a burden at the fireside and in the family of a struggling son.

When I first became Lloyd George's friend and active associate, more than fifty years ago, this deep love of the people, the profound knowledge of their lives and of the undue and needless pressures under which they lived, impressed themselves indelibly upon my mind. Most people are unconscious today of how much of their lives have been shaped by the laws for which Lloyd George was responsible. Health insurance, and old-age pensions, were the first large-scale State-conscious efforts to fasten a lid over the abyss without pulling down the structures of civilized society.

Now we move forward confidently into larger and more far-reaching applications of these ideas. I was his lieutenant in those bygone days, and shared, in a minor way, in the work. He was indeed a champion of the weak and the poor and I am sure that as time passes his name will not only live but shine on account of the grand, laborious, constructive work he did for the social and domestic life of our country.

But the second phase of his life's work, upon which his fame will rest with equal and even greater firmness, is his guidance of the nation in the First World War. Here I will venture to quote directly what I said ten years ago:

"Although unacquainted with the military arts, although by public repute a pugnacious pacifist, when the life of our country was in peril he rallied to the war effort and cast aside all other thoughts or aims. He was the first to discern the fearful shortages of ammunition and artillery and all the other appliances of war which would so soon affect, and in the case of Imperial Russia mortally affect, the warring nations on both sides. He saw it before anyone."

He presented the facts to the Cabinet even before he went to the Ministry of Munitions.

"Here he hurled himself into the mobilization of British industry. In 1915, he was building great war factories that could not come into operation for two years. There was the usual talk about the war being over in a few months, but he did not hesitate to plan on a vast scale for two years ahead."

In these and in many other matters which form a part of the story of these sombre and tremendous years we can observe and measure the debt we owe him.

"As a man of action, resource and creative energy he stood, when at his zenith, without a rival."

There is one further episode which I will mention. It fell to the lot of most of us who are here today to have to face a second world war. Lloyd George had been long out of office. Nearly a generation had passed since he ceased to be Prime Minister, but upon 3rd September, in the solemn debate which marked our entry into the new struggle, he spoke words which gave confidence to many and comfort to all. I will read them to the House:

"I have been through this before, and there is only one word I want to say about that. We had very bad moments, moments when brave men were rather quailing and doubting, but the nation was firm right through, from beginning to end. One thing that struck me then was that it was in moments of disaster, and in some of the worst disasters with which we were confronted in the war, that I found the greatest union among all classes, the greatest disappearance of discontent and disaffection, and of the grabbing for right and privileges. The nation closed its ranks then. By that means we went through right to the end, and after 4½ years, terrible years, we won a victory for right. We will do it again." . . .

When the history of Britain for the first quarter of the twentieth century is written it will be seen how great a part of our fortunes in peace and in war was shaped by this one man.

Sir Winston after his retirement from office, reviewing the guard of honour at Guildhall, where a statue of him was being unveiled (OVERLEAF), June, 1955.

After the unveiling of a bronze statue of him at Guildhall, 1955.

Receiving the Williamsburg Award from Winthrop Rockefeller.

LEFT: Being welcomed into the Company of Adventurers of England into Hudson's Bay, 1956.

A portrait of Sir Winston in his uniform as Lord Warden of the Cinque Ports is presented to him (ABOVE) in 1955, at a meeting of the Courts of Brotherhood and Guestling of the Confederation of Cinque Ports.

His enthusiasm for racing undiminished, Churchill moves through the crowds at Ascot (RIGHT) with Lady Churchill in 1956. ABOVE: The Queen arriving with the Royal party. OPPOSITE PAGE, BELOW: The Queen Mother and Princess Margaret in the Royal carriage.

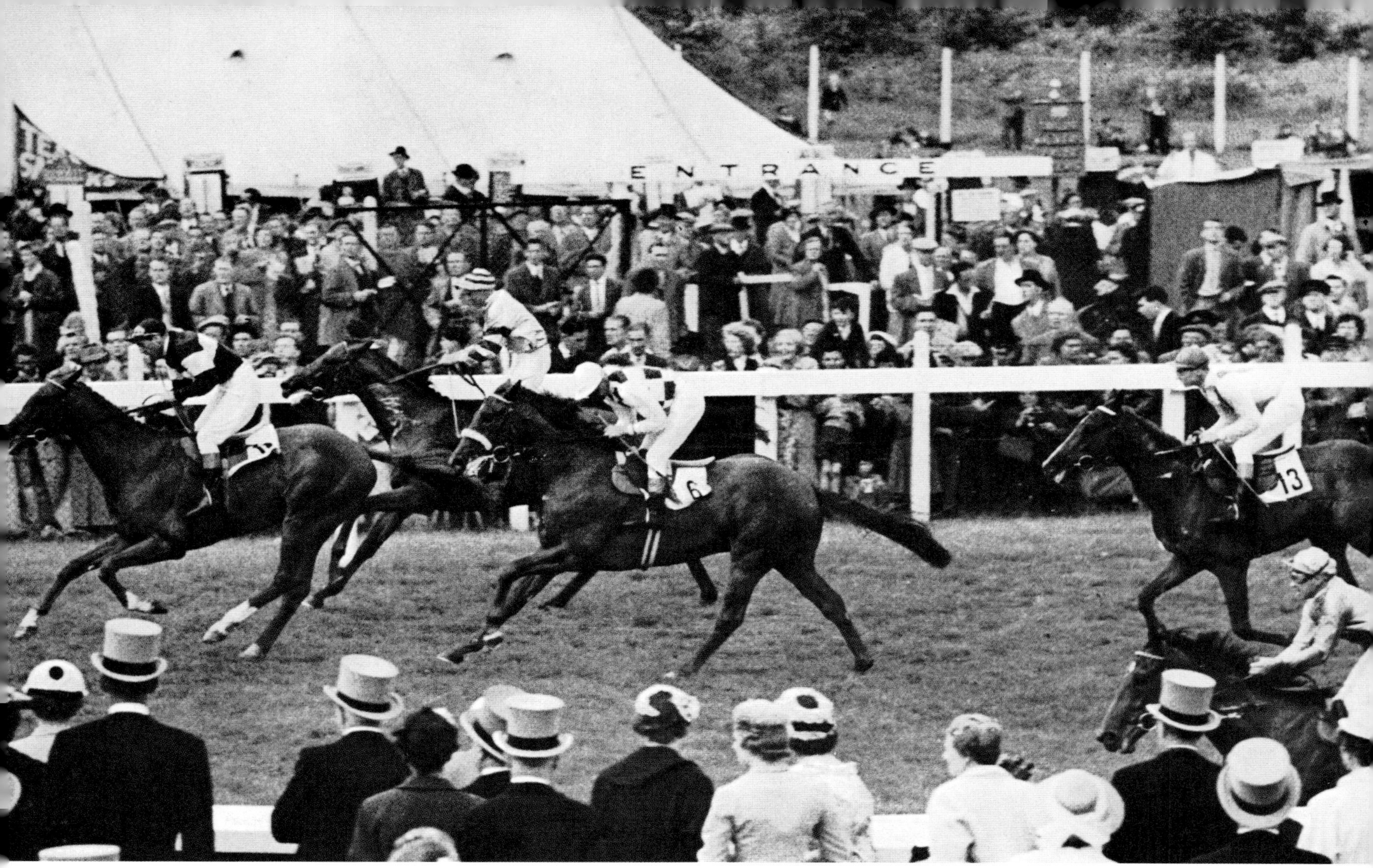
ENTRANCE
6
13

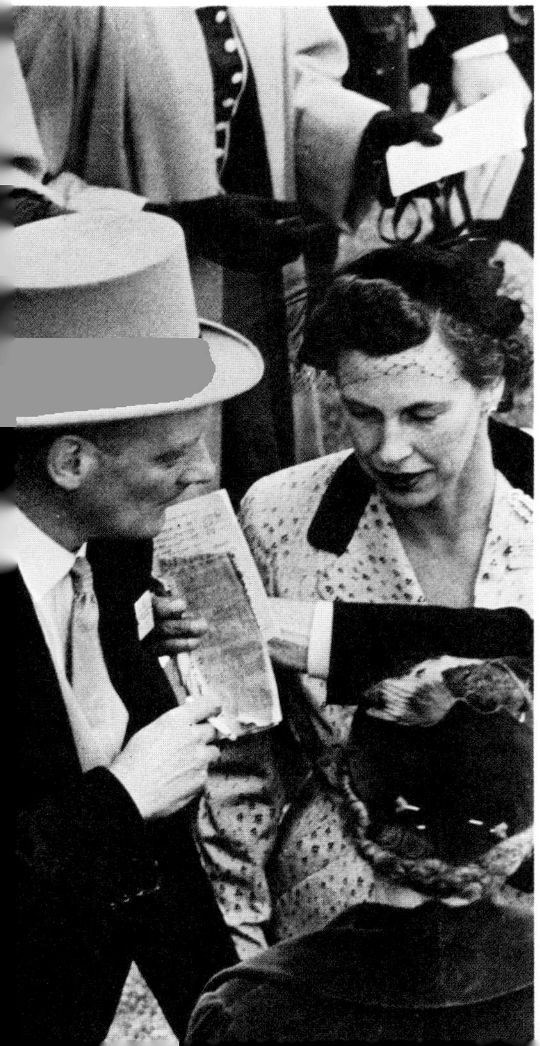

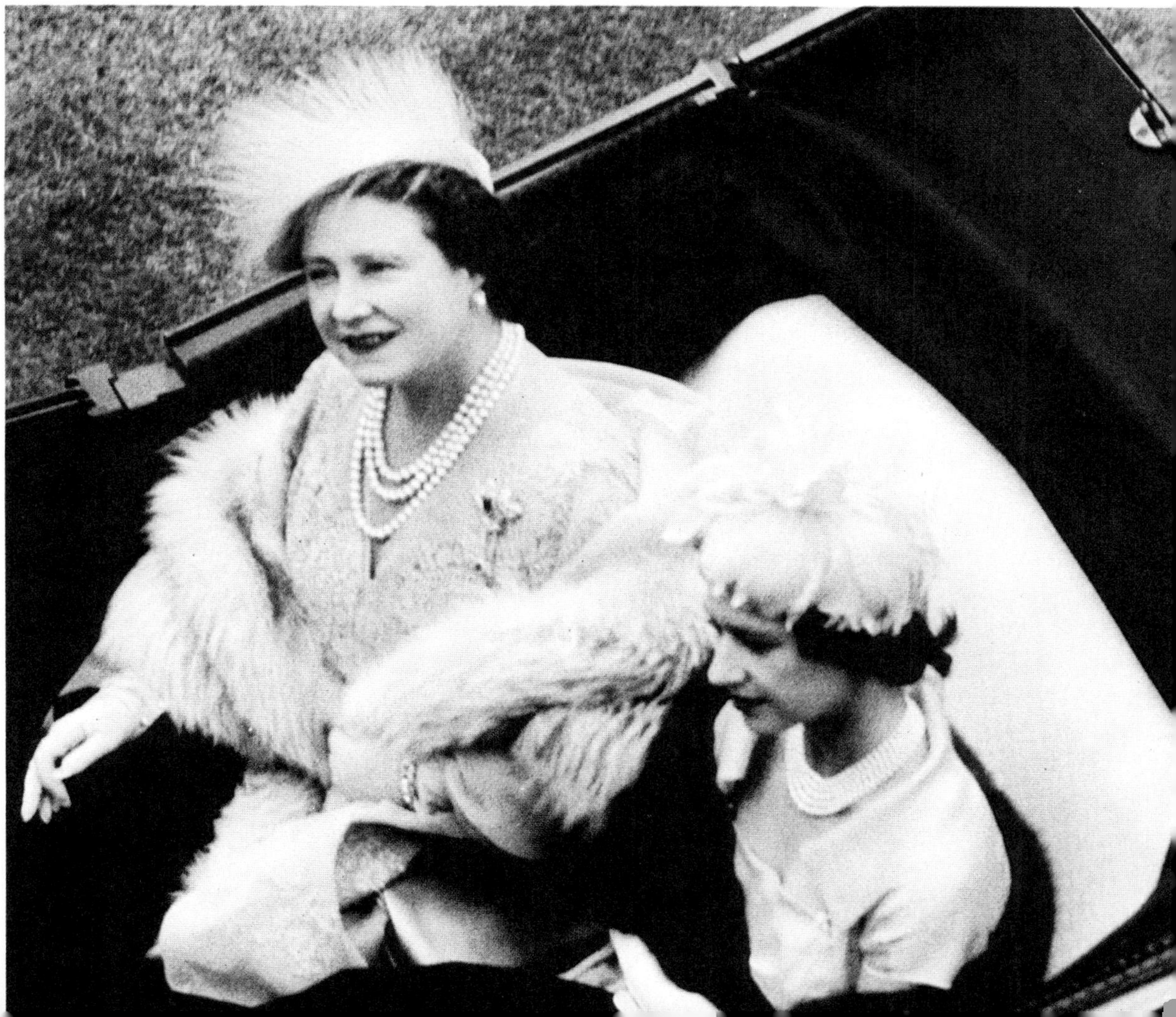

In the cemetery at Bladon, near Blenheim, where he himself was to lie, Churchill stands in the rain in 1958 among the graves of his Marlborough ancestors.

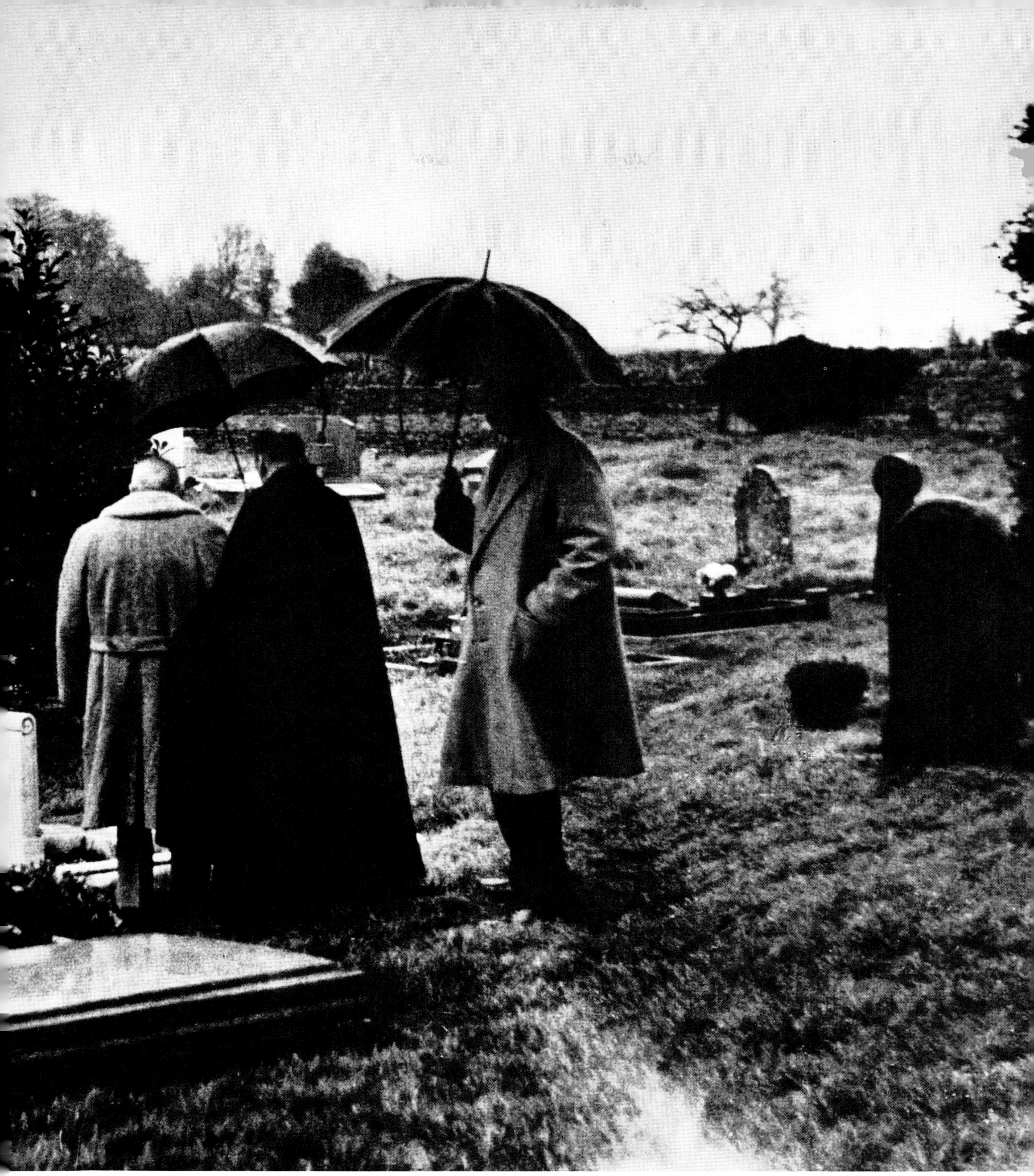

At the Royal Hospital, Chelsea, Churchill is greeted by his Soames grandsons Nicholas (OPPOSITE PAGE), 10, and Jeremy (RIGHT), 6, as he and Lady Churchill arrive (ABOVE, with granddaughter Charlotte, 4) for the christening in the Wren Chapel of their newest grandson, Rupert Christopher Soames (BELOW, with his parents, receiving a grandfather's kiss), July, 1959.

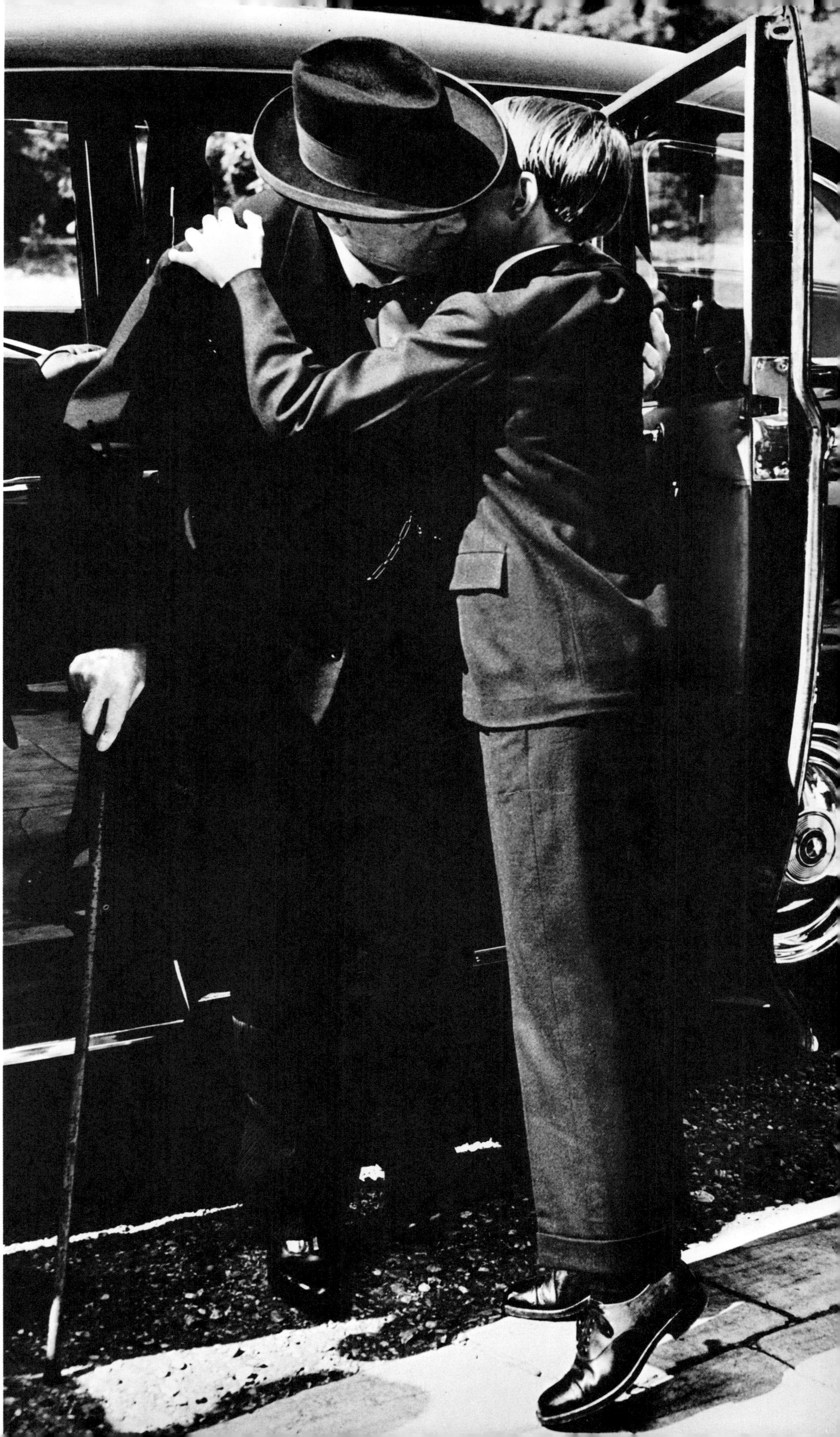

"Armed with a paint-box, one cannot be bored, one cannot be left at a loose end, one cannot 'have several days on one's hands'. Good gracious! what there is to admire and how little time there is to see it in! For the first time one begins to envy Methuselah. No doubt he made very indifferent use of his opportunities." At past 85, Churchill continued to paint whatever he saw: at Marrakech (BELOW), 1959; at Cap d'Ail (LEFT), 1960.

On a cruise aboard the yacht of Aristotle Onassis.

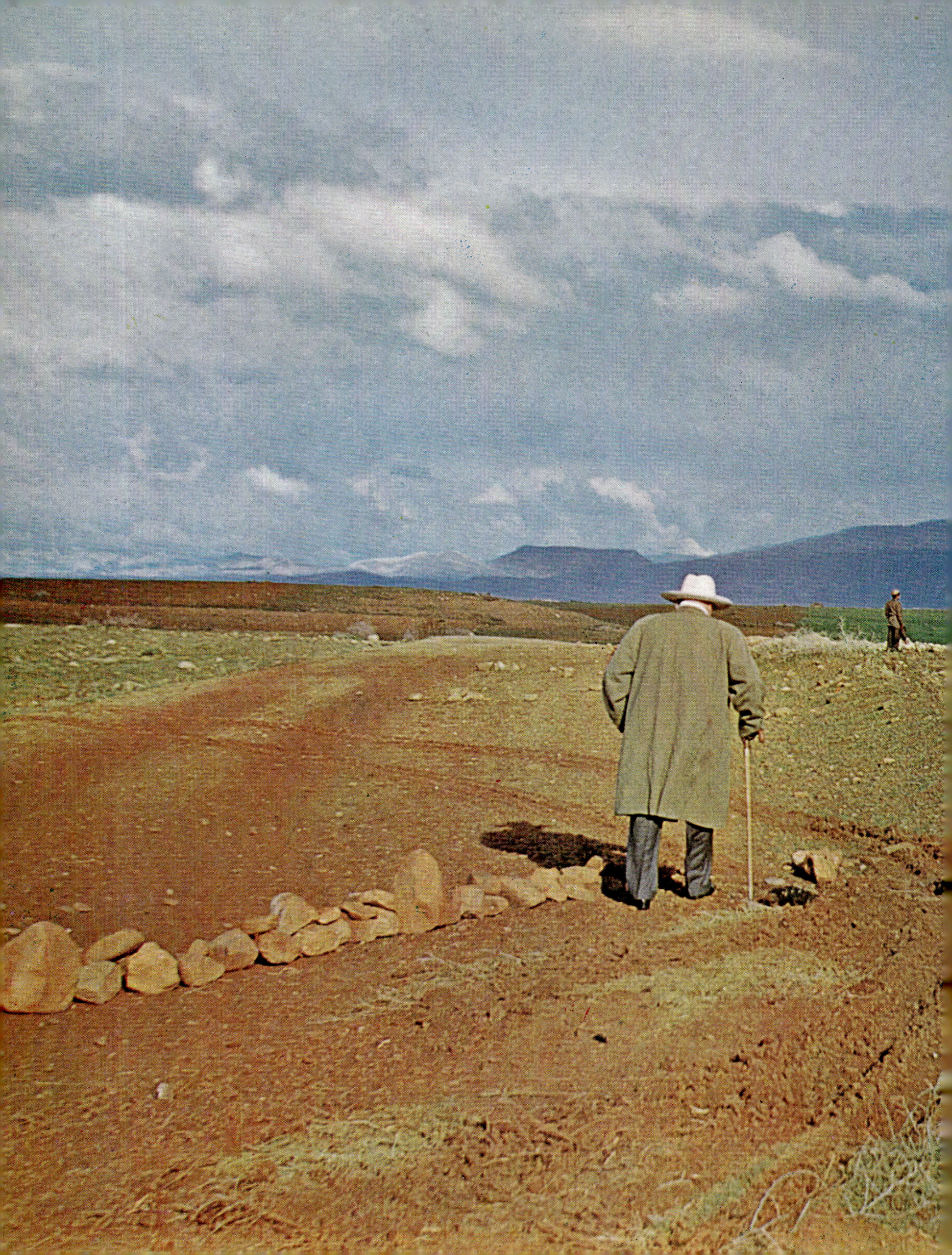

A last walk towards the Atlas Mountains, at Marrakech, 1959.

"It is foolish to waste lamentations upon the closing phase of human life. Noble spirits yield themselves willingly to the successively falling shades." Nearing 90, Churchill rests in the sun in the garden at Chartwell.

In the spring of 1956 he was awarded the Charlemagne Prize for services to Europe, at Aachen. That this should have gone to the man who was above all responsible for the overthrow of the German Reich was a sign of the rapidity with which the European scene had changed in 10 years. In his speech on that occasion he cast his last stone that was to ripple the surface of international waters. He spoke, as he had so often done before, of the grand design of a united Europe. Russia, he said, must play a part in the alliance that would guarantee the peace of Europe; if that position was first achieved, it might be that the reunification of Germany would be more easily effected. In Bonn the reaction was chilly to this strategy, which did not accord with the rigorous views held there about the steps by which reunification should be accomplished. During the Suez crisis Churchill, to the disappointment of many, was silent except for two letters to his constituents, in which he intimated that the Government's actions had his full support.

In the summer of 1962 he fell and fractured a thigh bone. About 12 months later he announced that he would not seek reelection in the next Parliament. On July 28, 1964, shortly before the dissolution of Parliament, the House of Commons accorded him the rare honour of passing a motion "putting on record its unbounded admiration and gratitude for his services to Parliament, to the nation and to the world. . . ." He did not take his seat in the Chamber that day. The motion was brought to him by the party leaders at his home at Hyde Park Gate, where he was soon to celebrate his ninetieth birthday.

RETIREMENT FROM PARLIAMENT

The honours that crowded upon him towards the end of his life are far too numerous to list. First in esteem was his honorary citizenship of the United States of America, which was declared by proclamation at a ceremony at the White House on April 9, 1963—an honour that has been bestowed on no one else in the history of the Union. In 1958 he was

"In the dark days and darker nights when England stood alone—and most men save Englishmen despaired of England's life—he mobilized the English language and sent it into battle," said President Kennedy, declaring Churchill an honorary citizen of the United States (RIGHT). "The incandescent quality of his words illuminated the courage of his countrymen. . . . By adding his name to our rolls, we mean to honour him—but his acceptance honours us much more."

decorated by General de Gaulle with the Cross of Liberation. He was made Grand Seigneur of the Company of Adventurers of England into Hudson's Bay; he was the first non-American to receive the Freedom Award; he was Lord Warden of the Cinque Ports and Grand Master of the Primrose League; he held honorary degrees at more than 20 universities and was a freeman of some 50 towns and cities from Thebes and Cap d'Ail to Harrow. Among the minor honours in which he took special delight was the annual invitation to song night at Harrow School.

© 1963 Toni Frissell

Lady Churchill on her seventy-eighth birthday, 1963. *"It would have been impossible for an ordinary man to go through what I have had to get through in peace and war without her devoted aid."*

232 OPPOSITE: At the window of his home in Hyde Park Gate on his ninetieth birthday, 1964.

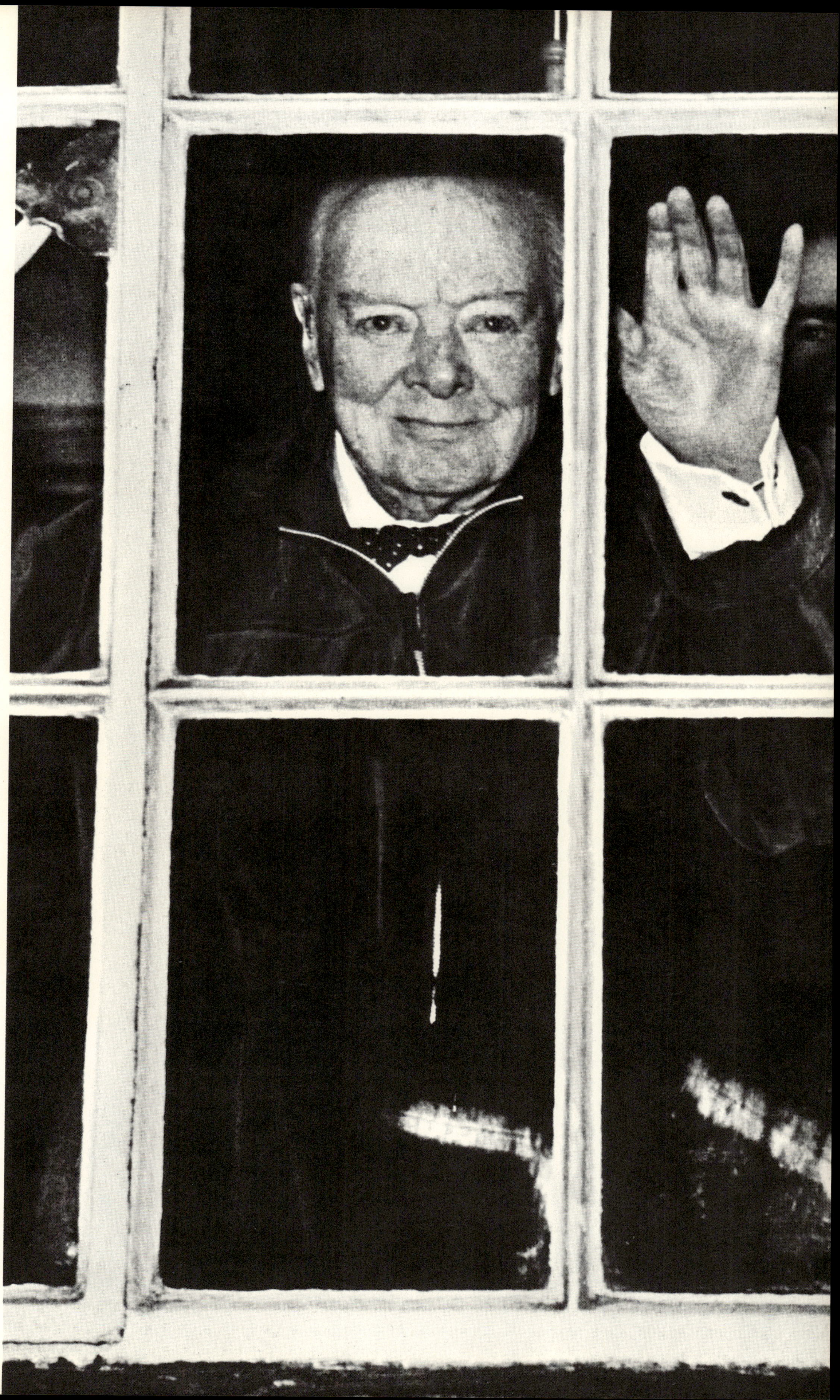

FAMILY
HAPPINESS
He married, as recorded earlier, Clementine, daughter of Colonel Sir Henry M. Hozier and Lady Blanche Ogilvy, and granddaughter of the seventh Earl of Airlie. From then on, he wrote in *My Early Life,* they "lived happily ever afterwards". That judgment, given in 1930, was not to be disturbed by time. Lady Churchill added grace and harmony to innumerable occasions in Sir Winston's public life, and made for him a secure and happy home at Chartwell. Three children of the marriage survive, and ten grandchildren.

"I am now nearing the end of my journey . . ." Lady Churchill watching as her husband sets out for a drive.

Stephen Fry

Susan McCartney

Stephen Fry

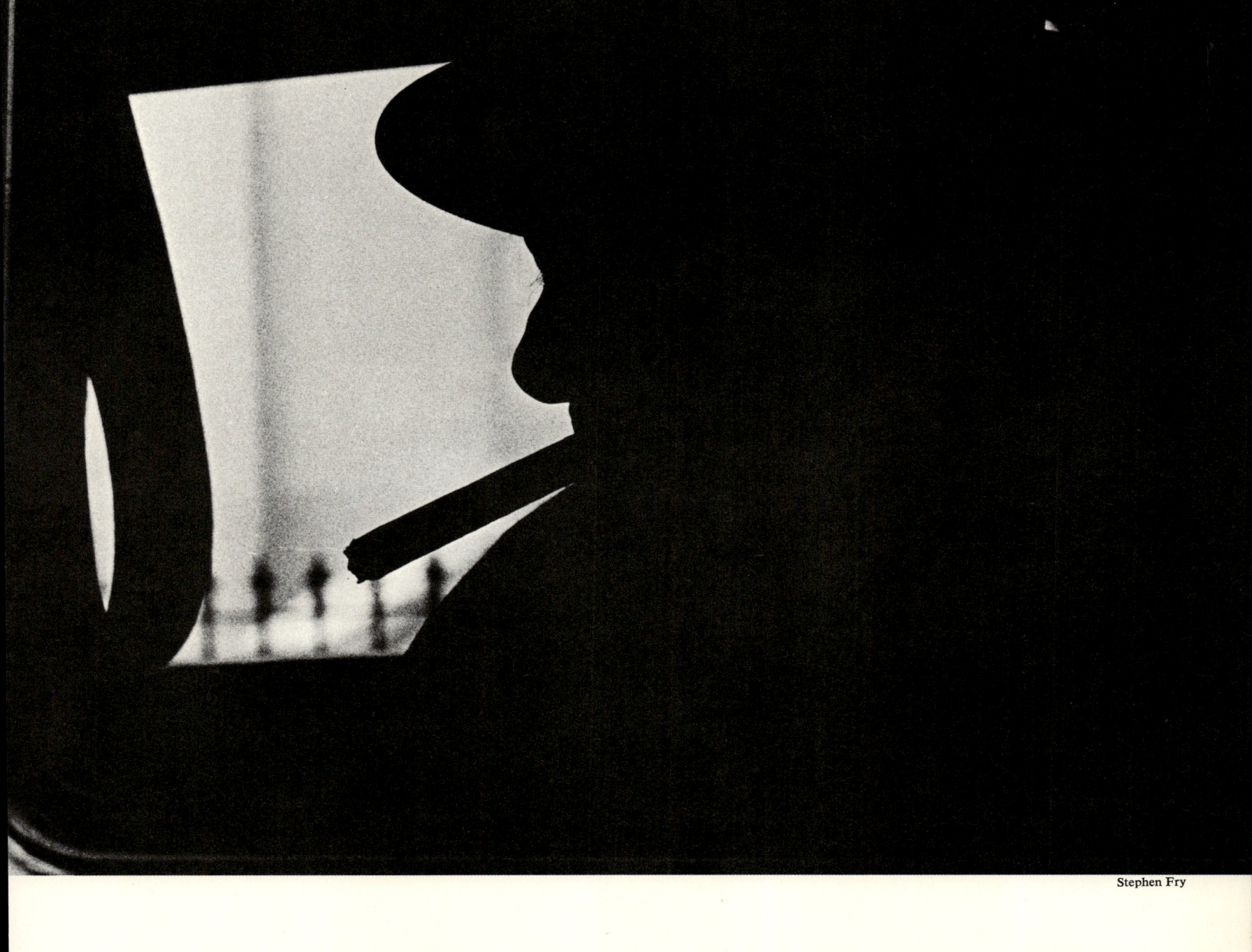

The proposal was made by Harold Laski in 1944 that a fund should be raised in token of the nation's gratitude to its Prime Minister. In thanking Laski, Churchill remarked that things of that kind were better left until a man is dead. "If, however", he added, "when I am dead people think of commemorating my services, I should like to think that a park was made for the children of London's poor on the south bank of the Thames, where they have suffered so grimly from the Hun."

THE GRATITUDE OF A NATION

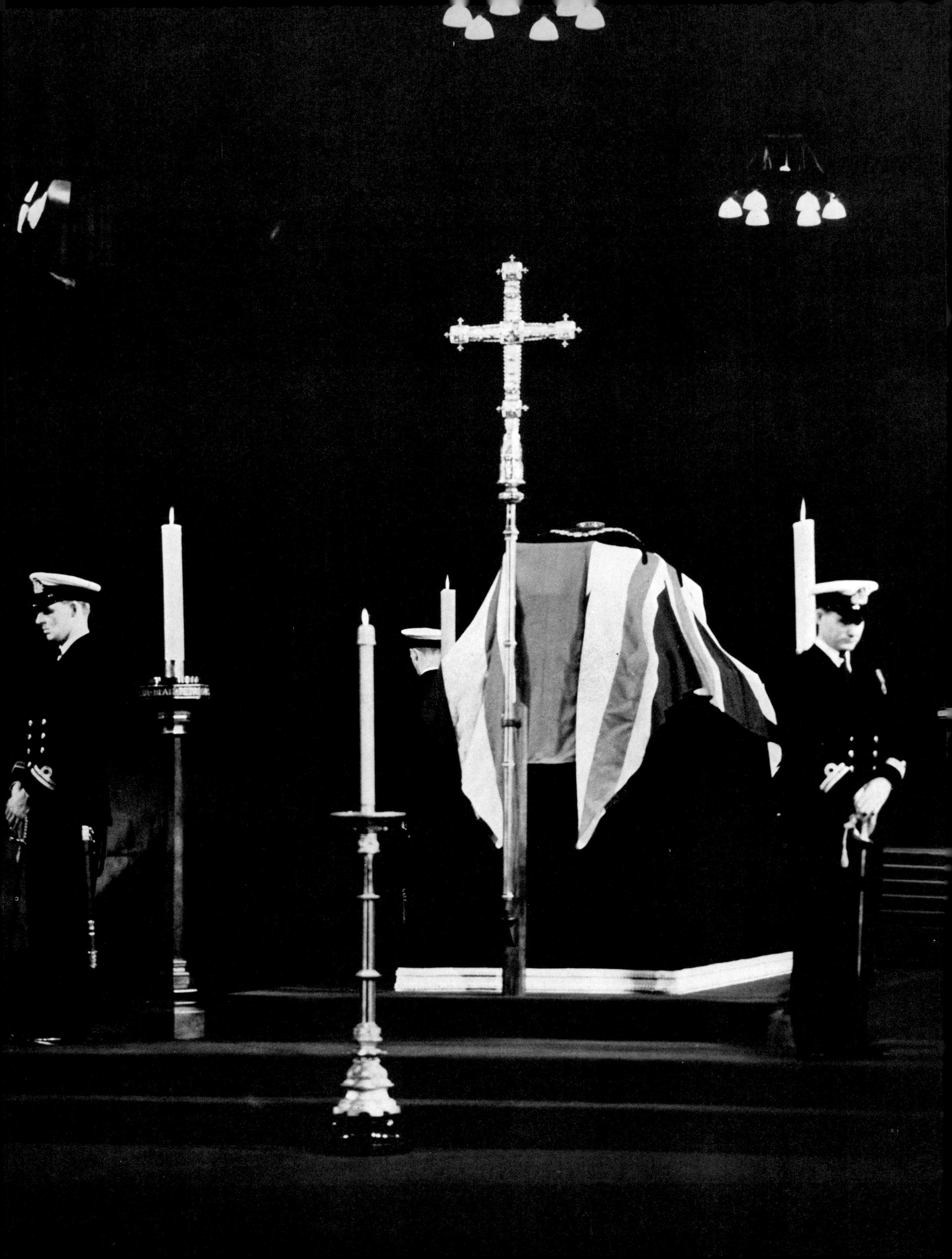

EPILOGUE: JANUARY 30, 1965

The long day had no beginning. It grew imperceptibly out of the third night of Sir Winston Churchill's lying-in-state at Westminster Hall. Great numbers of those who saw this memorable vigil—in the last hour, until six in the morning, there were more than 5,000, bringing the host to 321,360—joined the throng along the route to St. Paul's and the Tower, waiting again in dry, east wind, bitter nearly to freezing.

The body of Sir Winston Churchill lies in state in Westminster Hall (OPPOSITE), as lines of people waiting to view the coffin extend along the Embankment and (ABOVE) over Lambeth Bridge.

General Eisenhower arriving with Lady Elizabeth Gault to view the catafalque on January 29.

At the catafalque in the last half-hour the stream broadened beyond the carpeted path, so that the paving rang for the first time with the feet of people; and the press of those who stood to look back from the north door dissolved more and more reluctantly.

Now the naval guard over the coffin ended, and for nearly four hours, in private, the Queen's Royal Irish Hussars, successors of Sir Winston's first regiment, and the 17th/21st Lancers, with whose predecessors he charged at Omdurman, shared the vigil.

After daylight came the combined cadet contingent from Harrow School, who were to "keep the ground" in New Palace Yard. Wearing the uniforms of all three Services, they walked alone, bare-headed, past the candle-lit catafalque. From that moment the guard kept solitary watch until, with custodians of the royal palace and police excluded, the Earl Marshal, the Duke of Norfolk, escorted from their cars into the hall Lady Churchill, her son and daughters, and the other members of her family.

Waiting near by were the four chiefs of Staff—Admiral of the Fleet Lord Mountbatten of Burma, Chief of Defence Staff; Admiral Sir David Luce, Chief of Naval Staff and First Sea Lord; General Sir Richard Hull, Chief of the General Staff; and Air Chief Marshal Sir Charles Elworthy, Chief of the Air Staff, to whom, and to the family mourners, salutes were given.

IN NEW PALACE YARD

The guard of honour, nearly 100 strong, from the Brigade of Guards, in bearskins and greatcoats, occupied the centre; the Harrow School cadets ringed the yard, except where the ground was kept by a small contingent of the 4th/5th Royal Scots Fusiliers (T.A.), of which Sir Winston commanded a battalion in France in 1915-16.

To television viewers the military preparations gave a remote, ritualistic air to the scene; but to those standing in the shadow of Parliament buildings there was an intimacy in the ordering of the troops which made it at one with the solemn, private gathering inside the hall. This sense of fitness owed something to the bearing of the Royal Navy gun detachment as they brought their gun carriage at a slow, wheeling march from inside the palace. They stood eight abreast, their leading files turned inwards to face the carriage, and the rear files divided to give access.

At last came a signal from the Earl Marshal and the whole mass of naval ratings doffed caps with a whirr like a single beat of wings and, as one man, bowed their bared heads. At the same instant the coffin of Sir Winston, covered by the Union flag and surmounted by his Order of the Garter, could be seen under the white canopy of the north door.

Borne on the shoulders of eight tall guardsmen of the 2nd Battalion the Grenadier Guards, preceded by a company sergeant major and followed by a lieutenant, Sir Winston's coffin made the first short journey, carried with reverent, reluctant step, foot by foot, to the gun carriage, while guard of honour, escort party, and ground-keepers accorded it the General Salute.

Four naval ratings, relieving the Grenadiers with a precision worthy of a vigil-mounting, made all secure; the gun crew resumed their caps and took up position. As Big Ben, pointing to 9.45, chimed for the last time that day, five deep drumbeats sounded from Parliament Square, the first of 90 guns boomed from the park, and the gun carriage and coffin slowly moved from the precincts of the House of Commons which Sir Winston had served and loved since the century began. Every lighted window above showed other servants of Parliament, bidding him farewell.

In the train of the coffin and gun carriage came five carriages, drawn by Cleveland bays. Lady Churchill, accompanied by her daughters Lady Audley and Mrs. Christopher Soames, was in the first, driven by a red-cloaked coachman and postilions likewise in red. In the others were Mrs. Piers Dixon and Miss Celia Sandys; the Duke of Marlborough and Lady Avon; Miss Arabella Churchill and Mrs. John Churchill; and Mrs. Peregrine Churchill, Miss Emma Soames, and Miss Charlotte Soames.

In double file, Sir Winston's son, grandsons, kinsmen, and secretary, the youngest bareheaded, the others in top hats, began the long walk to St. Paul's. Led by Mr. Randolph Churchill and Mr. Winston Churchill, they were: Mr. Christopher Soames, Mr. Nicholas Soames, Mr. Jeremy Soames, Mr. Peregrine Churchill, Mr. Julian Sandys, Mr. Piers Dixon, Major John Churchill, and Mr. Montague Browne.

Meanwhile the procession was beginning to form, with the R.A.F. bands and a contingent of 300 R.A.F. men forming the head of the column just where Whitehall bends round into the Strand by Charing Cross. Contingent after contingent arrived behind and were guided into their place by the marshals, mostly drawn from the Brigade of Guards. At 9.40, just before the procession was due to move off, the leading contingent "reversed arms", and the movement was carried out all down Whitehall. The white helmets of the Marines lining the route were tilted as their wearers sunk their heads over their rifle-butts. The bickering and the chaffing in the crowds ceased.

THE PROCESSION UP WHITEHALL

The beat of a single drum, which was to haunt us all day, first made itself heard and, as the whole procession began to move forward in slow time, the strains of The Dead March were borne thinly up Whitehall on the cold morning air, to be taken up in turn by band after band.

And now, down this ancient thoroughfare of England, could be seen centuries of British history woven into a living, moving tapestry. The Earl Marshal of England and the insignia of medieval chivalry; regiments that first marched into London with Monk or clattered through Whitehall behind the second Charles; those that fought in Marlborough's wars, defended Hougoumont, and charged at Balaclava; impassive and apart, the Royal Navy, symbol of over a century of Britain's greatest days of power; the Battle of Britain pilots, who flew above London in Churchill's zenith, and the men of the civil defence services who battled beneath when there was "fire over England". In sombre ripples the colours changed from the khaki of the Territorials to the grey of the Foot

Guards' greatcoats, to the deep blue of the Navy and the spark of scarlet from the cloaks of the Household Cavalry.

The main group of the procession was headed by the great drum-horse with kettle-drums swathed in black crêpe, and the state trumpeters in their Georgian liveries. Hitherto, the procession had presented an anonymous, collective appearance. But now came pacing alone one of Churchill's most famous captains, Lord Mountbatten, with the Chiefs of Staff. Behind, red-capped and spurred, came the officers of the Queen's Royal Irish Hussars. They bore his insignia and his two banners, of the Cinque Ports and Spencer-Churchill.

Followed the Major-General of the Household troops and his staff and then, a solitary figure upon whom the burden of organizing this great ceremony of state rested, the Earl Marshal. He marched immediately in front of the great phalanx of seamen whose duty and privilege it is to draw the monarchs of Great Britain to their final resting place and, in this case, the great leader who, at two moments of most crucial decision, was, to Britain's good fortune, at the head of the Admiralty.

Behind the gun carriage walked the family mourners, led by Mr. Randolph Churchill; and in the tall coach with its scarlet-cloaked coachman on the box rode Lady Churchill, whose veiled face could be glimpsed through the window. The rear of the procession was brought up by the band of the Royal Artillery, in low-crowned shakos, and the police, the fire services, the Civil Defence Corps and the British Legion.

BEFORE THE CATHEDRAL

Up Ludgate Hill, and on the pavements round St. Paul's, the crowds had gathered early. Among the front rank, crushed hard against the barriers by the ten-deep pack behind, blankets and sleeping bags were carried like badges of honour from the long night vigil. Long before eight o'clock, when the route was closed to general traffic, the pavements could hold no more and movement ceased. There was nothing to do but stand and wait.

On the uncompleted skeleton of Juxon House, the new office block facing the cathedral, reporters and photographers clung to the scaffolding four floors up like frozen insects. Television cameras abounded; they ringed the rooftops and flanked the statue of Queen Victoria at the foot of the steps; they even hung, improbably, on the very summit of the great dome itself.

Soon began the orderly bustle in front of the cathedral. At 8.20, with more than two hours to go before the arrival of the procession, a line of women police of the W.R.A.C. took up their station in extended line before the west front, resplendent in green greatcoats and scarlet caps. Busily, they opened the doors of limousines and snapped to the salute as the first of the mourners arrived and filed into St. Paul's.

The flow of cars down Fleet Street and up Ludgate Hill began as a trickle and swelled quickly into a flood. Detachments of the W.R.N.S. and W.R.A.F. marched smartly up to "keep the ground" around the cathedral entrance, and, incongruously, council workmen began to spread the roadway with sand, swinging their shovels with proud rhythm before an unaccustomed audience.

The Archbishop of Canterbury, his purple cloak billowing in the chill breeze, mounted the steps. Only an hour to wait now, and the crowd quickened as a hundred transistors brought the news that the funeral procession was on its way from Westminster Hall.

The gun carriage bearing the coffin, drawn by seamen of the Royal Navy, on its way to St. Paul's.

Fixed patterns of colour began to form before the cathedral. The Household Cavalry, red greatcoats to the left and blue to the right, marched up in slow time and formed into two lines converging on the great main doors. The Queen's Colour Squadron of the R.A.F., bayonets fixed, made a guard of honour two deep across their front.

Familiar, famous faces were emerging now: Lord Avon with Sir Robert Menzies, Mr. Macmillan, Lord Attlee, and then, at 10 o'clock, Mr. and Mrs. Harold Wilson. Now, for the first time, the huge studded doors swung open to allow the crowd a glimpse of the pomp inside the cathedral. The Speaker of the House of Commons, Sir Harry Hylton-Foster, followed Mr. Wilson through the tall gateway, dressed in full ceremonial mourning; even in the thin light the mace of the House glittered as it was carried before him.

When the doors opened again it was to let out the Heralds, led by Garter King of Arms. Clad in their brilliant tunics of red and blue, embroidered in gold, they clutched their emblems of office draped with mourning black and formed an inner guard of honour within the lines of Household Cavalry. Old men some of them, but proud, their stance was individual rather than military.

ARRIVAL OF THE HEADS OF STATE

The scene was fully set. It was time for the arrival of heads of state, and promptly on cue they came sweeping in from the east to the roar of motorcycle engines as the police outriders preceded them. The crowd stirred, necks straining to see the new arrivals, and among them the figure of President de Gaulle was clearly visible as, tall and grave, stooping slightly in his khaki greatcoat, he mounted the steps.

Then came Queen Elizabeth the Queen Mother, serene in total black, but hardly had she entered the cathedral before the low insistent throb of drums announced the coming of the procession. The crowd fell silent, all conversation stilled, as with slow inevitable progress the column drew in sight and began to climb the hill. The funeral march, sad and solemn, filled the concourse before the cathedral.

The Lord Mayor of London arrived, went briefly inside, and then emerged again to stand, a lonely figure in scarlet and ermine, hands clasped over black-sheathed sword, in the centre of the great steps. He was waiting to welcome the Queen. When she came, with the Duke of Edinburgh and Prince Charles, there was, for once, no cheering, no waving. The crowd stared, quiet and still, as the royal party went gravely into St. Paul's to add their tribute to the thousands.

And all the while the procession passed by, the metronome tread of boots on the sanded road marking the seconds to its climax. It was not long in coming. Soon the last of the many bands had passed out of sight, and the Chiefs of Staff and the bearers of Sir Winston's decorations had reached the cathedral.

Preceded by the Earl Marshal, and drawn by the white-capped phalanx of naval ratings, the gun carriage bearing Sir Winston's coffin came steadily up the rise. There was movement in the crowd as hats were doffed and heads bowed, but there was no noise save the insistent beating of the draped drums.

Halted at last, the coffin with its covering flag and surmounting insignia of the Garter was eased from the gun carriage by the eight guardsmen of the bearer party and carried with slow solemnity into the cathedral. The family mourners followed. Theirs was the only movement. The guards of honour, the heralds, the gun crew with heads bowed and bared, the crowd itself—all stood like living statuary. And as Sir Winston's coffin passed inside there came through the open doorway the sound of singing.

Never before has St. Paul's been the scene of such an occasion. Monarchs and princes, presidents and prime ministers, chiefs of the armed Services, dignitaries of high and low degree and colleagues of the war years: some were there as old comrades or lifelong friends, others to pay tribute to a man they had never known and a few, no doubt, because their countries had felt that it would be politically correct for someone to attend.

Many of those in the cathedral that day were still unborn when Sir Winston, as President Kennedy had said, "mobilized the English language and sent it into battle— when Britain stood alone and most men save Englishmen despaired of England's life". There was young Prince Hassan of Jordan, only 18; King Constantine of the Hellenes, born in the same year that Sir Winston became Britain's war leader; Prince Taufa'ahan of Tonga, the grandson of Queen Salote; and the Crown Prince of Ethiopia.

Not since the state funeral of the Duke of Wellington in 1852 in this same St. Paul's had there been a ceremony to rival this one. Every nook and cranny of the cathedral was filled with chairs, closed circuit television screens showing the parts of the service which could not be seen from the more remote sectors of the cathedral.

In front of the congregation were three royal chairs, purple covered, for the Queen, the Duke of Edinburgh, and the Prince of Wales. Perhaps the greatest tribute to Sir Winston was the decision of the Queen to attend the service in person. Only Wellington and Gladstone in the past 112 years, other than royalty, have been accorded state funerals, and on neither occasion did the monarch attend.

The early arrivals, when the cathedral doors opened at 15 minutes to nine, were members of the Diplomatic Corps, Commonwealth High Commissioners and their suites, friends and relatives of the family. Then came the representatives of France, the United States and Russia, including Marshal Ivan Koniev, who led the offensive on Berlin in 1945, and General Eisenhower. Then the two processions up the nave of the Speaker and the Lord Chancellor. As the cathedral filled and the sound of shuffling feet grew less, a complete stillness came down, broken only by an occasional clatter as the scabbard or spur of one of the staff officers struck the stone slabs of the floor.

The doors of the cathedral were closed at 10 o'clock and shortly after the sword, targe, crest and spurs of the Garter were carried by the four senior Heralds in their gold and scarlet cloaks to the great west door to await the procession.

By this time, Mr. Harold Wilson, Sir Alec Douglas-Home, and Mr. Grimond, with their wives, had taken their seats; and now was the moment for the heads of state and royal representatives of heads of state to proceed to their seats facing the bier.

In front were the diminutive Prince Hassan of Jordan and the tall Prince of Liechtenstein. They were followed by Prince Bertil of Sweden, President Kaunda of Zambia, King Constantine of the Hellenes, Queen Juliana and Prince Bernhard of the Netherlands, King Olav of Norway, King Baudouin of Belgium, King Frederik of Denmark, the Crown Prince of Ethiopia, Grand Duke Jean of Luxembourg and the presidents of Iceland, Uruguay and Israel. Representatives of 110 nations were at the service, including four kings and a queen, five other heads of state, and 16 prime ministers. Of the countries invited only Mongolia and China were not represented.

Dwarfing the rest of the heads of state was President de Gaulle, who in the past had often viewed Sir Winston with mixed feelings but who had left old feuds behind him and was here to pay tribute to a wartime colleague.

WITHIN THE CATHEDRAL

While this assembly was continuing, not a sound had been heard from outside the cathedral.

ARRIVAL OF THE QUEEN

On the television screens the minute guns could be seen firing, but behind the great doors there was only the quiet organ music and the occasional rustling of cloth as a late-comer reached his seat. Then, faintly through the cathedral could be heard the shouts of command and the clatter of troops coming to attention, which signalled that the Queen had arrived. After shaking hands with the Archbishop of Canterbury, the Queen, the Duke of Edinburgh, and the Prince of Wales were conducted to the Chapel of St. Michael and St. George before proceeding down the nave to their seats, where the Lord Mayor of London placed the Black Sword of Mourning on a table in front of the Queen.

One minute later, the muffled beat of drums and the sounds of sombre music gave warning that the procession bearing Sir Winston's coffin was near the cathedral steps. The organ music died away and only the massive figure of General de Gaulle, towering over the other mourners, stood out clearly from the sea of faces. Almost at once the Chiefs of Staff, Sir Charles Elworthy, Sir David Luce and Sir Richard Hull, were conducted to their seats near the bier. The cathedral now appeared to be overflowing with high-ranking officers from field marshals downwards.

For a minute a great silence descended on the cathedral until, as the flag-draped coffin passed though the great west door, there was a glorious burst of song as the choir began the service with the familiar words of St. John, "I am the resurrection and the life, saith the Lord".

The procession forming in New Palace Yard; Westminster Hall in the background.

OPPOSITE: Lady Churchill and her son Randolph following the coffin, borne by Grenadier Guardsmen.

247

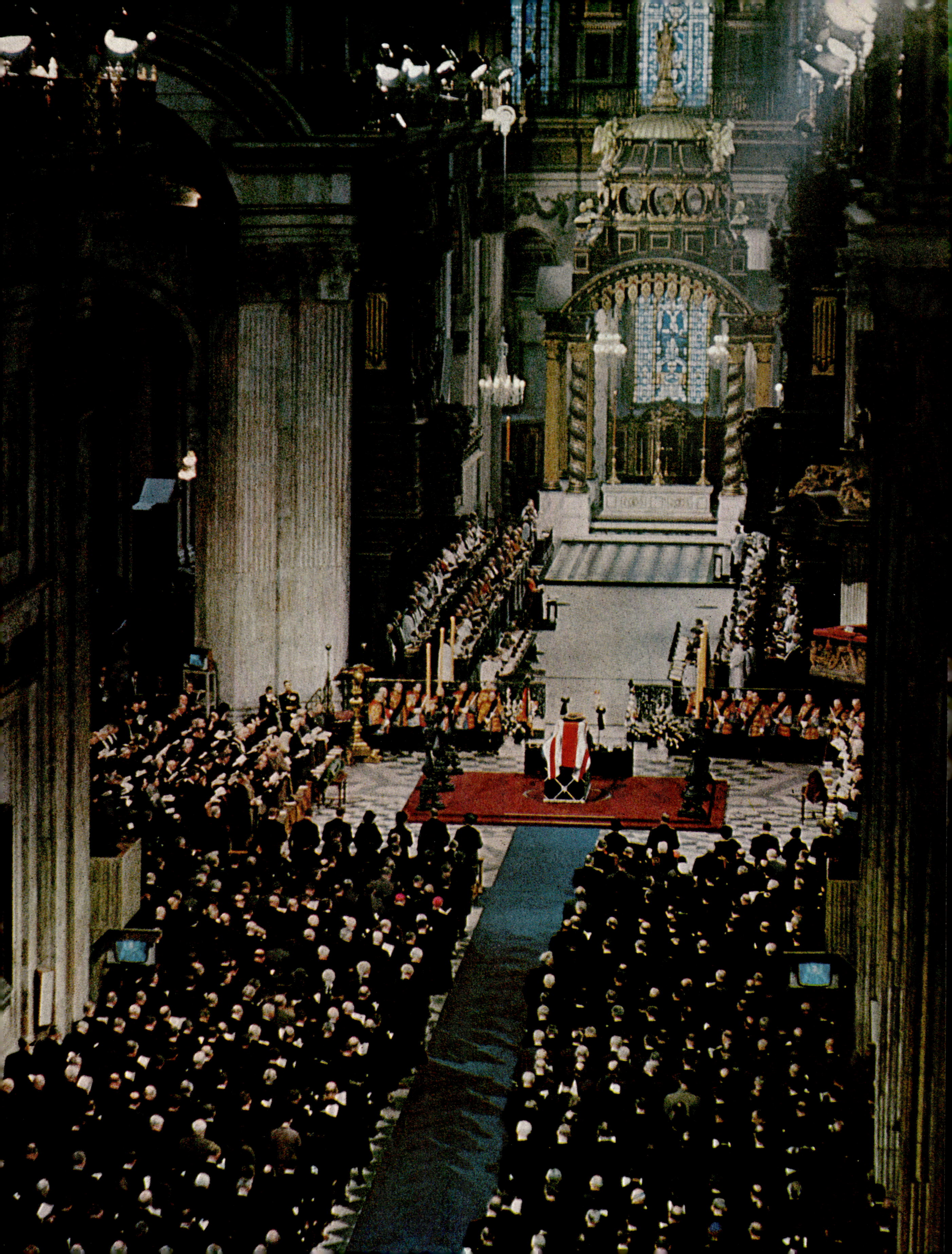

As the great procession, headed by the Earl Marshal, passed slowly up the nave, for a while only the golden banners of the Cinque Ports and of Spencer-Churchill, moving like tall sails above the sea of mourners, were an indication of the coffin's progress.

What a setting for this last farewell! On every side the nation's past heroes and glories—Nelson and Wellington, Abercromby and Cornwallis, Gordon and Howe, Roberts and Melbourne, Jellicoe and Beatty, Inkermann, Waterloo, Quatre-Bras and Salamanca, Crimea and Khartum, Corunna and Trafalgar.

As the procession came into view of those of the congregation seated about the catafalque, ahead of the coffin were seen the twelve pallbearers: old men now, some, like Lord Attlee, almost too old and fragile, others, like Sir Robert Menzies, Prime Minister of Australia, and Lord Mountbatten, still robust and full of years—all old comrades and wartime colleagues, of either the War Cabinet, Commonwealth, or the armed Services. Three former Prime Ministers, Lord Avon, Lord Attlee and Mr. Macmillan, were among the twelve. Slowly they came into sight like a page of history suddenly coming to life—Portal and Normanbrook, Ismay and Bridges, Slim and Templer.

THE PALLBEARERS AND THE FAMILY MOURNERS

Behind the coffin came the family mourners—at their head Lady Churchill, heavily veiled, and Mr. Randolph Churchill, followed by Sir Winston's two daughters, Lady Audley and Mrs. Christopher Soames.

The officers bearing Sir Winston's orders and decorations and the heralds bearing the achievements placed them on the black-draped table below the choir; and after the first hymn, the Dean of St. Paul's, the Rev. W. R. Matthews, read a prayer "on the occasion of the burial of a great man who has rendered memorable service to his country and to the cause of freedom".

The Earl Marshal, the Duke of Norfolk, leads the bearer party with the coffin on to Tower Pier.

OPPOSITE: The nave of St. Paul's Cathedral, with the coffin on the bier beneath the dome.

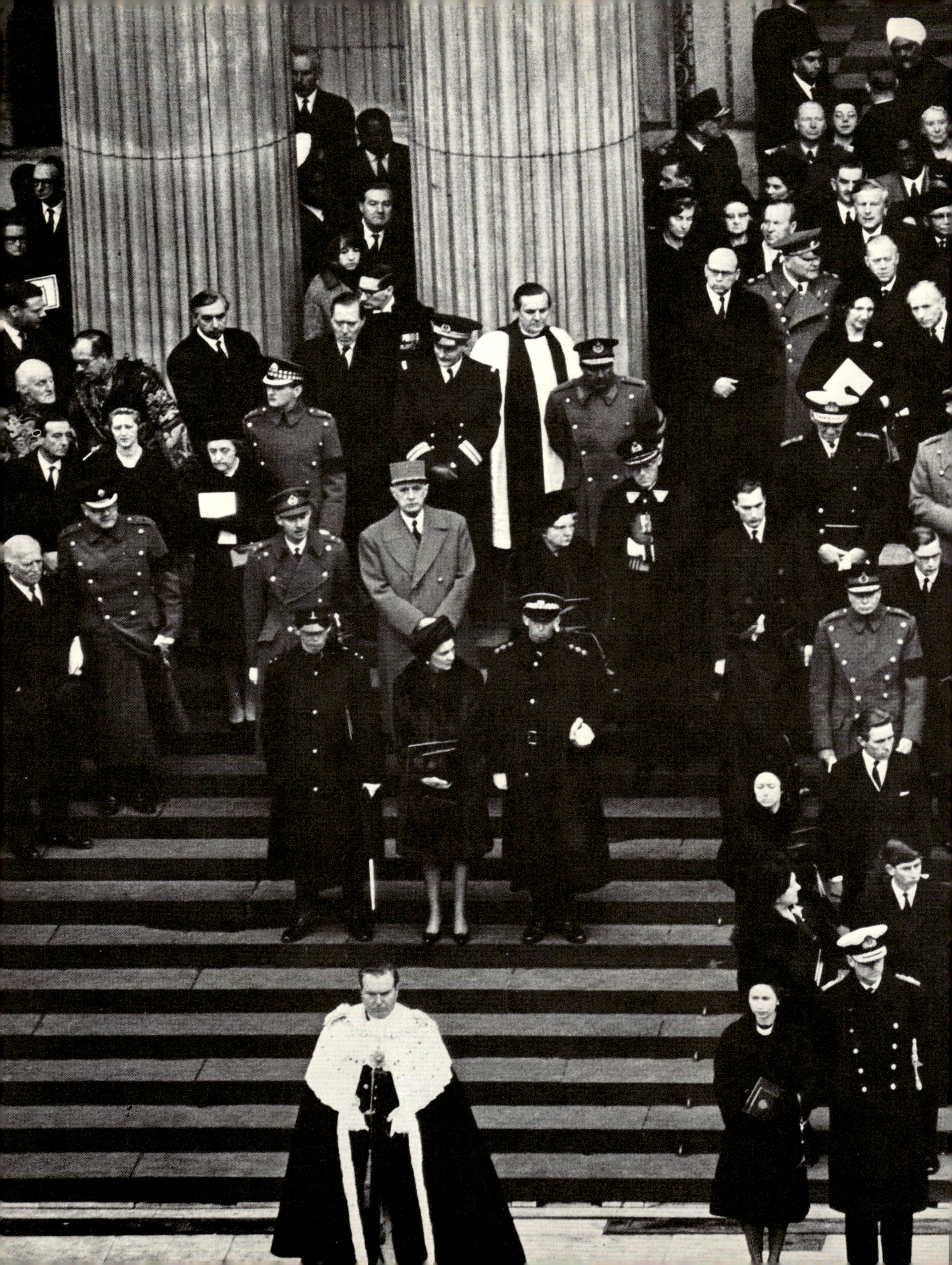

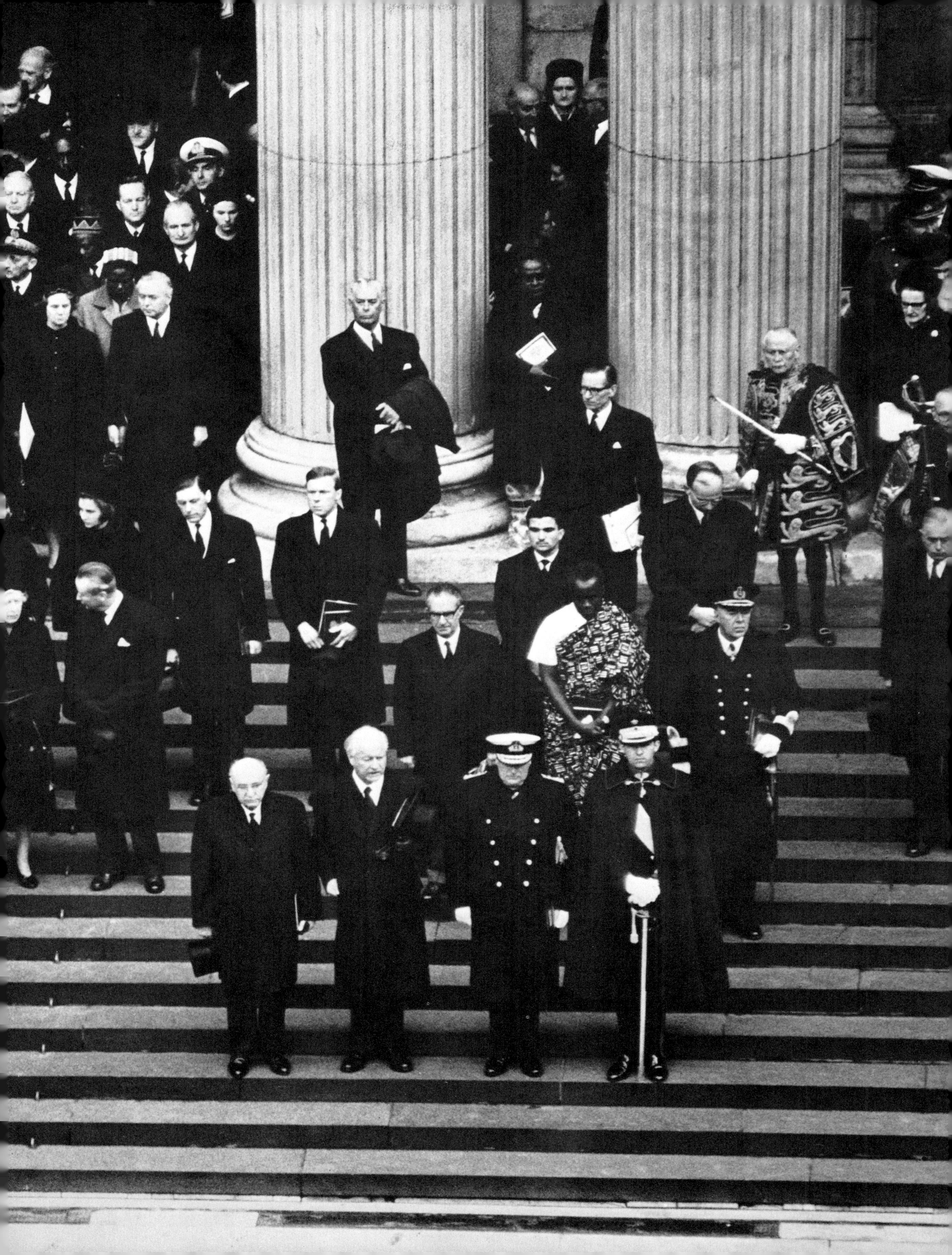

Not only the choice of St. Paul's but everything about the service showed the guiding hand of Sir Winston. The rollicking hymns could have been his selection alone. First, as the coffin was placed upon the bier, there was the John Bunyan hymn beginning:

Who would true valour see,

Let him come hither

followed shortly afterwards by the Battle Hymn of the Republic, "Mine eyes have seen the glory of the coming of the Lord", chosen as a tribute to Sir Winston's American mother. The last two hymns were "Fight the good fight with all thy might" and, as the coffin was carried out of the cathedral, "O God, our help in ages past".

It was a warrior's farewell in the warriors' church, and although it was officially a funeral service it was as much a service of thanksgiving. The orders of service and ceremonial were bordered in purple but they might, as appropriately, have been bordered in gold. There was sorrow, certainly, but for the great congregation of 3,500 people from every corner of the globe it was a sorrow mingled with joy that such a man had lived at such a time.

THE SERVICE IN ST. PAUL'S

As the 30-minute service continued there was many a moment of tearfulness from both within and without the close circle of family and friends. On the royal benches opposite, Queen Juliana sat with bowed head while Prince Bernhard remained deep in prayer. President de Gaulle and King Baudouin of Belgium sat erect, scarcely removing their gaze from the coffin. A few seats nearer to the choir, Mr. Macmillan sat deep in thought as he watched the last honours bestowed upon his old chief.

After the Archbishop of Canterbury had given his blessing from the high altar, a bugler, high in the Whispering Gallery, sounded Last Post.

The bugle notes echoed around the cathedral and then slowly faded away. After a moment's silence an answering bugle from over the great west door sounded Reveille. The heralds and officers regained their banners, insignia and decorations, the catafalque was rotated, the pallbearers took up their positions, and the procession slowly bore the coffin out of the cathedral.

The crowds in Fleet Street and Ludgate Circus had begun to fade away, but outside the cathedral and down Ludgate Hill they stayed on. The service over, they watched the Queen, the Prime Minister, and the host of other famous mourners stand sadly outside in the freezing air as the coffin was replaced on the gun carriage to continue its journey to Tower Pier.

During the service the procession had formed up east of St. Paul's, and already stretched half-way to the Tower down the ravine of Cannon Street running straight through the towering precipices of the City. The military bands laid their instruments down in front of them, and the sanded street sprouted exotically with rows of trombones and tubas, as if the streets of London were paved with brass.

The City police, in their heroic, Trojan war helmets, thumped their hands against their sides savagely to encourage circulation. The R.A.F. were lining the route from St. Paul's to Tower Hill, one of their officers roaming restlessly around, fussing about the ruler-straightness of his ranks, his sword protruding from an unglamorous grey coat.

The crowd listened to the service on transistor radios and joined in the singing. Down the long road every verse of "Mine eyes have seen the glory of the coming of the Lord" could be heard in different volumes and directions, from various radios and voices. The great offices, which on a normal Saturday morning are empty echoing mountains, were crammed on every floor with stockbrokers and insurance men, and their families, peering up at St. Paul's.

At last the long procession moved off from St. Paul's, led by R.A.F. bands playing solemn Handel and Mendelssohn. Work on a building site in Eastcheap stopped, cranes petrified in mid-air, as the slow column moved down towards Julius' Tower, the silent sentinel keeping watch and ward on the Thames.

THE PROCESSION TO THE TOWER

Down on Tower Hill the crowd were crushed up against the barriers by a sudden flood of spectators, who had watched the first half of the procession, and had now hurried down during the service to see the end, and were piled 30 deep around the walls. The pipers, drawn from the Guards, from the Lowland Brigade, and from the Inniskillings, were waiting to join the procession here, feather bonnets and pipebanners fluttering furiously in the wind. The Yeomen Warders "keeping the ground" jealously outside their white tower, punctuated the grey day with gaudy exclamation marks of Tudor scarlet and gold.

At Tower Wharf, in the middle of that mysterious forest below London Bridge, the first hint of the approaching procession was a distant drum, beating slowly. Tower Bridge, and the forbidding battlements of the Tower itself, had acquired what looked like intricate new castellations, but turned out on closer inspection to be rows of closely packed heads. Suddenly, with a thump to make the heart jump, the saluting battery of the Tower fired, and spouted a gout of smoke out over the Thames. The gunners, kneeling stiffly in splendid uniforms beside their artillery, looked like a print of some Crimean cannonade.

With a flash of coachman's red cloak the carriages drew up at the gate of the pier, and the family mourners, led by Lady Churchill and her son Randolph, arm in arm, walked over the bridges in a tight close group, the two little granddaughters at the end looking frozen. Half of them boarded the *Havengore,* the Port of London Authority's survey launch, which was to carry Sir Winston to Festival Hall pier. It fluttered the flag of the Lord Warden of the Cinque Ports, encrusted with heraldic emblems. The rest of the family went aboard the *Thames,* moored just behind. Both launches faced head downstream, because it was flood tide, and London's great street paved with water was smooth and dark, oily and uninviting. Sweet Thames was running softly.

The other launches, the fussy little black police boats, took up their positions in midstream, for the first river procession of this sort since the funeral of Nelson. The bagpipes broke into their most evocative, hair-bristling laments—"My Home", "The Flowers of the Forest", and "Lochaber no More"—and yet again scattered clouds of startled gulls and pigeons down the sky. The bearer party carried the coffin down Tower Hill, and along the narrow twisting gangways of the pier, led by the small, solitary, sturdy figure of the Earl Marshal, clutching his baton, the organizer and marshal of the whole day.

Once the Duke turned anxiously as the Grenadiers, faces strained rigid with effort and concentration, had to stop and adjust their hold. Behind came the pallbearers and the Chiefs of Staff. As the coffin was laid on the bier on the deck of *Havengore* the bagpipes stopped, and the thin pipes of the Navy shrilled like a night wind in a waste land. The herd of cranes on Hay's Wharf opposite started dipping their long necks, like dinosaurs, in an eery, impressive civilian salute.

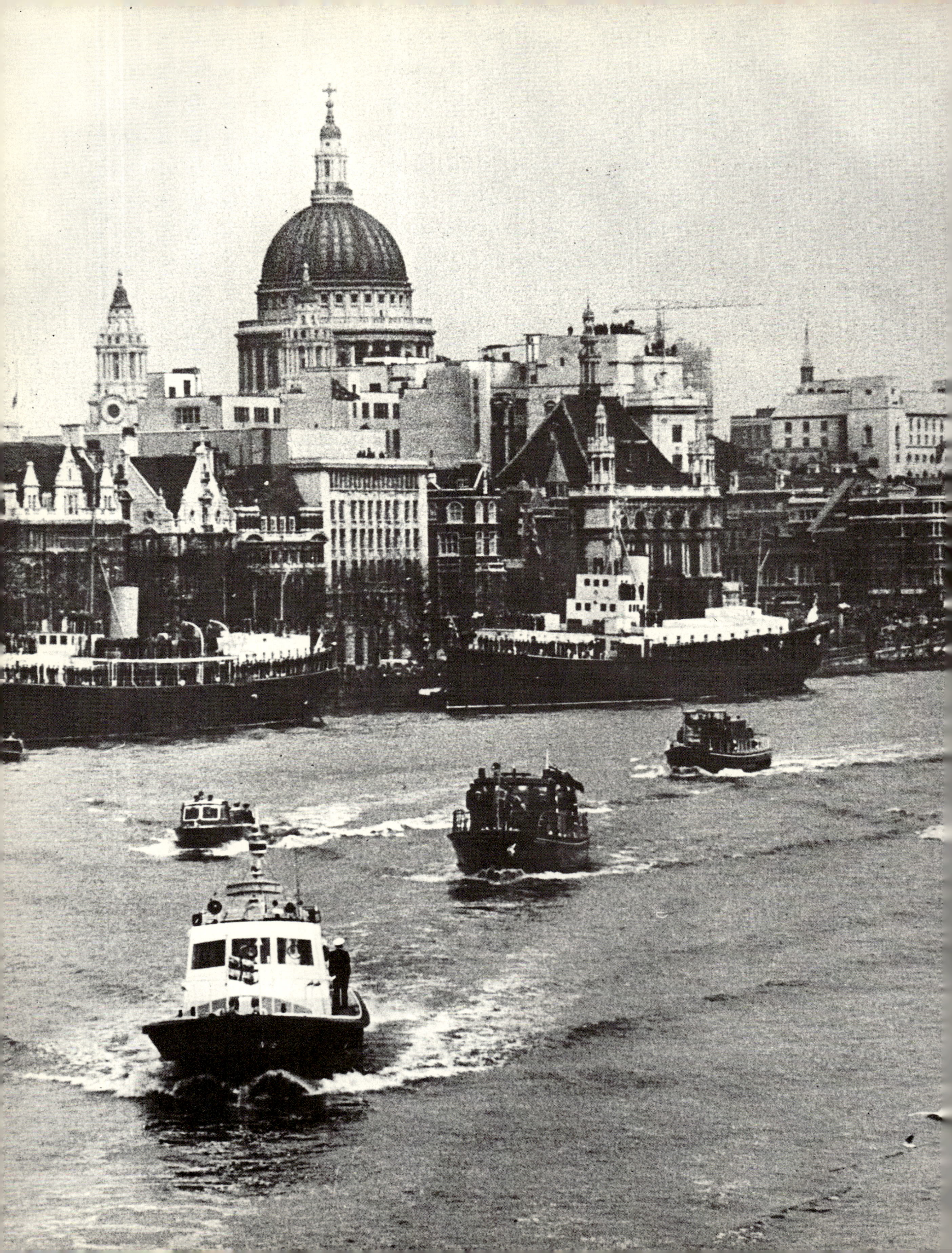

Cranes along the Thames dipping in homage; R.A.F. Lightnings over Tower Bridge.

The launch turned out from the pier, slowly, upstream, and the Royal Marine band burst into "Rule Britannia" in sudden contrast to all the solemn, slow music. A 19-gun salute rolled and rattled up the wharves. Suddenly from nowhere R.A.F. jets swooped almost between the towers of the bridge. The "former naval person", the First Lord of the Admiralty in two wars, Lord Warden of the Cinque Ports, Elder Brother of Trinity House, was leaving the City most suitably by the dark river. The launch became a black dot beneath the congested arches of London Bridge.

Sixteen Lightning aircraft of Fighter Command, darting from the sky in box formations of four and roaring up the Thames to the north-west, heralded the approach of the *Havengore* to the Festival Hall pier. The jets dipped in a swift 400-foot-high salute, thin, grey exhaust trails scarring the sky behind them.

The *Havengore*, accompanied by its tiny flotilla of craft, passed beneath the wide arch of Waterloo Bridge, moving up King's Reach then rippling at full flood. The famous fretwork of buildings from Westminster to the City made an impressive backdrop. The boat moored at the pier, where twin flags were flying at half mast, and rocked gently as the bearers gently and firmly lifted the coffin, still flag-draped and bearing the black cushion on which rested the insignia of the Most Noble Order of the Garter.

The family, led by Lady Churchill and her son Randolph, followed. Hundreds of people, including workers from the South Bank development site, watched silently as the coffin was placed inside a motor hearse. This moved off towards Waterloo Station, followed by a convoy of cars.

At Waterloo the broad road approach to platform 11 was clear and crowd-lined. The coffin was placed on the special train, drawn by the Battle of Britain locomotive *Winston Churchill*. Members of the family entered their carriage and with a hiss of steam the train drew slowly from the platform, on its way to Bladon, the resting place chosen by Sir Winston himself in the Blenheim countryside of his beginnings.

The massive demonstration of homage and thanks was over.

UP THE THAMES TO WATERLOO

The body of Sir Winston Churchill is borne up the Thames towards Festival Pier by the launch *Havengore* (OPPOSITE), as St. Paul's and the City of London recede in the distance.

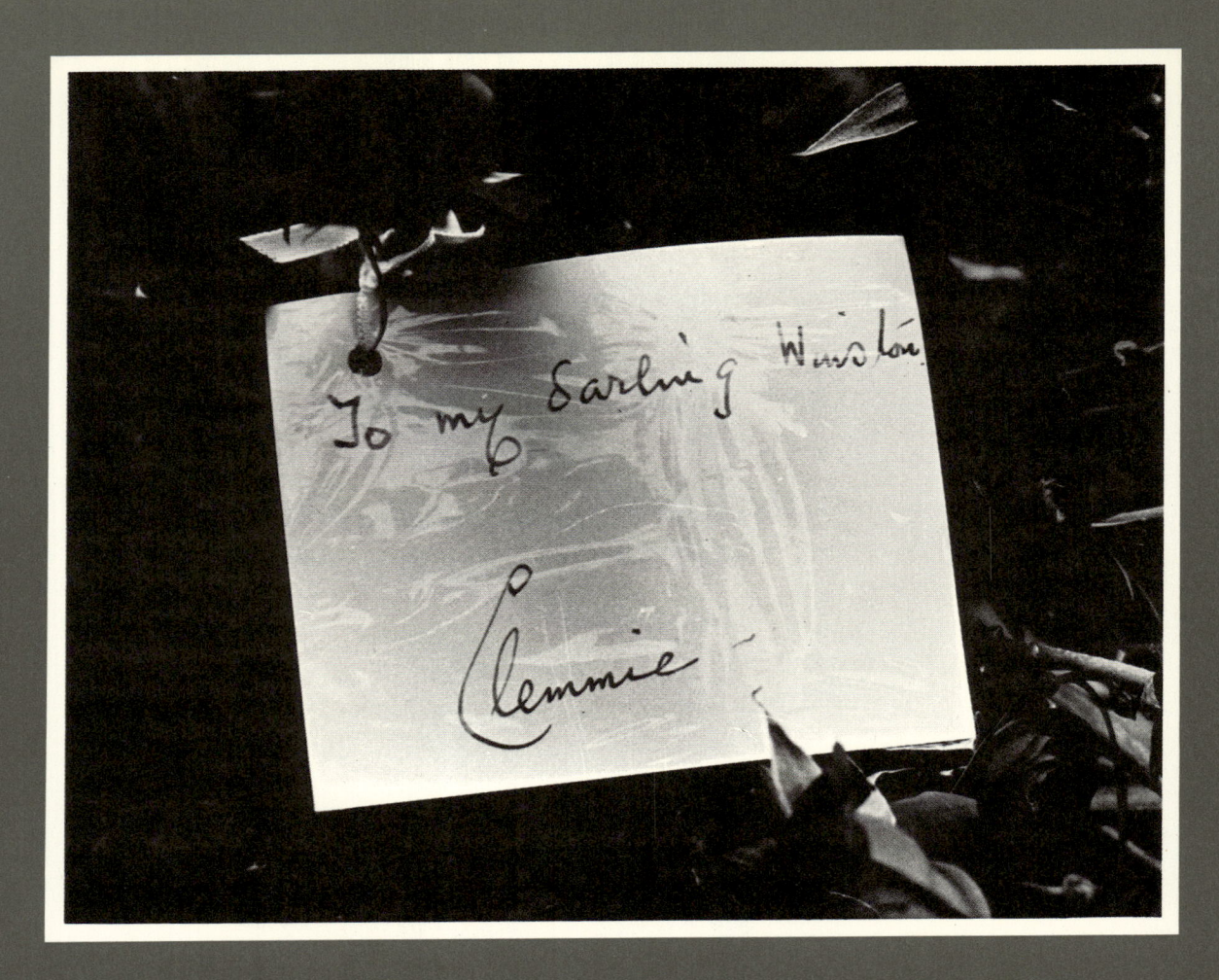

Two wreaths on Churchill's grave at Bladon.

Attendance at the Funeral Service

Among those who accepted invitations to attend the funeral service in St. Paul's Cathedral were the following:—
The Queen and the Duke of Edinburgh
Queen Elizabeth the Queen Mother
The King of Norway
The Queen of the Netherlands and the Prince of the Netherlands
The King of Denmark
The King of the Belgians
The King of the Hellenes
The Grand Duke of Luxembourg
The Prince of Liechtenstein
The Prince of Wales
The Crown Prince of Ethiopia
Prince Bertil of Sweden
Prince Hassan of Jordan
Prince Taufa'ahan of Tonga
Princess Margaret, Countess of Snowdon, and the Earl of Snowdon
The Duke and Duchess of Gloucester
Prince William and Prince Richard of Gloucester
The Princess Royal
Princess Marina, Duchess of Kent
The Duke and Duchess of Kent
Princess Alexandra and the Hon. Angus Ogilvy
Prince Michael of Kent
Colonel Sir John Aird (representing the Duke and Duchess of Windsor), and Captain R. F. Abel Smith (representing Princess Alice, Countess of Athlone)
FAMILY MOURNERS.—Lady Churchill (widow), Mr. Randolph Churchill (son), Lady Audley (daughter), Mr. Christopher Soames, M.P., and Mrs. Soames (son-in-law and daughter), Mr. Julian Sandys, Mr. and Mrs. Piers Dixon, Mr. Winston Churchill, Miss Celia Sandys, Mr. Nicholas Soames, Miss Arabella Churchill, and Emma, Jeremy, and Charlotte Soames (grandchildren), the Duke of Marlborough, Major and Mrs. John Churchill, Mr. and Mrs. Peregrine Churchill, and the Countess of Avon (nephews and nieces), the Marquess and Marchioness of Blandford, Lord Charles Spencer-Churchill, Lady Sarah Russell, Major Hugo and Lady Caroline Waterhouse, Mr. Robin and Lady Rosemary Muir, Lady Ivor Spencer-Churchill, Robert Spencer-Churchill, the Earl of Sunderland, Earl and Countess Spencer, the Hon. Mrs. Anthony Henley, Miss M. H. Whyte, Miss Grace Hamblin, Mr. Anthony Montague Brown (private secretary).
PALL BEARERS.—Sir Robert Menzies (Prime Minister of Australia), Mr. Harold Macmillan, Field Marshal Sir Gerald Templer, Lord Normanbrook, Lord Bridges, Lord Ismay, Field Marshal Viscount Slim, Marshal of the R.A.F. Viscount Portal of Hungerford, the Earl of Avon, Earl Attlee, Field Marshal Earl Alexander of Tunis, and Admiral of the Fleet Earl Mountbatten of Burma (Chief of the Defence Staff).
FOREIGN AND COMMONWEALTH REPRESENTATIVES.—President de Gaulle of France, and Admiral G. Cabanier, Chief of French Naval Staff; President A. Asgeirsson of Iceland; President Z. Shazar of Israel, and Mr. D. Ben-Gurion; President K. Kaunda of Zambia, and Mr. S. Kapwewe, Foreign Minister; President L. Giannatasio of Uruguay; Mgr. Cardinale, Apostolic Delegate, representing the Pope.
Mr. Keith Holyoake, Prime Minister of New Zealand; Mr. Lester Pearson, Prime Minister of Canada, and Mr. J. G. Diefenbaker, Leader of the Opposition; Mr. Ian Smith, Prime Minister of Rhodesia; Dr. G. Borg Olivier, Prime Minister of Malta; Sir Roland Symonette, Prime Minister of the Bahamas; Mr. Forbes Burnham, Premier of British Guiana.
Mr. S. Singh, Indian Minister for External Affairs; Mr. Z. A. Bhutto, Pakistan Minister for External Affairs; Mr. K. Ofori-Atta, Minister of Justice of Ghana, and Major-General Otu, Chief of the Defence Staff; Dr. T. O. Elias, Attorney-General and Federal Justice Minister of Nigeria, and Alhaji S. Shagari, Minister of Internal Affairs and Communications; Mr. O. Kambona, Minister of External Affairs of Tanzania; Mr. A. Araouzos, acting Foreign Minister and Minister of Commerce of Cyprus, and Mr. T. Papadopoulos, Minister of Labour; Mr. R. Lightbourne, Jamaican Minister of Trade and Industry, and Mr. D. C. Tavares, Minister of Housing; Mr. Oginga Odinga, Vice-President of Kenya; Mr. Z. A. Baharoon, Chief Minister of Aden; Chief Justice Earl Warren, of the United States of America, and General Dwight D. Eisenhower.
Mr. E. Gerhardsen, Prime Minister of Norway; Dr. J. M. A. H. Luns, Foreign Minister of the Netherlands; Mr. J. O. Krag, Prime Minister of Denmark; M. P.-H. Spaak, Foreign Minister of Belgium; M. P. Werner, Prime Minister of Luxembourg.
Mr. K. Rudnev, a Deputy Prime Minister of the Soviet Union, and Marshal I. Koniev; Mr. A. Quaison-Sackey, president of the United Nations General Assembly; Dr. L. Erhard, Federal German Chancellor, and Dr. G. Schröder, Foreign Minister; Dr. J. Klaus, Austrian Chancellor.
Mr. J. Virolainen, Prime Minister of Finland; Mr. M. Tshombe, Prime Minister of the Congo; Mr. Chung Il-Kwan, South Korean Prime Minister; Mr. N. Kishi, of Japan.
Signor M. Brosio, Secretary-General of the North Atlantic Treaty Organization; Mr. K. Suphamonghkon, Secretary-General of the South-East Asia Treaty Organization; Senhor V. Leitao da Cunha, Foreign Minister of Brazil.
Dr. P. T. Pereira, member of the Council of State of Portugal; Signor G. Andreotti, Italian Minister of Defence; Señor I. I. Borges, Foreign Minister of Venezuela; Señor G. Valdes, Foreign Minister of Chile.
Señor V. Ortiz, Argentine Foreign Minister; Mr. H. Bourguiba, jun., Foreign Minister of Tunisia; Mr. E. Kardelj, President of the Yugoslav Federal Assembly; Senator J. de Klerk, South African Minister of the Interior, and Sir de Villiers Graaff, Leader of the Opposition.
Mr. F. Aiken, Minister for External Affairs, Republic of Ireland; Mr. K. Satir, Deputy Prime Minister of Turkey; Mr. E. Seaone, Vice-President of Peru; Dr. F. Wahlen, Foreign Secretary of Switzerland.
Mr. E. Pelaez, Vice-President of the Philippines; Mr. C. B. Rogers-Wright, Minister of External Affairs of Sierra Leone, and Mr. J. Nelson-Williams, Minister of Information and Broadcasting; Dr. A. C. Flores, Foreign Minister of Mexico; Mr. J. Rudolf Grimes, Foreign Minister of Liberia.
Mr. L. Motyka, Polish Minister of Culture and Art; Mr. L. Koné, Foreign Minister of Upper Volta; Mr. C. Alliali, Foreign Minister, Republic of the Ivory Coast; U Thi Han, Burmese Foreign Minister.
Dr. A. A. Khalatbary, Secretary-General, Central Treaty Organization; Mr. I. d'Eeckhoutte, Secretary-General, Western European Union; Dr. E. N. van Kleffens, representing the three European Communities; as well as Ambassadors, High Commissioners, and other members of the Diplomatic Corps who attended on behalf of their nations.

The Earl Marshal and the Duchess of Norfolk, the Duchess of Beaufort, the Duke and Duchess of Fife, Dr. J. C. Heenan (Roman Catholic Archbishop of Westminster), Admiral the Hon. Sir Alexander and Lady Patricia Ramsay, Captain and the Hon. Mrs. Alexander Ramsay, the Lord Great Chamberlain and the Marchioness of Cholmondeley, the Marquess and Marchioness of Abergavenny.
The Earl and Countess of Harewood, Countess Alexander of Tunis, the Countess of Swinton, Lady Dorothy Macmillan, Lady Moyra Hamilton, Lord and Lady Adam Gordon, Viscount and Viscountess Tenby, Viscount and Viscountess Boyd of Merton, Viscountess Slim, Viscount Rothermere. the Dowager Viscountess Hambleden, Viscount Knollys, Allison Viscountess Dunrossil, Viscount Chandos.
Lord Cobbold (Lord Chamberlain), Lord and Lady Moran, Lord and Lady Casey, Baroness Asquith of Yarnbury, Lady Gardiner, Hope Lady Dynevor, Lord and Lady Hailes, Lady Normanbrook, Lady Ismay, Lady Bridges,

the Dowager Lady Digby, the Hon. Mrs. Leyland Heywood, Lady Juliet Duff, the Hon. Gerald and Mrs. Lascelles, Lady Helen Nutting, Lieutenant-Colonel the Hon. Sir Martin and Lady Charteris, Lady Rose Baring, the Hon. Lady Hylton-Foster, the Hon. Lady Milbank, Sir Shane and Lady Leslie, Sir Max and Lady Aitken.

Admiral Sir David Luce (Chief of Naval Staff and First Sea Lord) and Lady Luce, General Sir Richard Hull (Chief of the General Staff) and Lady Hull, Air Chief Marshal Sir Charles Elworthy (Chief of the Air Staff) and Lady Elworthy.

Sir Anthony Wagner (Garter Principal King of Arms) and Lady Wagner, Sir John Heaton-Armstrong (Clarenceux King of Arms), Mr. A. J. Toppin (Norroy and Ulster King of Arms), Mr. R. P. Graham-Vivian (Windsor Herald), Mr. M. R. Trappes-Lomax (Somerset Herald), Mr. J. R. B. Walker (Lancaster Herald), Lord Sinclair (York Herald), Mr. W. J. G. Verco (Chester Herald), Mr. R. de la Lanne Mirrlees (Richmond Herald), Mr. J. P. B. Brooke-Little (Bluemantle Pursuivant), Mr. A. C. Cole (Portcullis Pursuivant), Lieutenant-Colonel R. O. Dennys (Rouge Croix Pursuivant), Mr. C. M. J. F. Swan, (Rouge Dragon Pursuivant), Mr. Francis Jones (Wales Herald Extraordinary), Mr. Dermot Morrah (Arundel Herald Extraordinary), Mr. G. D. Squibb (Norfolk Herald Extraordinary), Mr. C. W. Scott-Giles (Fitzalan Pursuivant Extraordinary).

Lieutenant-General Sir Ian and Lady Jacob, Lady Birley, Lady Fielden, Major Sir D. J. Morton, Sir Leslie and Lady Rowan, Lieutenant-Colonel Sir Martin Gilliat, Sir Edward and the Hon. Lady Ford, Brigadier Sir James Gault, Lady Templer.

The Lord Chancellor, Lord Gardiner, attended in state with the Permanent Secretary, Sir George Coldstream, Q.C., the Serjeant-at-Arms, Captain K. L. Mackintosh, R.N., and other officers. The Speaker of the House of Commons, Sir Harry Hylton-Foster, also attended in state with the Serjeant-at-Arms (Rear-Admiral A. H. C. Gordon Lennox), the Speaker's Secretary (Brigadier Sir Francis Reid) and the Speaker's Chaplain (Canon M. S. Stancliffe).

The Lord Mayor, Sir James Miller, attended in state with the sheriffs, Alderman A. C. Trinder and Mr. A. H. Ley.

The Prime Minister came with Mrs. Wilson, and other members of the Cabinet present included:—

The Lord President of the Council and Mrs. Bowden, the Lord Privy Seal and the Countess of Longford, the First Secretary of State and Mrs. Brown, the Chancellor of the Exchequer, the Secretary of State for Foreign Affairs and Mrs. Stewart, the Secretary of State for Defence and Mrs. Healey, the Secretary of State for the Home Department and Lady Soskice, the Secretary of State for Commonwealth Relations and Mrs. Bottomley, the Secretary of State for Scotland and Mrs. Ross, the Secretary of State for Wales and Mrs. Griffiths, the Chancellor of the Duchy of Lancaster.

The Secretary of State for the Colonies and Mrs. Greenwood, the President of the Board of Trade and Mrs. Jay, the Secretary of State for Education and Science and Mrs. Crosland, the Minister of Housing and Local Government and Mrs. Crossman, the Minister of Labour and Mrs. Gunter, the Minister of Technology and Mrs. Cousins, the Minister of Agriculture, Fisheries and Food and Mrs. Peart, the Minister of Power, the Minister of Transport, the Minister of Overseas Development and Mr. Castle.

The Minister of Health and Mrs. Robinson, the Minister of Pensions and National Insurance, the Minister of Aviation and Mrs. Jenkins, the Postmaster General and Mrs. Wedgwood Benn, the Minister of Public Building and Works, the Minister of Land and Natural Resources and Mrs. Willey, the Deputy Secretary of State for Defence and Minister of Defence for the Army and Mrs. Mulley, the Minister without Portfolio and Lady Fletcher, the Minister without Portfolio (Lord Champion), the Paymaster General, the Chief Secretary, Treasury, and Mrs. Diamond.

The Minister of Defence for the Royal Navy and Mrs. Mayhew, the Ministers of State for Foreign Affairs (Mr. George Thomson, Lord Caradon, Mr. Walter Padley, and Lord Chalfont), Lady Chalfont, the Minister of State for Commonwealth Relations and Mrs. Hughes, the Ministers of State, Board of Trade (Mr. George Darling, Mr. Edward Redhead and Mr. Roy Mason), Mrs. Darling, the Minister of State Department of Education and Science and Mrs. Prentice, the Minister of State, Department of Economic Affairs and Mrs. Albu, the Attorney General and Lady Jones, the Solicitor General and Lady Foot.

Sir Alec Douglas-Home (Leader of the Opposition) was present with Lady Douglas-Home, and Mr. Joseph Grimond attended with Mrs. Grimond. Members of the Shadow Cabinet and of all parties in the House of Commons who attended included:—

Mr. Julian Amery, Sir William Anstruther-Gray, Mr. John Boyd-Carpenter, Sir Edward Boyle, Mr. Henry Brooke, Mr. R. A. Butler, Mr. Robert Carr, Mr. William Deedes, Mr. Edward Du Cann, the Hon. Hugh Fraser, Mr. Joseph Godber, Mr. Edward Heath, Mr. Wyndham Henderson, Mr. Quintin Hogg, Dame Patricia Hornsby-Smith, Mr. Aubrey Jones, Sir Keith Joseph, Mr. Ernest Marples, Mr. Reginald Maudling, Mr. Michael Noble, Sir Richard Nugent, Sir Kenneth Pickthorn, Mr. Enoch Powell, Mr. James Ramsden, Sir Peter Rawlinson, Q.C., Sir Martin Redmayne, Sir David Renton, Brigadier Sir John Smyth, V.C., Mr. Peter Thomas, Sir John Vaughan-Morgan, Sir Derek Walker-Smith, the Hon. Richard Wood.

Commander Sir Peter Agnew, Mr. Michael Alison, Mr. James Allason, Mr. S. Scholefield Allen, Q.C., Miss Harvie Anderson, Mr. Ernest Armstrong, the Hon. John Astor, Mr. Humphrey Atkins, Mr. W. H. K. Baker, Lord Balniel, Sir John Barlow, Mr. Joel Barnett, Mr. Brian Batsford, Colonel Sir Tufton Beamish, Mr. Ronald Bell, Mr. C. R. Bence, Mr. Humphrey Berkeley, the Hon. Anthony Berry, Mr. Peter Bessell, Mr. W. J. Biffen, Mr. John Biggs-Davidson, Mr. E. S. Bishop, Sir Cyril Black, Mr. P. A. R. Blaker, Mr. Harold Boardman, the Hon. Clive Bossom, Mr. Terence Boston, Captain E. R. Bowen, Q.C., Mr. Donald Box, Mr. Bernard Braine, Dr. Jeremy Bray, Sir Esme Brinton.

Lieutenant-Colonel Sir Walter Bromley-Davenport, Dr. A. D. D. Broughton, Sir Edward Brown, Mr. R. W. Brown, Mr. J. Bruce-Gardyne, Mr. Paul Bryan, Mr. Alick Buchanan-Smith, Mr. Antony Buck, Wing Commander Eric Bullus, Mr. F. F. A. Burden, Sir Herbert Butcher, Mr. Mark Carlisle, Mr. Lewis Carter-Jones, Sir Robert Cary, Mr. Paul Channon, Mr. Donald Chapman, Mr. Christopher Chataway, Mr. Robert Chichester-Clark, Mr. William Clark, Mr. N. J. Cole, Mr. Bernard Conlan, Mr. J. H. Cordle, Mr. F. V. Corfield, Mr A. P. Costain, Commander A. T. Courtney, Sir Beresford Craddock, Mr. Aidan Crawley, Mr. Richard Crawshaw, Mr. F. Petre Crowder, Q.C., Sir Knox Cunningham, Q.C.

Mr. Charles Curran, Mr. G. B. H. Currie, Mr. James Dance, Mr. Harold Davies, Mr. Ifor Davies, Dr Wyndham Davies, Sir Henry d'Avigdor-Goldsmid, Sir Geoffrey de Freitas, Mr. Edmund Dell, Mr. Simon Wingfield Digby, Mr. Douglas Dodds-Parker, Mr. Desmond Donnelly, Mr. Charles Doughty, Q.C., Mr. G. B. Drayson, Mr. Tom Driberg, Sir Rolf Dudley Williams, Mr. Jock Dunnett, Mr. Maurice Edelman, Sir John Eden, Captain Walter Elliot, Mr. R. W. Elliott, Mr. Peter Emery, Mr. Michael English, Mr. David Ennals, Sir Eric Errington, Mr. John Farr, Mr. Anthony Fell, Mr. Nigel Fisher, Mr. Alan Fitch, Sir John Fletcher-Cooke, Mr. Bernard Floud, Mr. B. T. Ford, Sir John G. Foster, Q.C., Mr. Ian Fraser.

The Hon. Thomas Galbraith, Lady Gammans, Mr. Edward Gardner, Q.C., Lady Megan Lloyd George, Mr. David Gibson-Watt, Rear-Admiral M. C. Morgan Giles, Sir John Gilmour, Mr. David Ginsburg, Colonel Sir Douglas Glover, Mr. Victor Goodhew, Mr. Harry Gourlay, Mr. J. A. Grant, Mr. R. G. Grant-Ferris, Mr. Arnold Gregory, Mr. R. Gresham Cooke, Mr. C. F. Grey, Mr. Percy Grieve, Q.C., Mr. Eldon Griffiths, Mr. Harold Gurden, Mr. John Hall, Mr. A. G. F. Hall-Davis, the Marquess of Hamilton, Mr. W. W. Hamilton, Mr. Joseph Harper, Mr. F. W. Harris, Mr. R. Reader Harris, Mr. Brian Harrison, Colonel Sir Harwood Harrison, Mr. Stephen Hastings.

Mr. Paul Hawkins, Mr. John Hay, Mr. F. H. Hayman, Lieutenant-Colonel A. Forbes Hendry, Mr. Terence Higgins, Mr. J. Hiley, Mr. John Hill, Mr. H. Emlyn Hooson, Q.C., Mr. Alan Hopkins, Mr. P. M. Hordern, Mr. Richard Hornby, Mr. Geoffrey Howe, Mr. Denis Howell, Mr. J. L. Hunt, Mr. A. E. Hunter, Mr. M. Clark Hutchison, Mr. Henry Hynd, Mr. T. L. Iremonger, Mr.

258

A. J. Irvine, Q.C., Mr. B. Goodman Irvine, Mr. Sydney Irving, Mr. Colin Jackson, Sir Barnett Janner, Mr. Patrick Jenkin, Mr. John Jennings, Mr. Carol Johnson, Mr. James Johnson, Mr. Russell Johnston, Mr. Arthur Jones, Mr. Idwal Jones, Mr. T. W. Jones, Mr. Michael Jopling.
Mr. Clifford Kenyon, Mrs. A. P. Kerr, Dr. D. L. Kerr, Sir Hamilton Kerr, Mr. Anthony Kershaw, Mr. J. A. Kilfedder, Mr. E. M. King, Dr. Horace King, Mr. T. P. G. Kitson, Mr. Godfrey Lagden, Viscount Lambton, Colonel C. G. Lancaster, Sir John Langford-Holt, Sir Harry Legge-Bourke, Mr. Leslie Lever, Mr. N. H. Lever, Mr. Kenneth Lewis, Mr. Ron Lewis, Captain John Litchfield, Mr. Ian Lloyd, Mr. Charles Longbottom, Mr. Gilbert Longden, Mr. Walter Loveys, Mr. Eric Lubbock, Sir Jocelyn Lucas, Sir Hugh Lucas-Tooth, Dr. J. Dickson Mabon, Sir Stephen McAdden, Mr. Ian MacArthur, Mr. John McCann, Mr. J. E. MacColl, Mr. George Mackie, Mr. John Mackie, Mr. Martin McLaren, Sir Fitzroy Maclean, Mr. Frank McLeavy, Mr. Patrick McNair-Wilson, Mr. Malcolm MacPherson, Commander Sir John Maitland, Mr. E. L. Mallalieu, Q.C.
Mr. Charles Mapp, Mr. A. A. H. Marlowe, Q.C., Mr. Neil Marten, Mr. Robert Mathew, Mr. Angus Maude, Mr. Robert Maxwell-Hyslop, Lieutenant-Commander S. L. C. Maydon, Mr. Robert Mellish, Mr. John Mendelson, Sir Anthony Meyer, Mr. W. Stratton Mills, Mr. E. J. Milne, Mr. N. Miscampbell, Mr. David Mitchell, Mr. William Molloy, Mr. Hector Monro, Mr. Walter Monslow, Mr. Jasper More, Mr. W. G. O. Morgan, Mr. Alfred Morris, Mr. John Morris, Mr. C. A. Morrison, Sir Charles Mott Radclyffe, Mr. H. O. Murton, Mr. Airey Neave, Sir Harmar Nicholls, Sir Godfrey Nicholson, Mr. C. B. B. Norwood, Mr. Eric Ogden, Mr. Brian O'Malley.
Mr. Cranley Onslow, Sir Ian Orr-Ewing, Mr. John Osborn, Sir Cyril Osborne, Mr. John Page, Mr. Derek Page, Mr. R. Graham Page, Mr. R. T. Paget, Q.C., Mr. George Pargiter, Mr. Trevor Park, Mr. Laurence Pavitt, Sir Frank Pearson, Mr. John Peel, Mr. Ian Percival, Q.C., Mr. E. G. Perry, Mr. John Peyton, Miss Mervyn Pike, Dame Edith Pitt, Mr. Rafton Pounder, Mr. David Price, Mr. Francis Pym, Miss J. M. Quennell, Mr. H. E. Randall, Mr. W. R. Rees-Davies, Mr. Ivor Richard, the Hon. Nicholas Ridley, Mr. Julian Ridsdale, Sir William Robson-Brown, Sir John Rodgers.
Mr. William Roots, Q.C., Mr. Christopher Rowland, Sir Ronald Russell, Mr. Norman St. John Stevas, Mr. James Scott-Hopkins, Mr. Richard Sharples, Mr. Robert Sheldon, Mr. William Shepherd, Mrs. Renée Short, the Hon. Samuel Silkin, Q.C., Sir George Sinclair, Mrs. Harriet Slater, Mr. Dudley Smith, Mr. Ellis Smith, Mr. Julian Snow, Sir Alexander Spearman, Mr. Keith Stainton, the Hon. Richard Stanley, Mr. J. A. Stodart, Mr. John Stonehouse, Sir Samuel Storey, Sir Henry Studholme, Sir Spencer Summers, Dr. Shirley Summerskill, Mr. Thomas Swain, Mr. John Talbot, Sir Charles Taylor, Mr. Edward Taylor, Mr. Frank Taylor, Sir William Teeling, Mr. John Temple, Sir Leslie Thomas, Sir Richard Thompson.
Mr. Jeremy Thorpe, Mr. John Tilney, Mr. Frank Tomney, Mr. Raphael Tuck, Lady Tweedsmuir, Mr. W. R. van Straubenzee, Dame Joan Vickers, Mr. David Walder, Mr. Peter Walker, Mr. Patrick Wall, Mr. Dennis Walters, Dame Irene Ward, Mr. Bernard Weatherill, Mr. David Weitzman, Q.C., Mr. John Wells, Mr. W. T. Wells, Q.C., Mr. William Whitelaw, Mr. W. C. Whitlock, Mr. W. T. Williams, Q.C., Sir Gerald Wills, Mr. Geoffrey Wilson, the Hon. Christopher Woodhouse, Mr. Woodrow Wyatt, Mr William Yates, the Hon. George Younger.

Sir Barnett Cocks (Clerk of the House of Commons) with Mr. D. W. S. Lidderdale (Clerk-Assistant) and Mr. R. D. Barlas (Second Clerk-Assistant), Sir Robert Speed, Q.C. (Counsel to the Speaker), Mr. S. C. Hawtrey, Mr. C. A. S. S. Gordon, Lieutenant-Colonel P. F. Thorne, Mr. E. S. Taylor, Mr. A. A. Birley, Mr. C. A. James, Mr. M. T. Ryle, Mr. C. J. Boulton, Mr. A. A. Barrett, Mr. R. K. Middlemas, Mr. C. B. Winnifrith, Major G. V. S. Le Fanu, and other officers of the House of Commons.

Mr. Averell Harriman, M. Jean Monnet, M. Paul Reynaud, Major-General John and Lady Jane Nelson, Mr. J. R. and Lady Margaret Colville, Mr. Aristotle Onassis, Mrs. Montague Browne, Commander C. R. Thompson, Mrs. June Churchill, Mr. and Mrs. Anthony Moir, Brigadier Green, Mr. and Mrs. D. B. Pitblado, Mr. B. Goddard, M. André de Staerke, Mr. R. V. Vanderfelt (Secretary-General, Commonwealth Parliamentary Association).
Commander Sir Douglas Marshall, Mr. C. F. H. Gough, Sir David Robertson, Mr. I. Bulmer-Thomas, Mr. J. A. Leavey, Mr. Somerset de Chair, Brigadier C. H. M. Peto, Mrs. Nigel Fisher, Dr. Robert McIntyre, Dr. Alan Glyn, Lord St. Helens, Commander R. T. Bower, Sir Martin Lindsay of Dowhill, as well as many members and officers of the House of Lords.

Chronological Summary of the Life of Sir Winston Churchill

1874 Born at Blenheim Palace, November 30.

1888 Enters Harrow School in the fourth form.

1893–94 At Sandhurst, in training for the cavalry.

1895 Death of his father, January 24. Commissioned in the 4th Hussars. Covers the insurrection in Cuba for the *Daily Graphic;* is under fire for the first time on his twenty-first birthday.

1896–98 At Bangalore, India, with the 4th Hussars. With the Malakand Field Force on the North-West Frontier, 1897. Joins Kitchener's Army in Egypt as correspondent for the *Morning Post;* charges with the 21st Lancers at Omdurman, September, 1898. Publication of his first book, *The Malakand Field Force.*

1899–1900 Resigns his commission to enter politics; defeated in a by-election at Oldham. Goes to South Africa to cover the Boer War as a correspondent, is captured by the Boers and makes a daring escape, December, 1899. Serves with the South African Light Horse through the relief of Ladysmith and the entry into Pretoria, June 5, 1900. Returns to England; elected to Parliament in the "Khaki Election". Lectures in the United States and Canada, December.

1901–04 Makes his maiden speech in the House of Commons as Conservative Member for Oldham, February 18, 1901. Becomes a Unionist Free Trader and is disowned by the Oldham Conservative Association, 1903. Crosses the Floor of the House, May 31, 1904, to join the Liberals.

1905–07 Becomes Under-Secretary of State for the Colonies, December, 1905. His biography of Lord Randolph Churchill published, 1906. Is made a Privy Councillor; tours East Africa, 1907.

1908–09 Promoted to the Cabinet as President of the Board of Trade. Defeated in a by-election at North West Manchester; is later returned at Dundee. Marries Clementine Hozier, September 12, 1908. Supports Lloyd George's People's Budget, 1909, and begins his long association with the Welsh leader. Birth of his daughter Diana.

1910–11 As Home Secretary, helps to launch the movement for penal reform. Takes command of the police at the battle of Sidney Street, January 3, 1911. Birth of his son, Randolph. Appointed First Lord of the Admiralty, October 23, with a mandate to maintain the Fleet in readiness for war with Germany.

1912–14 Learns to fly, 1913; sets up the Royal Naval Flying Corps. At the outbreak of war, August 4, 1914, mobilizes the Fleet on his own responsibility; leads the expedition to Antwerp. Birth of his daughter Sarah.

1915–16 Failure of the campaign in the Dardanelles; is forced to resign from the Admiralty, May, 1915, and accepts the Chancellorship of the Duchy of Lancaster. Resigns to rejoin the Army, November 11, and is sent to France with the 2nd Grenadier Guards. Commands a battalion of the Royal Welsh Fusiliers at the front, 1916.

1917–18 Exonerated by the report of the Dardanelles Commission, February, 1917; serves as Minister of Munitions in Lloyd George's Coalition Government from July 15, 1917, through the end of the war.

1919–20 Secretary of State for War and Air; appeals for volunteer force to cover withdrawal of British troops from Bolshevist Russia.

1921 As Colonial Secretary, helps negotiate peace with leaders of the Irish Rebellion; at Cairo Conference negotiates a Middle East settlement, with T. E. Lawrence as adviser.

1922 Defeated at Dundee in the general election in which Conservatives return to power. Is made a Companion of Honour. Birth of his daughter Mary.

1924–29 Defeated in a by-election in the Abbey Division, Westminster; standing as a Constitutionalist, is returned at Epping in the 1924 general election. Chancellor of the Exchequer in the Baldwin Government; his first Budget, 1925, announces a return to the gold standard. Publishes the *British Gazette* for the Government during the General Strike, 1926. Standing once again as a Conservative, is returned at Epping in 1929, when his Party loses in the general election.

1931 Resigns from the Conservative "Shadow Cabinet" on the issue of India.

1933–38 Publication of his four-volume life of Marlborough. In the House, advocates preparedness, particularly in the air, as Hitler rises to power. Advises and supports Edward VIII in the Abdication crisis, 1936. Decries policy of appeasement as Munich pact is signed, 1938.

1939–40 Again becomes First Lord of the Admiralty as war is declared on Germany, September 3, 1939. Norway, Denmark, and the Lowlands invaded; Chamberlain resigns and a Coalition Government is formed, May 10, 1940, with Churchill as Prime Minister and Minister of Defence. Allied troops are evacuated from Dunkirk, France falls, and the Battle of Britain begins.

1941–42 British withdraw from Crete, June, 1941. Germany invades Russia, June 22. Churchill meets Roosevelt in mid-ocean and signs the Atlantic Charter, August 12. Japanese attack on Pearl Harbor brings the United States into the war, December 8; Churchill visits Washington, addresses the U.S. Congress, signs United Nations Pact, January, 1942. Singapore falls to the Japanese, February; Burma overrun. Churchill views desert war in North Africa; to Moscow for meeting with Stalin, August. British victory at El Alamein, October; allied landing in North Africa, November 8.

1943–44   Churchill confers with Roosevelt at Casablanca, January, 1943; Nazis surrender to Russians at Stalingrad. Rommel's Afrika Korps defeated in the Western Desert, June. Allied landings in Sicily, July 10. Churchill attends Quebec Conference, August. Italy surrenders unconditionally, September 8. Teheran Conference, November. Monte Cassino captured, May, 1944. Allied landings in Normandy, June 6; Churchill visits the beachhead, June 10. Paris liberated, August 25. Churchill attends second Quebec Conference, September; meets Stalin in Moscow, October; visits Paris, November 11.

1945   Attends Yalta Conference, February, 1945; death of Roosevelt, April 13. Visits the front in Germany as allied forces cross the Rhine, March 25. Announces unconditional surrender of German forces in Europe, May 8. Attends Potsdam Conference, July. Conservatives defeated in general election, July 25; Churchill resigns as Prime Minister. Atomic bombs dropped on Japan, August 6–9; war ends with surrender of the Japanese, September 2.

1946–50   Leader of the Opposition in the House of Commons. Makes "Iron Curtain" speech at Fulton, Missouri, March, 1946; urges creation of a United States of Europe in a speech at Zürich, September. Receives the Order of Merit; made Lord Warden of the Cinque Ports, August 15. Addresses the Congress of Europe, May, 1948. Begins publication, 1948, of his memoirs of the Second World War. Is returned at Woodford, 1950.

1951–55   Labour Party defeated in the general election of 1951; Churchill is once more asked to form a Government, October 25. Death of King George VI, 1952. Churchill is knighted by Queen Elizabeth, April 24, 1953; awarded the Nobel Prize for Literature. Celebrates his eightieth birthday, 1954. Announces his retirement as Prime Minister, April 5, 1955.

1956–63   Publication of his four-volume *History of the English-Speaking Peoples*. Returned once more as Member for Woodford, 1959. Declared Honorary Citizen of the United States, 1963. Announces his intention not to stand for re-election to Parliament.

1964   The House of Commons accords him a vote of gratitude for his services "to Parliament, the nation, and the world", July 28. Celebrates his ninetieth birthday, November 30.

1965   Dies at his home in Hyde Park Gate, London, January 24.

Churchill's Books and Speeches

The Story of the Malakand Field Force: An Episode of Frontier War. London: Longmans, Green, 1898.
The River War: An Historical Account of the Reconquest of the Soudan (2 vols.). London: Longmans, Green, 1899; New York: Scribner's, 1933.
Ian Hamilton's March. London: Longmans, Green, 1900.
Savrola: A tale of the Revolution in Laurania. London: Longmans, Green, 1900; New York: Random House, 1956.
Mr. Brodrick's Army. London: Arthur L. Humphreys, 1903.
For Free Trade: A Collection of Speeches . . . Preceding the Late General Election. London: Arthur L. Humphreys, 1906.
Lord Randolph Churchill (2 vols.). London and New York: Macmillan, 1906.
For Liberalism and Free Trade: Principal Speeches . . . during the campaign in Dundee. May, 1908. Dundee: John Leng, 1908.
My African Journey. London: Hodder and Stoughton, 1908.
Liberalism and the Social Problem. London: Hodder and Stoughton, 1909.
The People's Rights: Selected from his Lancashire and other recent Speeches. London: Hodder and Stoughton, 1910.
The World Crisis (6 vols.). London: Thornton Butterworth; New York: Scribner's; 1923-31.
My Early Life: A Roving Commission. London: Thornton Butterworth; New York: Scribner's; 1930.
India: Speeches and an Introduction. London: Thornton Butterworth, 1931.
Thoughts and Adventures. London: Thornton Butterworth, 1932. (Published in U.S. as *Amid These Storms: Thoughts and Adventures.* New York: Scribner's, 1932.)
Marlborough: His Life and Times (4 vols.). London: Harrap, 1933-38; New York: Scribner's (5 vols.), 1933-37.
Great Contemporaries. London: Thornton Butterworth; New York: Putnam; 1937.
Arms and the Covenant: Speeches. Compiled by Randolph S. Churchill. London: Harrap, 1938. (Published in U.S. as *While England Slept.* New York: Putnam, 1938.)
Step by Step: 1936-39. London: Thornton Butterworth; New York: Putnam; 1939.
Into Battle: Speeches. Compiled by Randolph S. Churchill. London: Cassell, 1941. (Published in U.S. as *Blood, Sweat and Tears.* New York: Putnam, 1941.)

The Unrelenting Struggle: War Speeches. Compiled by Charles Eade. London: Cassell; Boston: Little Brown; 1942.

The End of the Beginning: War Speeches. Compiled by Charles Eade. London: Cassell; Boston: Little Brown; 1943.

Onwards to Victory: War Speeches. Compiled by Charles Eade. London: Cassell; Boston: Little Brown; 1944.

The Dawn of Liberation: War Speeches. Compiled by Charles Eade. London: Cassell; Boston: Little Brown; 1945.

Victory: War Speeches. Compiled by Charles Eade. London: Cassell; Boston: Little Brown; 1946.

Secret Session Speeches. Compiled by Charles Eade. London: Cassell; New York: Simon and Schuster; 1946.

The Sinews of Peace: Post-War Speeches. Edited by Randolph S. Churchill. London: Cassell, 1948; Boston: Houghton Mifflin, 1949.

Painting as a Pastime. London: Odhams Press, Ernest Benn, 1948; New York: McGraw-Hill, 1950.

The Second World War (6 vols.). London: Cassell, 1948-54; Boston: Houghton Mifflin, 1948-53. Volume I—*The Gathering Storm* (1919–May 10, 1940). Volume II—*Their Finest Hour* (May 11, 1940–January 5, 1941). Volume III—*The Grand Alliance* (January 6, 1941–January 16, 1942). Volume IV—*The Hinge of Fate* (January 17, 1942–June 3, 1943). Volume V—*Closing the Ring* (June 6, 1943–June 5, 1944). Volume VI—*Triumph and Tragedy* (June 6, 1944–July 26, 1945).

Europe Unite: Speeches, 1947 and 1948. Edited by Randolph S. Churchill. London: Cassell, Boston: Houghton Mifflin; 1950.

In the Balance: Speeches, 1949 and 1950. Edited by Randolph S. Churchill. London: Cassell, 1951; Boston: Houghton Mifflin, 1952.

War Speeches: Definitive Edition (3 vols.). Compiled by Charles Eade. London; Cassell, 1952; Boston: Houghton Mifflin, 1953. Volume I—From the rise of Hitler to the invasion of Russia, June 22, 1941. Volume II—From June 25, 1941, to September 6, 1943. Volume III—From September 11, 1943, to August 16, 1945.

Stemming the Tide: Speeches, 1951 and 1952. Edited by Randolph S. Churchill. London: Cassell, 1953; Boston: Houghton Mifflin, 1954.

History of the English Speaking Peoples (4 vols.). London: Cassell; New York: Dodd, Mead; 1956-58. Volume I—*The Birth of Britain.* Volume II—*The New World.* Volume III—*The Age of Revolution.* Volume IV—*The Great Democracies.*

The Unwritten Alliance: Speeches, 1953-1959. Edited by Randolph S. Churchill. London: Cassell, 1961.

Photographic Credits

ACME: 128 bot. l. AIRD & TAYLOR LTD: (Malcolm Aird), 248. ASSOCIATED NEWSPAPERS LTD: 233, 256. BARRATT'S PHOTO PRESS LTD: 43. CECIL BEATON: 101, 123 bot. BETTMANN ARCHIVE: 23 bot. r., 64 top r. BROWN BROTHERS: 17 top & bot., 23 top l. & bot. l., 25 top l. & r., 31 l., 33 bot., 41 bot. l., 44 top, 50 l., 59 top, 135. ROMANO CAGNONI: 246. CAMERA PRESS LTD: 20, 63, 64 bot., 136 l., 238; (Stephen Fry), 234, 235, 237, CENTRAL PRESS PHOTOS LTD: 19 bot. l., 53, 80, 116. COMBINE: 70, 72 l., 74-75, 100 top, 108 top l., 140 l. & r., 141 bot. l., 146, 185, 195, 204, 205, 211, 212 bot., 217. CULVER PICTURES INC: 32 bot. EUROPEAN PICTURE SERVICE: 35, 42 top r., 52, 57, 59 bot., 61 r., 65, 82, 126 bot., 156, 164, 167, 177 bot., 194, 196 top, 206 l., 207, 208, 213, 214 bot., 215 bot., 224 top r., 225, 239, 243, 252. FOX PHOTOS LTD: 92, 99 r. TONI FRISSELL: 112, 184, 192, 193, 202, 203, 232. H. M. STATIONERY OFFICE: 79 bot. l. HALLMARK GALLERY: 24 bot. l., 29 r., 41 r., 42 l., 69, 89. C. G. HOLME: 68. IMPERIAL WAR MUSEUM: 24 top l., 25 bot. l., 28 top l., 60, 106, 107 bot., 108 bot. l. & bot. r., 109 bot. r., 111, 113, 114, 115, 131, 132, 133, 134, 139, 141 top & bot. r., 142 bot., 143 bot., 144-45 top, 144 bot. l., 145 bot. r., 147, 151 r., 152, 154, 155, 158, 159, 160 top, 168, 169, 172 bot., 173, 176 bot., 179 top. INTERNATIONAL NEWS PHOTO: 124 top r., 125 top l., 163 bot. I.P.S.: 179 bot. KEYSTONE PRESS AGENCY LTD: 110, 190 top, 191, 198, 212 top. FREDERIC LEWIS INC: 32 top. LONDON EVENING STANDARD: 126 top (Low cartoon reproduced from August 26, 1940, issue). MIRRORPIC: 38, 39, 50 bot. r., 73 bot. r., 76 top r., 86, 91 top, 215 top. ODHAMS PRESS: 209. PHOTO RESEARCHERS INC: (Susan McCartney), 236. PICTORIAL PARADE INC: 64 top l., 142 top. PRESS ASSOCIATION PHOTOS LTD: 40 r., 48, 83, 94 top, 162 bot., 190 bot., 224 top l. RADIO TIMES HULTON PICTURE LIBRARY: 23 top r., 24 top r. & bot. r., 26 bot., 27 top r. & bot., 31 top r. & bot. r., 37, 40 top l. & bot. l., 41 bot., 44 bot., 45 top & bot. l., 47 bot. r., 49, 50 top r., 51, 54, 58 bot., 66, 67, 72 r., 76 l. & bot. r., 81, 85, 87 l., 90 top & bot. l., 94 center & bot., 95, 98 top l., 100 bot., 118, 119, 120, 121, 122, 129 bot. r., 172 top, 180, 181, 187, 188, 189, 196 bot., 197, 200, 201, 206 top r. & bot. r., 220, 221. FRANKLIN D. ROOSEVELT LIBRARY: 42 bot. r., 127, 128-29 top, 136 top r., 137, 143 top l. & top r., 160 bot., 161 top & bot. l. EDVARD STEICHEN: 10. THOMSON NEWSPAPERS LTD: (Topix), 73 top, 77, 78, 79 bot. r., 177 top, 214 top, 222-23, 226; (Sunday Times), 210, 227, 228-29, 249, Copyright © Sunday Times, London, 1965; (Jack Esten), 230; (Peter Jones Griffiths), 247, THE TIMES of London: 18 l., 19 r., 71 top, 84, 104, 117, 170-71, 174, 182-83, 217, 218, 219, 224 bot. l., 250-51. UNDERWOOD & UNDERWOOD: 26 top, 34, 45 bot. l., 46, 47 top l. & bot. l., 55, 58 top, 61 bot. l., 62, 79 top, 87 r., 90 bot. l., 91 bot., 93, 98 bot. l., top r. & bot. r., 99 top l., 103, 105, 109 top, 124 l., 125 r., 129 bot. l., 150 top & bot l., 153, 161 bot. r. UNITED PRESS INTERNATIONAL: 71 bot., 88, 107 top, 123 top, 130, 138, 144 bot. r., 186, 199, 212 bot. l., 231, 240, 255. U. S. ARMY: 61 top l., 150 bot. r.; (Air Forces), 124 bot. r., 148, 162-63 top, 178; (Signal Corps), 149, 157, 165, 166. VOGUE photograph: 17 center, 19 top l., Copyright © by The Conde Nast Publications Inc.

Index

Airlie, 7th Earl of, *see* Ogilvy, Walter
Aitken, William Maxwell (Baron Beaverbrook), 116, 117
Alanbrooke, Viscount, *see* Brooke, Field Marshal
Albert, Prince, *see* George VI, King
Alexander, A. V. (Viscount Alexander of Hillsborough), 117
Alexander, Field Marshal Harold (Earl Alexander of Tunis), 132, 134, 143
Alexandra, Queen, 41
Anderson, Sir John, 116
Anne, Princess, 204
Anne, Queen, 16, 17
Asquith, Herbert Henry (Earl of Oxford and Asquith), Prime Minister, 21, 36, 40, 43, 60, 62, 72
Asquith, Margot, Countess of Oxford and Asquith, 21
Athlone, Earl of (Sir Alexander Cambridge), 143
Attlee, Clement R. (Earl Attlee), 7, 116, 117, 177, 179, 180, 198, 244, 249
Audley, Lady, *see* Churchill, Sarah
Avon, Earl of, *see* Eden, Anthony
Avon, Lady (Clarissa Churchill), 241

Baldwin, Stanley (Earl Baldwin of Bewdley), Prime Minister, 72, 77, 89, 96
Balfour, Arthur James (Earl Balfour), Prime Minister, 36, 72
Battenberg, Prince Louis of, 12, 58
Bayerlein, General Fritz, 135
Beatrice, Princess, 26
Beaverbrook, Lord, *see* Aitken, William Maxwell
Bell, Gertrude, 69
Bevan, Aneurin, 7, 194
Bevin, Ernest, 116
Birkenhead, Lord, *see* Smith, F. E.
Birley, Sir Oswald, 174
Botha, Louis, 27
Bridges, Edward, 1st Baron, 249
Brodrick, William St. John (Earl of Midleton), 36
Brooke, Field Marshal Alan Francis (Viscount Alanbrooke), 8, 143, 179
Bryant, Sir Arthur, 179
Burghley, William Cecil (Baron of Burghley), 22

Campbell-Bannerman, Sir Henry, Prime Minister, 36, 40
Canterbury, Archbishop of (Most Rev. A. M. Ramsey), 242, 246, 252
Carol, King of Roumania, 93
Cecil, Lord Hugh Richard, 36, 40
Chamberlain, Sir Austen, 72
Chamberlain, Joseph, 21, 27, 35, 36
Chamberlain, Neville, 96, 98, 100, 116
Chaplin, Charles, 89
Charles, Prince of Wales, 204, 244, 245, 246
Chatham, Lord, *see* Pitt, the elder
Chiang Kai-shek, General, 142
Churchill, Arabella (granddaughter), 241

Churchill, Charles Richard John Spencer, *see* Marlborough (9th Duke of)
Churchill, Lady Clementine, 40, 42, 45, 50, 51, 52, 69, 73, 76, 85, 87, 111, 119, 141, 158, 185, 192, 193, 196, 200, 202, 204, 208, 215, 220, 224, 232, 234, 240, 241, 242, 246, 249, 253, 255, 257
Churchill, Diana (daughter) (Mrs. Duncan Sandys), 85
Churchill, John, *see* Marlborough (1st Duke of)
Churchill, John Winston Spencer, *see* Marlborough (7th Duke of)
Churchill, Major John (nephew), 241
Churchill, Mrs. John, 241
Churchill, Mary (daughter) (Mrs. Christopher Soames), 77, 141, 185, 187, 224, 241, 249
Churchill, Peregrine (nephew), 241
Churchill, Mrs. Peregrine, 241
Churchill, Lord Randolph (father), 8, 16, 22, 23, 36, 37, 75, 87, 140, 180
Churchill, Lady Randolph (mother), 22, 23, 24, 48, 252
Churchill, Randolph F. E. (son), 85, 87, 241, 242, 246, 249, 253, 255
Churchill, Sarah (daughter) (Lady Audley), 85, 185, 249
Churchill, Winston (grandson), 190, 241
Clemenceau, Georges, 64
Collins, Michael, 69
Cornwallis West, Mrs. George, *see* Churchill, Lady Randolph
Cradock, Admiral Sir Christopher, 58
Cunningham, General Sir Alan G., 143

de Gaulle, General Charles, 136, 158, 231, 244, 245, 246, 252
de Rougemont, Denis, 188
Devonshire, Spencer Compton, 8th Duke of, 36
Dill, Field Marshal Sir John Greer, 117
Disraeli, Benjamin (Earl of Beaconsfield), Prime Minister, 8, 22, 180
Dixon, Piers, 241
Dixon, Mrs. Piers, *see* Sandys, Edwina
Douglas-Home, Sir Alec, Prime Minister, 245

Earl Marshal, the, *see* Norfolk, Duke of
Eden, Anthony (Earl of Avon), 116, 117, 143, 177, 195, 198, 244, 249
Edinburgh, Duke of, *see* Philip, Prince
Edward VII, King, 41, 44
Edward VIII, King (formerly Prince of Wales and later Duke of Windsor), 21, 45, 64, 70, 89, 90
Eisenhower, General Dwight D. (later President), 143, 168, 175, 194, 240, 245
Elizabeth, the Queen Mother, 220, 244
Elizabeth II, Queen, 14, 16, 21, 91, 198, 200, 201, 203, 204, 211, 213, 214, 215, 220, 244, 245, 246, 252, 257

Elliott, Maxine, 50
Elworthy, Sir Charles, 240, 246

Fisher, John (Baron Fisher of Kilverstone), 58, 59, 60, 62
Foch, Marshal Ferdinand, 64
Friedeburg, Admiral Hans Georg von, 169

Gault, Lady Elizabeth, 240
George V, King, 45, 46, 47, 54, 61, 75
George VI, King, 14, 21, 41, 91, 100, 102, 185, 198, 211
Gibbon, Edward, 181
Gibbons, Grinling, 19
Giraud, General Henri, 136
Gladstone, William Ewart, Prime Minister, 56, 76, 245
Greenwood, Arthur, 116
Grey, Edward (Viscount of Fallodon), 36, 42
Grimond, Joseph, 245

Haig, Douglas (1st Earl of Bemersyde), 64
Haldane, Richard Burdon (Viscount Haldane of Cloan), 36
Halifax, Edward Wood, Earl of, 116
Hamilton, General Sir Ian, 93
Harington, General Sir Charles, 69
Harwood, Rear-Admiral Sir H. H., 100
Herbert, Lord David, 122
Hitler, Adolf, 89, 98, 102, 107, 120, 126, 164, 176
Hoare, Samuel (Viscount Templewood) (First Lord of the Admiralty), 96
Hollis, Colonel Sir Leslie, 117
Home, 14th Earl of, *see* Douglas-Home, Sir Alec
Hozier, Clementine, *see* Churchill, Lady Clementine
Hozier, Colonel Sir Henry M., 234
Hull, General Sir Richard, 240, 246
Hylton-Foster, Sir Harry, 244

Ibn Saud, King of Saudi Arabia, 160
Inskip, Sir Thomas (Minister for Defence), 96
Ismay, General Hastings Lionel (Baron of Wormington), 116, 117, 249

Jerome, Jennie, *see* Churchill, Lady Randolph
Jerome, Leonard, 22, 23
Joynson-Hicks, William (Viscount Brentford), 40

Kennedy, John Fitzgerald, President, 8, 231, 245
Kerstens, Dr. P. A., 188
Keynes, Lord John Maynard, 77
King, W. L. Mackenzie, Prime Minister, 143, 180
Kitchener, Horatio Herbert (1st Earl Kitchener of Khartoum), 21, 27, 56
Koniev, Marshal Ivan, 245

Laguerre, Louis, 19

263

Laski, Harold, 22, 237
Law, Andrew Bonar, Prime Minister, 60, 64
Lawrence, T. E., 69
Leahy, Admiral William D., 158
Lloyd George, David (Earl of Dwyfor), 12, 35, 36, 40, 42, 43, 56, 60, 62, 64, 69, 72, 116, 213, 216
Lord Mayor of London, see Miller, Sir James
Luce, Admiral Sir David, 240, 246

Macaulay, Sir Thomas Babington, 87, 181
Macmillan, Sir Harold, Prime Minister, 244, 249, 252
Mahdi, the (Mohammed Ahmed ibn Seyyid Abdullah), 21, 27
Malenkov, Georgi M., 194
Margaret, Princess, 91, 220
Margesson, Captain Henry D. R., 117
Marlborough, John Churchill, 1st Duke of, 16, 17, 22, 87, 241
Marlborough, John Winston Spencer Churchill, 7th Duke of, 22, 23
Marlborough, Charles Richard John Spencer Churchill, 9th Duke of, 44, 87
Marlborough, John Albert Edward William Spencer Churchill, 10th Duke of, 241
Marshall, General George C., 143, 158
Mary, Queen, 41, 45, 47, 91
Mary, Princess (Princess Royal), 45
Masterman, C.P.G., 43
Matthews, Rev. W. R., 249
McKenna, Reginald, 43
Menzies, Sir Robert, 244, 249
Michael, Prince, of Roumania, 93
Miller, Sir James (Lord Mayor of London), 244, 246
Mohammed Riza Pahlavi (Shah of Persia's son), 126
Molotov, Vyacheslav Mikhailovich, 126
Montague Brown, Anthony, 241
Montgomery, Field Marshal Sir Bernard Law (Viscount Montgomery of Alamein), 8, 62, 132, 134, 142, 243, 156, 168, 169, 177
Morley, John (Viscount Morley), 36, 56
Morrison, Herbert (Baron Morrison of Lambeth), 180
Morrison, W. S. (Viscount Dunrossil), 213
Mountbatten, Louis (Earl Mountbatten of Burma), 240, 242, 249
Mussolini, Benito, 97, 98
Mustapha Kemal, 69

Norfolk, Duke of (Bernard Fitzalan-Howard) (the Earl Marshal), 240, 241, 242, 244, 249, 253
Normanbrook, Lord (Norman Craven Brook), 249

Ogilvy, Lady Blanche, 234
Ogilvy, Walter, 7th Earl of Airlie, 234
Onassis, Aristotle, 227
Orlando, Vittorio Emanuele, 64

Palmerston, Henry John Temple (Viscount Palmerston), Prime Minister, 11
Pembroke, Countess of, 122
Philip, Prince (Duke of Edinburgh), 198, 201, 214, 244, 245, 246
Pitt, William, the elder (Earl of Chatham), 7, 12, 22, 100
Pitt, William, the younger, 11, 12, 22
Portal, Air Chief Marshal Sir Charles, 117, 249
Pound, Admiral Sir Dudley, 117

Ramadier, Paul, Premier, 187, 188
Rawlinson, General Lord Henry, 64
Retinger, Dr., 188
Reynolds, Sir Joshua, 18
Riza Khan, Shah of Persia, 126
Rockefeller, Winthrop, 218
Rommel, Field Marshal Erwin, 132, 135
Roosevelt, Franklin D., President, 11, 13, 126, 127, 128, 131, 132, 136, 137, 138, 142, 143, 156, 158, 160, 161, 175, 179
Runciman, Walter (Viscount Runciman), 27

Samuel, Herbert Louis (Viscount Samuel), 91
Sandys, Celia (granddaughter), 241
Sandys, Edwina (granddaughter) (Mrs. Piers Dixon), 192, 241
Sandys, Julian (grandson), 241
Simon, Sir John, 87
Simpson, Mrs. Wallis Warfield, 90

Sinclair, Sir Archibald, 117
Slim, Field Marshal Sir William J., 249
Smith, F. E. (1st Earl of Birkenhead), 54, 72
Smuts, Field Marshal Jan Christiaan, 62, 180
Soames, Christopher, 224, 241
Soames, Mrs. Christopher, see Churchill, Mary
Soames, Charlotte (granddaughter), 224, 241
Soames, Emma (granddaughter), 202, 241
Soames, Jeremy (grandson), 224, 241
Soames, Nicholas (grandson), 220, 224, 241
Soames, Rupert Christopher (grandson), 224
Stalin, Marshal Josef, 142, 143, 160, 168, 179
Sutherland, George Granville, 5th Duke of, 82
Sutherland, Millicent, Duchess of, 51
Sutherland, Graham, 8, 212

Tedder, Air Chief Marshal Sir Arthur William (Baron of Glenguin), 143
Templer, Field Marshal Sir Gerald, 249
Truman, Harry S., President, 175, 179, 185
Twain, Mark (Samuel L. Clemens), 32

Vanbrugh, Sir John, 18
Victoria, Princess, 26
Victoria, Queen, 14, 16, 26, 27, 242

Webb, Beatrice (Mrs. Sidney Webb), 40
Wellington, Arthur Wellesley, 1st Duke of, 245, 249
Weygand, General Maxime, 102
Wilhelm II, Kaiser of Germany, 12, 54
Wilson, Sir Arthur, 60, 64
Wilson, Harold, 244, 245, 252
Wilson, Mrs. Harold, 244
Wood, Sir Kingsley, 116

Zhukov, Marshal Grigori Konstantinovich, 142
Zog, King of Albania, 97